THE TUAREGS

Their Islamic Legacy and Its Diffusion in the Sahel

H.T. NORRIS

ARIS & PHILLIPS LTD., Teddington House, Warminster, Wilts, England

ISBN 0 85668 031 1

Printed in England by Fyson & Co. Ltd. Bath.

Book cover written by one of the scholars of the Kel Es-Suq. The Arabic repeats the name of God, affirms His uniqueness and invokes blessings upon His Prophet.

CONTENTS

LIST OF ILLUSTRATIONS

PREFACE

The aim of this book is to provide an introduction to the Islamic life, culture and history of the Tuaregs, more particularly those in the Sahelian states of Mali and Niger. It is not a sociological study. There are several good books about the life of the Tuaregs as a whole, and some of the most noted are listed in the Bibliography. Names such as H. Duveyrier and H. Barth are world famous. Other research workers and specialists, Professors Nicolaisen and Prasse in Denmark, Edmond and Suzanne Bernus in France, to name only a few, have made valuable and detailed studies of Tuareg social, cultural and linguistic life today. For the past history of the Tuaregs, the works of Urvoy, Nicolas and Lhote are stimulating and authoritative, even if doubts may sometimes exist as to the accuracy of their conclusions. Lord Rennell Rodd's impressive work on the Tuaregs of Air is still of great value regarding their history.

My book is essentially an Islamist's assessment of the contribution made by the Muslim scholars and leaders of the Tuaregs to the cultural life of the Sahel. At the outset it should be stressed that access to material in order to make this assessment is very limited. To my knowledge no anthropological study of a Tuareg *Ineslemen* community has yet been attempted, nor, because of Sahelian disaster conditions, is it likely to be easy, and may now already be too late. A second obstacle is the lack of accessible Tuareg Arabic texts. The collections of manuscripts formerly housed in the Assemblée Nationale in Niamey and in certain private collections in the Sahel are the most valuable sources of documentation, but often difficult to consult. In the circumstances I have largely drawn upon my own collection of relevant texts photographed or copied in the field with the help of several Tuareg friends and scholars of repute.

I am grateful to the following for their hospitality and for giving me of their valuable time - Shaykh Muḥammad Ibrahīm and Shaykh Muḥammad al-Mu'min of Abalagh, Muḥammad 'Abd al-Raḥmān and Muḥammad al-Mukhtār, teachers of Arabic at Abalagh and Tchin Tebaraden respectively; Professor Qāsim al-Bayhaqī and his colleagues at the Lycée Franco-Arabe in Niamey, and al-Ḥājj 'Abdu Malam Mūsā, Secretary in the Niger Embassy in Algiers. I owe a particular debt to Ghubayd agg Alojaly of ORTN, Agades, a friend and correspondent of several year's standing. I also wish to thank a number of drought refugee scholars of the

Kel Intasar and Kel Es-Suq in Lazaret Camp, Niamey.

Several members of the Niger Government and its cultural Institutes were very helpful to me. I specially wish to thank M. Issaka Dankoussou, Executive Secretary, and M. Altinine ag Arias, Transcripteur Tamashek, both of the Centre for Oral Traditions, Niamey. Without assistance from The School of Oriental and African Studies, University of London, the research undertaken would not have been possible. Several British scholars have helped me in various ways, and in particular I am grateful to Professor J. Hunwick, Dr. J. Bynon and Dr. E. Sartain for their views and criticism.

Where for linguistic or other reasons Arabic and Tuareg names or words have been transcribed, particularly from manuscripts, then diacritics, macrons and other symbols which appear in the system of transcription in my other Saharan books has been followed.

Many of the theories and deductions I have expressed have not been arrived at after discussion with Tuareg scholars. Others have been duly acknowledged although I take due responsibility for any misinterpretation of their views. Long talks into the Sahelian and Saharan nights are among the most stimulating experiences of my life. Among the Niger Tuaregs I have been given some of the most generous hospitality I can recall, hospitality made all the more precious in the knowledge that its bestowers have been living through terrible times of dearth and misery.

H. T. Norris

November, 1974

ABBREVIATIONS

A.	*Abalagh,* Niger Republic, where the private collection of manuscripts owned by Shaykh Muhammad Ibrāhīm al-Aghlālī is located.
A.C.	*Agades Chronicles.* The texts in the private collection of the Sultan of Agades, Ibrāhīm b. ʻUmaru, unless otherwise stated.
A.N.	*Assemblée Nationale,* Niamey. The collection of manuscripts formerly housed in this building under the supervision of ex-President Boubou Hama.
B.I.F.A.N.	Bulletin de l'Institut fondamental d'Afrique Noire.
C.A.	*Chroniques d'Agadès,* translated by Y. Urvoy, Journal de la Société des Africanistes IV, pp. 145-177. Paris, 1934.
D.G.	The *De Gironcourt Collection* of papers preserved in the Bibliothèque Nationale de l'Institut de France, Paris. See Research Bulletin, Vol. 3, No. 2, July 1967, Centre of Arabic Documentation, Institut of African Studies, University of Ibadan.
E.C.P.T.	*The Ecology and Culture of the Pastoral Tuareg* by Johannes Nicolaisen, National Museum, Copenhagen, 1963.
I.M.	*Infāq al-Maysūr* by Shaykh Muḥammad Bello al-Fulānī.
N.A.	*Notes Africaines.*
N.T.	*Notes* on a late fifteenth century document concerning 'al-*Takrūr*' by John Hunwick in *African Perspectives,* C.U.P., 1970.
N.U.	*Naṣīḥat al-Umma* fī istiʻ māl al-rukḫsa by Sīdī Mawlay Muḥammad al-Hādī, (document no. 94, *A.N.*)
P.V.	*People of the Veil* by Francis Rennell Rodd, Macmillan, 1926.
T.D.N.C.A.	*Travels and Discoveries in North and Central Africa* by Henry Barth, Minerva Library, Ward Lock, 1890.
T.F.	*Tārīkh al-Fattāsh* by Ibn al-Mukhtār, Ar. text and Fr. tr. by O. Houdas and M. Delafosse, Paris 1913.
T.N.	*Tadhkirat* al-*Nisyān* fī Akhbār Mulūk al-Sūdān, Ar. text and Fr. tr. by O. Houdas, Paris, 1901.
T.S.	*Tārīkh al-Sūdān* by al-Saʻdī. Ar. text and Fr. tr. by O. Houdas, Paris, 1911.

INTRODUCTION

LINKS BETWEEN THE TUAREGS AND THE ANCIENT NEAR EAST AND THEIR FIRST CONTACT WITH THE ARABS.

Not so long ago it was seriously suggested that the Tuaregs of the Sahara were descendants of the Vandals or the Crusaders. Few, if any, would hold this view today. Yet the fanciful ideas which lay behind the conjecture should not be dismissed with contempt. Until recently little was known about the physical characteristics of the Saharan peoples and even now there are wide gaps in our knowledge which are still unfilled. The archaeology of the Tassili frescoes, the Garamantian Fezzan and Libya in general is of comparatively recent date. Perhaps the Egyptologists were the first to appreciate soundly based social and cultural parallels between the nomads of the Libyan interior, their Ancient Eastern predecessors and the civilisation of the Nile. It was they who were to provide major arguments for the establishment of the Tuaregs as an individual people in the 'Hamito-Semitic' world.

When the explorer Henri Barth visited the Sahara and the Sudan about 1850 he seemed to detect some continuous link between the peoples on the northern bank of the Niger and the ancient dwellers on the Nile. At Bourem (Būghem), not far from Gao, he made the following observation (1):-

> 'There is a remarkable tradition that a Pharaoh once came from Egypt to this spot, and again returned. This story would at least imply an early intercourse with Egypt, and should not I think, be viewed incredulously; for, if it had no foundation whatsoever, it would certainly attach to the capital of the nation itself, and not to a place which possesses no great historical importance. But on the other hand it is highly interesting to observe, that this is the spot where the great river which here makes a bend from a west-easterly into a southerly direction, is nearest to Egypt. Let it be further taken into account, that the inhabitants of the oasis of Aújila, which lies on the great commercial road from Egypt to these regions were the first who opened this part of Negroland to the intercourse of the Arabs. The whole history of Songhay points to Egypt; the itinerary of the route of the Nasamones, if rightly understood, inclines to this quarter, and it is easily to be understood how Herodotus, on receiving the news that so large a river was running eastward, in such a northerly latitude as nearly 18°, could conceive the opinion that this was the Upper Nile. Even in more modern times, we find Egyptian merchants established from the eleventh century in the town of Bíru or Waláta, side by side with those of Ghadamés and Tafilélet; the principal commerce of Gágho and Kukia was directed towards Egypt, and the large commercial entrepôt - Súk - of the tribe of the Tademékka, about one hundred miles from Burrum, on that great highroad, was evidently founded for that purpose.'

Among the most noted contributions to the thesis that the Tuaregs, the ancient Libyans and ultimately their Egyptian neighbours were once cloesely related, ethnically, culturally, linguistically and historically, was that of Oric Bates, who in his distinguished classic, 'The Eastern Libyans', written just before the First World War, brought to light many cultural resemblances which could only be explained by some common origins. The name of Meshwesh which occurs in Ancient Egyptian hieroglyphs seemed to indicate a powerful confederation of allied tribes to the west of the Nile. Bates suggested that Meshwesh was related morphologically to *MŠU* or *MZGH*, these latter radicals forming, so to speak, the common ethnic nomenclature of the Berbers, more particularly the 'free' or 'noble' people, the title of *Imashaghen* which, with its variants, has come to be applied by the Tuaregs, not only to their aristocracy, but also occasionally to themselves as a people.

The deductions of Oric Bates manifested certain customs common to the Tuaregs and the Ancient Libyans. He chose the Azgar confederation of the Tuareg peoples to illustrate many of his discoveries. He argued the similar status between the Libyan women and the Tuareg women and the common rights they enjoyed where these touched on the laws of succession and of inheritance. The councils or counsellors of the chiefs of the Libyan tribes and confederations, sometimes ten in number, seemed to be paralled in the Azgar confederation. The Libyan prince or Meryey, like a Tuareg *Amenukal* could be deposed and would commonly be succeeded by a kinsman on the distaff side. Chieftainship was of different grades. The 'Great Chief of the Meshwesh' was styled 'Great Chief of Chiefs' or as the Tuaregs would call him an *Amenukal*. Libyan chieftainship was often associated with the priesthood. One of them called Wayheset was termed in the Dakhila Stela of the XXIIIrd Dynasty as 'the prophet and chief Wayheset'. His office would thus combine that of *Amenukal* and *Imām/Kāhin*, a state of affairs by no means unknown to the Tuaregs, particularly in medieval times, and not unknown even today. (2)

In a lecture about the origin of the Tuaregs, read at the Royal Geographical Society in 1925, (3) Lord Francis Rennell Rodd highlighted, expanded and reinterpreted many of the points of identity which Oric Bates had discovered. Rodd had reservations about whether *MZGH* and *Imashaghen* were related. He sensed that the Tamashegh root *Ahegh* 'to raid' or 'to plunder' had far greater relevance to the function and the very earliest names of the Tuaregs, their nobility in particular. To date there is no final agreement in the debate although the opinions of Berberists tend to favour the views which Rodd had expressed. (4) Rodd stressed Tuareg diversity. 'The origin of their culture is one of the most interesting problems in North Africa, for not all of it seems derivable from Egypt. Its elucidation may ultimately provide an explanation of the identity and history of the Garamantes.' (5) This diversity of origin applied equally to the stratum of population in the Tuareg communities, excluding the negroid elements which were to feature prominently at a later age when intermarriage with slaves became so common. Therefore it would be an over-simplification to conclude that no element other than the Mediterranean type entered into the composition of the ancient Libyans and through them to their Tuareg descendants. (6)

Rodd, on balance, found it difficult to accept the view that the Tuaregs were all descended from a single stock. He inclined to the supposition that they stood apart from the sedentary Libyans. One theory he did not dismiss was that embodied in many legends about the origin of the Lemta who were undoubtedly held by the Arabs to be among the forebears of the Tuaregs. Lemta was one of the earliest names to appear in Arabic geographical and historical records. He felt that there were some grounds for believing that ancient Semitic Himyaritic or Mahri South Arabians had crossed from that peninsula to Africa as they had done in Ethiopia, and as part of the Lemta had penetrated into Sahelian regions via Darfur, Wadai and Bornu. The earliest trend of Tuareg migrations had been from east to west. It was the ultimate cause for the expulsion of Tuaregs from Bornu into Air and beyond it towards the territory of the Iwillimeden north of the Niger buckle. The flaw in his argument is now seen to be in the Arabic documentary evidence. This indicates that several respected Arab genealogists of early date dubbed all these South Arabian stories and epics as fiction, fabricated for purposes of lineal prestige and attributable to Yemenite authors whose writings had been diffused among the lettered Arabs in Africa. This seriously weakened the case for some genuine pre-Islamic Arabian origin for the Tuaregs of pre-history.

However, Rodd did not overstress his arguments. At the same time he held that some link between the Ancient Egyptian Temehu and the Tuaregs was beyond doubt. He also saw links between the Tuaregs and the Meshwesh and the Imukehek, a Libyan people who were defeated and captured by Amenhotep I. Their name seemed to recall the title of *Imohagh* or *Imashegh*, the Tuareg aristocratic class or 'caste'. The Ancient Libyans appeared from Egyptian art to have certain physical characteristics found among the Tuaregs, particularly the nobles. There was evidence for both curly or straight black hair, and dark brown eyes. A superficially mongoloid high-cheekboned person of low stature lived with another who was Mediterranean in appearance, long faced and so tall as to appear like a giant. The contrast has provoked diversity of opinion among physical anthropologists. Sir Denison Ross and Sir Flinders Petrie, who were present to hear Rodd's stimulating paper, had unusual observations to make on his theories from the points of view of the Oriental linguist and the Egyptologist.

The petroglyphs or rock engravings of horses and chariots in the Adrar-n-Ifoghas, suggest that the Tuaregs occupied the Central Sahara in the first millenium BC. They reached the Sudan by horse but subsequently they adopted the camel which enhanced their mobility. They were nomadic and advanced increasingly southwards. As the gradual dessication of the Sahara progressed, they hastened the retreat of the earlier negro sedentary population to more habitable regions. The horse and 'chariot' routes established high-ways for trans-Saharan commerce. The Roman punitive expeditions of Cornelius Balbus, Septimius Flaccus, Julius Maternus and others against the Garamantes of the Fezzan assuredly left their mark on the life and habits of the earliest Tuaregs in those regions.

Apart from the Romans, the Byzantines were to spread their culture and beliefs deep into the Sahara along these ancient routes. According to Procopius (c.558 AD) the inhabitants of Awjila and Ghadames were converted to Christianity under Justinian, and in 569 the Garamantes adopted the faith. It has been conjectured that certain Christian elements in Tuareg culture came from this quarter, the cross motif, social customs, names like Samuel, Saul and Daniel and words in Tamashegh like *mess* (God or master), *angélus* (angel), *abekkadh* (sin), and the season of spring *tafsit* (pl. *tifessai*).

Byzantine rule succumbed to the Islamic conquest in Egypt, Libya and Tunisia. In 640 AD 'Amr b. al-'Āṣ and the Arab armies invaded Egypt. He then advanced into Cyrenaica, and the task of conquest and occupation of large tracts of North Africa was to be achieved later by generals such as 'Uqba b. Nāfi', 'Abdullāh b. Sa'd b. Abī Sarḥ, 'Abdullāh b. Zubayr and others. Nowhere are the Tuaregs specifically mentioned in these wars and battles which were centred in the North African littoral. But it is reasonable to assume that at least some of them joined the military class of *mawālī*, the recruits of the Berber peoples. This recruiting occurred prior to 739 AD. Around the year 700 AD the beginning of the Islamisation of the Tuaregs of the Fezzan and its borders probably began.

The Danish anthropologist Johannes Nicolaisen who has studied the Northern Tuaregs has argued the case for the correlation of black-skin tents raised on T-shaped posts and dromedary herds. These are pointers to culture contact with Arabic-speaking peoples who had entered the territories of the Tuaregs at a date not long after first Arab conquests, Arabs who influenced Tuareg desert habits in these respects. (7) The theory is an interesting one and on the face of it plausible but conclusive proof is ruled out by the almost total lack of early Arabic documentary evidence before the tenth century to corroborate it. Following the arguments of Stephane Gsell that black tents were late-comers to Berber Africa, were possibly unknown to them before the Arab invasion, but were in common use in the eighth century and were almost indistinguishable from tents of the Arabs, Nicolaisen has suggested that -

> 'We cannot disregard the possibility that black tents were known in Northern Africa before the first Arab invasion. But there can be little doubt that outside of the Atlas black tents are characteristic of Arabic-speaking people, and we seem to be on safe ground if we state that the Arabs are responsible for the present fairly large distribution of black tents in the desert regions between the Red Sea and the Atlantic.'

If it is possible to trace any direct link between the first impact of the Arabs and their Islamic way of life on the Tuaregs then it may have begun with the adoption of elements of material culture and breeding habits. Little by little, social institutions were copied or adapted. Inevitably, there was some comprehension of the religion which had reformulated pre-Islamic beliefs in the Arabian peninsula. Some of these pre-Islamic beliefs were also adopted and the new faith was modified by the cults and social systems of the Ancient Libyans and their descendants. Material culture presaged later borrowings from every form of Islamic culture. It is surprising that early evidence is so lacking, yet it is even more surprising that despite the scanty evidence, both documentary and archaeological, there seems sufficient grounds for drawing parallels between Ancient Libyan peoples and the Tuaregs and to accept some unbroken legacy of ancient customs and ideas. (8)

NOTES

1) See Barth, *T.N.C.A.*, p. 427
2) See Oric Bates, *The Eastern Libyans*, pp. 110-117, and references in his book under *Imushagh* and *Azgar.*
3) The *Geographical Journal*, Vol. LXVII(I), January, 1926, pp. 27-52.
4) See K.G. Prasse, *L'origine* du mot Amāziy. *Acta Orientalia*, 3-4. pp. 197-200. Copenhagen 1959.
5) Rodd, *op. cit.*, p. 33
6) *ibid*, pp. 34-36, 43-46.
7) Johannes Nicolaisen, *Folk*, Vol. 1, 1959, Copenhagen, pp. 115-127.
8) See in particular the contributions to J. and Th. Bynon, *Hamito-Semitica*, Mouton, 1975.

CHAPTER I

TUAREG CENTRES AND SOCIETIES

The peoples who speak the Tamashegh tongue, known to the Western world as the Tuaregs, inhabit the Sahara and Sahel between Timbuctoo and Bilma , In Salih in Algeria and Kano in Nigeria. They are nominally Muslim and share many customs and ways of life with other Sahelian peoples who are their neighbours, the Moors, the Fulani and the Teda. Yet they are among the most distinct people in the Muslim world. The agile and proud veiled cameleer, sword-girt and seated upright in a chair-like saddle is as bold an individual as any who made his mark on African history. Some of them still use their unique *Tifinagh* script, which links them to societies and syllabaries of the ancient world. Many a traveller has reckoned their customs to be something alien in the world of Islam. Tuareg mobility, their combination of harshness and a dignified gentleness, have earned them much praise and an equal amount of distrust and abuse. Yet, are they as unique as is sometimes claimed?

Much depends on where they live. In the Sahel states of Mali and Niger they are a substantial part of a very mixed sedentary or nomadic population. In the north, in parts of Algeria and the Libyan Fezzan, they are scanty in number with Arab nomads and few sedentaries as their neighbours. Their distinction from the Arabs, which was once strongly stressed by their champions, has of late been re-appraised by knowledgable scholars who know the Algerian Tuaregs well. Johannes Nicolaisen has proposed that some of the dominating noble Tuaregs emigrated from Libya after the Arabs had arrived. It is probable that the political systems and material culture of these northern Tuaregs were influenced by the Arabs at an early date. (1)

There are marked differences in day to day life between the Tuaregs in the northern deserts and those of the Sahelian region. The latter has ancient commercial routes running west to east and east to west. Politically, the Tuaregs there have been subject to, or have cooperated with, negro empires of major power and wealth in Mali and in Niger. The habitat of the southern Tuaregs has been centred in two Massifs, the Adrar-n-Ifoghas and Air, and in the adjacent deserts, plains and valleys of Azawagh, Tagedda, Azawād and the southlands near the Niger river and in Hausaland.

The Adrar-n-Ifoghas is a chain of mountains in the Sahara of Mali. It varies in height between 1600 and 2600 feet. Amidst the mountains there are gravel plains and wadi beds. The Adrar is within the region of the autumn monsoon rains, and its vegetation is typically Sahelian, annual and perennial grasses, thorny shrubs and trees. Most pasture and drinking water for humans and animals depend directly on regular rainfall. (2)

The ruined town of Tadamakkat in the Adrar-n-Ifoghas is of peculiar significance to the Tuaregs. This is not only because of its bygone commercial importance, but because it provided some sort of spiritual and academic home. In semi-legendary Tadamakkat the Tuareg Islamic scholars of the Central Sahara - the *Ineslemen* Kel Es-Suq - located many of their epics and through it they attached their traditions to those of the world-wide Muslim community.

Tadamakkat - believed by many to be buried beneath the ruins of a site known nowadays as As-Sūq - the market - was a second Mecca to the Muslim Tuaregs. In their belief the sanctified hooves of the steed of 'Oqba, the Arab conqueror of Africa had hallowed its sand and rock. The miraculous bones of the Prophet's Companions and Helpers had been interred in its graveyards. The town was sited between two mountains, exactly like Mecca. The Arab geographer al-Bakrī recorded that in his day (d. 1094) Tadamakkat signified in Berber 'the image or replica of Mecca'.

The Air Massif in Niger is on a far grander scale. Here the peaks rise to 6000 feet or more, and the whole of the Air is a kind of island some 300 miles long and 150 miles broad. The valleys are green with fan palms, acacias and scattered palms. The monsoon rains may come as a raging torrent. To the north of Agades, capital of Air, there are gardens of wheat, onions and tomatoes. The crops are irrigated from permanent wells. At Iferouane in the north of Air camels may find rich grazing and in the past, though to a lesser degree in the present day, the Air Massif was able to support a semi-nomadic Tuareg population of between 10,000 and 20,000 people. At the end of each year hundreds of Air camels were involved in the caravan which crossed over 400 miles of the eastern Tenere desert to the oasis of Bilma. The camels were loaded with rock salt which was mined by hand from water-filled pits. The salt was carried back to Air and from thence to Hausaland where it was in great demand. Despite recent drought much of this commerce still survives.

The salt pans at Tagedda are of more ancient date than those at Bilma. The salt-workings of Tagedda-n-Tesemt are situated some 180 kilometers to the north west of Agades. They lie to the south of the Eghazar Wa-n-Agadez, a shallow wadi which drains the depression of Tagedda, a natural basin of wide horizons edged by sandstone rocks and beds of dry sand. Behind the village of Tagedda-n-Tesemt is a hill called Bogonuten. It is artificial, raised by the labours of men from the salt pans.

Local tradition maintains that these salt workings were only discovered about 1750, though they would seem to be older than this. Behind Bogonuten is an area of small craters and pools, man-made, for the exploitation of the salt. Saline soil is soaked in large basins. The water which is then saturated with the salt is diverted and drained into smaller basins and pools where it is allowed to evaporate in the wind and heat of the sun, a two-day operation. Then, the salt is collected and made into 'loaves' and triangular plaques which are marked with a cross - the *tanasafut* - camel mark of the Inussufen tribe, or the mark of the Ishsherifen, the Iswaghen, or the Sultan of Agades who owns the salt workings. The bars are ready to be sold, a regular occupation from the autumn onwards. They are sold to caravans bringing millet from the south, or local caravans going to Hausaland for commercial exchange. At times as many as 5,000 bars of salt a year leave for the south.

To the north of Bogonuten, the route to Algeria leads into the peaks of the Hoggar, bounded to the west by the Tanezrouft, the waste which seems to correspond to the territory of the medieval Guenziga (Wanziga), the deserts between Tilimsān and Timbuctoo in which was located the waterless stretch of 'Gogdem'. Thus named by the traveller Leo Africanus, it would apparently indicate a terrain of 'shaven headed' plateaux (Ag(Agadem)), or perhaps *Agogdan (m)* a Tamashegh word made up from a command to take sufficient supply of water or provisions for a dangerous crossing, (*Agu aygdan*). To the east of Bogonuten are the levels of the Eghazar - the *Bādiyat Tageddā* of Arabic texts - and faintly visible on the horizon the outliers of the Air massif, hills and slopes which define the boundaries of the whole region of 'medieval Tagedda'. For the latter was not one town, but a region, a province of three *Quṣūr*, to quote Malfante who visited Tuwāt in 1447. Tagedda was not only Tagedda-n-Tesemt, but Tagedda-n-Tagheyt (of the fan palm), Tagedda-n-Adrar (of the mountain) and several other villages and small towns, among them Anū-Ṣamman, quite close to Agades.

Azawagh is totally different. The name indicates a type of plain, but more especially it denotes all the country between the Adar plateau in southern Niger and the valleys of Air. Azawagh is divided between a region of dead dunes in the centre, the Saharan Tenere of Tamesna in the north, and the sandstone plateaux of Tagama to the north-east where are to be found large trees and the monsoon water pools and broad lakes. Azawagh is an open land, in contact with the millet lands of the south and the northern desert routes. To the Iwillimeden Tuaregs who dwell in it, Azawagh is a beautiful land, a land of rocks like tree trunks, game, even fish it is said, and there are potsherds and ruins which tell of former habitations and tombs of men long forgotten or held in sanctity.

One further region in which the Tuaregs, side by side with the Kunta Moors, established ancient centres of Islamic learning is that known as Azawād. It is situated to the north of Timbuctoo and adjoins the present frontier between Mali and Mauritania. In it is to be found a decayed caravan town called Arawān, and it was in this far west of the Tuareg homeland that the Kel Intasar were to evolve their highly original society. They borrowed many ideas from their Moorish neighbours but succeeded in preserving a genuinely Tuareg personality. In Azawād the Moors and Tuaregs competed for supremacy.

One of the simplest descriptions of present-day Tuareg society is to be found in a grammar of the Tamashegh dialect of Air. (3) The unnamed informant, in a passage of dialogue, gives a Tuareg view of the distribution of his people, its principal divisions and a summary of its chiefly authorities:-

'At the present time during which we live, the noble *Imashaghen* (var. *Imajaghen*) are not many in number. The drum (*eṭṭebel*) of the *Amenukal* has only one tribe (which can choose it.). The *Amenukal* is chosen (chief) in a specific tribe. After the nobles come the vassals (*Imghad*). After the vassal comes the slave *(Akli).* Each slave has his master, so does the woman slave or servant. He abides in his tent, he pastures his herd of animals, he goes to water, and he carries out his work and labour.

The artisans (*Ineden*) are in the wild and in the villages. They make swords and saddles. The *Ighawalen* are slaves who have obtained their liberty.

The tribes in the countries of the Tuaregs are many in number. The names of the tribes in the Ajjer and the Fezzan (*Targa*) are the Uraghen, the Imeqqeghesen, the Imenan and the Ihadanaren. The Ahaggar have numerous tribes. Their chief is the *Amenukal.* He is one of the Kel Ghela. Also to be found are the Taytoq, Dag-Ghali, Ajuh-n-Tele, Ayt Loayen, Iseqqemaren and others.

As for the people of Air (Kel Ayr), their chief is the *Amenukal* (Sultan) of Agades. Their tribes are the Kel Ferwan, Kel Tadele, Kel Fadey, Igdalen, Kel Gharus, Ikazkazen and Iberdiyanan. But one tribe is very important. It is named the Kel 'We (Kel Away). Their chief is called the *Anastafidet.* In this tribe are the Kel Ghazer, Kel Tafidet, Kel Timia, Kel Bagzan, Kel Aziny-Eres and others.

In the land of the Adrar (-n-Ifoghas) there is only one *Amenukal.* Its chief is the chief of the Ifoghas and the Ednan. The districts of the Sudan are very many, and there are numerous Tuaregs in them; those of Zinder, Tahoua, Filingué, Menaka and up to and beyond Timbuctoo. Their name is Iwillimeden. The tribes are many, Tademaket, Kel Intasar, Tangeregif, Tagaregare, Kel Geres (their head, Tanbari.)

The chief of these tribes is an *Amenukal.* I have heard it said that the Iwillimeden have two chiefs, but I know not whether it be true or false.'

The highly stratified class structure of Tuareg society bears a resemblance to that of the Moors in the adjacent regions of the Hodh and Timbuctoo. Some parallels are historically plausible, and there may well be substance in the argument for a common kinship in the early medieval period, if not earlier. The aristocracy of the Mauritanian Banū Ḥassān or Ma'qil, or the Bdūkalen Ṣanhāja, who, it is believed, preceded them, seem to pair the *Imashaghen* nobles in Sahelian Tuareg society.

The lettered Islamic Tuaregs, known as the *Ineslemen* seem to pair the *Murābiṭīn* or Zwāya among the Moors, but it is far from certain that a parallel is apt. In the west, among the Moors, the Zwāya virtually compete with the Banū Ḥassān in power and status. Their role in many regions is clearly defined. Among the Tuaregs the *Ineslemen* do not seem to correspond to a comparable coherent body or class. Only in a few areas do they wield any authority, and by and large the Tuaregs deem them to be semi-vassals. 'The path followed by the *Imashaghen* leads one way, the way of the 'marabout' is another.' However, in certain places and at certain times, the *Ineslemen* wrested authority from the *Imashaghen* nobility, and in such instances their influence has been dynamic and profound, not merely an Islamic influence, amorphous and ineffectual, but like a yeast leavening the dough.

Beneath the *Imashaghen* and the *Ineslemen* are the *Imghad* vassals and the *Iklan* slaves. Some similarities may be detected between them and the *Laḥma, Ḥarāṭīn* and the *'Abīd* in Mauritanian communities.

The Tuaregs, more particularly the Ahaggaren, once categorised slaves into two types. The *Iklan* were in general household slaves, the *Ighawalen* were preoccupied with out-of-door activities. *Iklan* (singular *Akli*) comes from a root meaning 'to be black'. In origin they were negros captured in the Sudan. In the Hoggar they formed a separate class which was not tribal, while elsewhere in the Sahel this was by no means the case. Among the Ahaggaren, slaves were well treated and shared meals with their masters, and their children were brought up together. The *Iklan* could inherit, they could possess animals and had a right to their produce. Slaves could not marry without the consent of their masters. The Ahaggaren took slaves as concubines. The offspring were free but were not of the same class as their father although they could inherit from him. Some *Iklan* were half-manumitted. They became herders and were known as *Iklan-n-Egaf* or 'dune captives'. They carried out arts and crafts, were organised into tribes, were endogamous and remained subject to a vassal or a noble tribe. In Air, the *Iklan* were primarily concerned with garden cultivation and pastoral duties. They were in practise permitted to own property and always had hope of manumission with a consequent change to status of *Imghad* or vassals.

The *Ighawalen* are often called Bella or Buzu by non-Tuaregs. They are herders of live stock, especially camels, and seem higher up the social ladder than the *Iklan*. They have a greater proportion of Tuareg blood, and because of their mobility they have found freedom in the Sahelian cities of the south, or a richer life there. Barth visited the town of Bichi, now in Northern Nigeria. The Buzu of the Itisen there born of free mothers cultivated fields around the town for their overlords. The south also offered employment in a military capacity, a profession which would automatically change the status of the Buzu, bring them wealth and ensure them their freedom.

There is insufficient documentary evidence to show conclusively Tuareg borrowing from the Moors to an extent which permits no independant evolution in Tuareg societies, one unconnected with the evolution of the class structures among the Moors, the Rgaybāt, and other Saharan and Sahelian peoples.

Yet it is precisely such borrowing from the Mauritanian Moors which has been the cornerstone of the theories of Francis Nicolas and others who have tried to trace the historical evolution of Tuareg institutions. In their view two systems compete. The first maintains descendence through the male line and brother's son. The second maintains descendence through the female line, through the *teġeze*, that is to say, 'mother's house'. In the latter succession, after a brother, it is the eldest son of the maternal aunt or the eldest son of the eldest sister who have preference in the political power of the *eṭṭebel*.

This Tamashegh word has many senses. It is derived from an Arabic word (*ṭabl*) denoting a drum, tribute, or a man's kinship group. This latter sense of *ṭabl* is certainly pre-Islamic, and it is recorded in early Arabic lexicons. But the *eṭṭebel* among the Tuaregs seems to denote not only the drum of chiefly authority, but 'drum chief' and 'drum group'. Some women have the power to transmit the right of succession, and they are said to have the *eṭṭebel*. The power to transmit the right of succession is inherited by the daughters of a woman who has it, and in turn by her daughters and so on, with priority in order of seniority.

The gulf between the 'patrilineal system' and the 'matrilineal system' in the view of Nicolas is a tribal one. The Iwillimeden, the Kel Es-Suq and Kel Intasar owe their system directly to the Moors, while the Kel Ahaggar, Kel Air and Kel

Geres have stubbornly followed what he believed to be a traditional and ancient succession.

'The tendency of present groups to switch more and more into the rule of patriarchal devolution is to be noticed, on the one hand among those whose affinities link them with the West (peoples who have their origin in the veiled Ṣanhāja of Mauritania or of the Mali Adrar) and on the other among those who have been Islamized the most.' (4) In short, the switch in succession is a prime indicator of the force of Tuareg Islam, an Islam which owes its vitality and power to elements entirely outside the natural habitat and social systems of the Tuareg peoples. This theory is clearly an over-simplification. Tuareg society has always been highly varied, and a society open to ideas from every quarter. Historical records and oral traditions reveal the reality to be complex and diverse in date, character and degree.

In the pages which follow, some light may be cast on this and other aspects of Muslim practise in Tuareg society. Perhaps the story of their past will never be sufficiently known to uncover all the motives behind their social and politicial history. Any record, however, demands a written format and a script and language to record it. Since Arabic is that language in all the societies of the Sahel, it is through Arabic records alone, it would seem, that the evolution can be cautiously traced and its landmarks eventually established.

NOTES

1. For varied views on this whole question see:-

   Folk, Copenhagen, pp. 115-127.
   W. Robertson Smith, *Kinship and Marriage in Early Arabia*, Cambridge, 1885, p. 95.
   'The Origin of the Tuareg', by Francis Rodd, *The Geographical Journal*, Vol. LXVII (1), January 1926, p. 49.
   Emrys Peters, 'The Proliferation of Segments in the Lineage of the Bedouin of Cyrenaica', Curl Bequest Prize Essay, 1959. *Journal of the Royal Anthropological Institute*, Vol. 90, Parts I and II, 1960, pp. 29-53.
   Lloyd Cabot Briggs and Marceau Gast, 'Descent, Inheritance and Succession among the Tuareg of the Ahaggar', paper presented to the IXth International Congress of Anthropological and Ethnological Sciences, Chicago, Aug. to Sept. 1973, pp. 1-15.

2. Jeremy Swift, 'Disaster and a Sahelian nomad economy.' Report of the 1973 Symposium, *Drought in Africa,* SOAS, pp. 71-78.

3. *Initiation à la langue des Touaregs de l'Aïr*, published by the Fraternité Charles De Foucauld, Agades (Niger), 1968, pp. 81-84.

4. See Francis Nicolas, 'Etude sur la coutume et la tradition. Matriarcat et Patriarcat, Mémoires de l'Institut Français d'Afrique Noire (Contribution à l'Etude de l'Aïr), pp. 491-496. Paris, 1950.
   For further details on Tuareg societies, class names and major tribal divisions see the appendices of this book, pp 221-226.

CHAPTER II

THE 'EQUESTRIAN DIVINER' AND THE 'GARAMANTIAN CHARIOTEER'.

'The noise of a whip, and the noise of the rattling of the wheels, and of the prancing horses, and of the jumping chariots.' Nahum III, v.2.

It is commonly held that the Tuaregs have been given their name by the Arabs. There is a root in the Arabic language which indicates 'he abandoned' *(taraka).* The Tuaregs are the 'abandoners of the Islamic faith'. Some North African Arabs, for pejorative reasons, have spread this report. (1) But the views of the origin of the abandonment, what was abandoned, and who were the abandoners, often differ.

One legend from the Libyan oasis of Ghadames has no apparent connection with Islam. The Tuaregs had been involved in an abandonment for different reasons. To introduce the tale basic material from the Arabian saga of the Banū Hilāl has been used. (2)

'As for their being named 'Tawārik' it was that in bygone years there was a man who was called Dhiyāb al-Hilālī. He was near Tunis with his tribe and pasturing herds. They were fearful. He posed a choice to his herders, 'To keep the camels or else preserve the tribe?' 'Keep the camels,' they replied. So he took with him forty men of his tribe, and he left in their company to go to the camels.'

'Dhiyāb had a mare which drank the milk of a certain camel. It was smitten by an *'ifrīt* of the jinn', and its milk diminished. Dhiyāb was informed of this misfortune, so he set out to find the *'ifrīt*, going from one place to another. One day he passed by a certain town. At its gate he saw a bowl of food and a very young girl. Each day the town gave to the *'ifrīt* a bowl of food and a young girl. Dhiyāb pondered the affair, then suddenly he heard a noise like a storm of thunderbolts, and he saw the *'ifrīt* approaching. He smote it with a mighty blow and killed it.'

'The town was full of joy, and its inhabitants said to him, 'Ask what you will.' 'Give me forty virgins.' They were presented, and he brought them to his companions. For some time they remained married to them. Then when Sa'd al-Labīb came for them Dhiyab and his companions returned to his tribe. The women remained behind and alone. Those who were pregnant and gave birth after their husbands' departure called their offspring 'Tawārik', because their fathers had abandoned and forsaken them'

Among the themes of this legend are two which shed light on the ideas of social relationship which, it was believed, brought Tuareg society into being. The first is the common lineal bond of all the Tuaregs through their mothers, for, if the legend were true, paternal relationship was either unknown or of wholly subordinate significance. The second theme has a historical hypothesis at its heart. At some point of time there was allgedly an intermarriage between incoming Arabian nomads and the autocthonous dwellers in the desert. Unlike the countless patrilineal lineages which were later devised, this intermarriage was of no eponymic consequence in the evolution of Tuareg social systems. The importance lay in the foundation of a ruling house or class by a stranger of Arabian blood and by the implication that the Tuaregs had once lived in an environment urban in part or in whole. Something of this idea survives in the name of Massūfa or Inussufen - one frequently given by medieval Muslim writers to the Tuaregs. They are said to have been called thus because they were dwellers in the desert, but were not 'of the desert'. Deep down there was a belief that these desert men once knew a more settled habitat, and that in some way they were heirs to Byzantium or to Imperial Rome.

The Tuaregs, the Fulanis, the Hausa and the Arab tribes of Lake Chad and Bornu have adopted this Hilālī story and have rephrased its theme. Borrowed from the sophisticated epics of the Banū Hilāl in North Africa, 'master of propagation', Abū Zayd, (Bā Yazīd), or his kinsman Dhiyab became the legendary founder of the Hausa and other Sahelian states or tribes.

The story has been diffused from the Empty Quarter of Arabia to Tunisia, then to the Sahel. (3) The warrior on a horse, father of a people who have been 'abandoned' or who allege that their lineage begins in the progeny of this equestrian commander will be seen to emerge as a hero among the Tuaregs.

As for the 'abandoned' (*tawārik*) the lettered of the Sahel hardly know them. The Arabic letters in their texts are fairly consistently TRQ/ṬRQ/TRG. These show no connection whatsoever with the deprecatory Arabic root. It is likely that a tribe, confederation, perhaps a people who dwelt in the Fezzan called either the Targa or the Uraghen, is the most plausible origin for the Tuaregs. (4)

The use of one proper name to indicate all the Tuaregs was common practise among Arabic writers. In the medieval period two names were frequently used to denote them. While the 'veiled Peoples' from the Atlantic to Libya were of the family of Ṣanhāja (Ṣanāhija in more recent texts), the Central Saharan region and its borders were the particular domain of either the Lamṭa or the Massūfa. These names also indicated nomads elsewhere but the region between Timbuctoo and the Fezzan, Tuwāt and Agades - the heartlands of the Tuaregs of today - were the central domain of the Lamṭa and the Massūfa.

It is now impossible to know what was the clear difference between these peoples. The Lamṭa at one time may have meant all the Tuaregs, the Massūfa more specifically certain along the southern fringe of the Sahara and the Sahel border, particularly on the Mali and Mauritanian frontier and in parts of Air.

When the earliest Arabic records refer to them the Lamṭa and the Massūfa were desert dwellers. The former made, and carried, giant oryx-skin shields, and they were well established in parts of the Fezzan. It seems from the *Kitāb al-Buldān* (5) by Aḥmad b. Abī Ya'qūb al-Ya'qūbi (d. 897/905) that in the remoter regions of the Fezzan in the ninth century, the nomadic population was essentially Tuareg, or akin to the Tuaregs:-

'Further to the south is found the country of Zawīla, inhabited by Muslims all Ibāḍīs who perform the pilgrimage. They indulge in the commerce of Sudanese slaves, whom they have reduced into captivity. These belong to the tribes of the Mīra, Zaghāwa, Maruwa and to other negro peoples in their vicinity. I have been assured that the Sudanese princes sell their subjects without juridical pretext and without any motive, following the shares and spoils of war. It is from Zawīla that the Zawīla hides come. It is a region of palm-groves, millet crops and other cereals. There are to be found individuals who come from Khurasan, Basra and Kufa. Beyond Zawīla, a distance of some fifteen days march is to be found the town of Kuwwār. (6) It is inhabited by a very mixed Muslim population, mostly Berber, who sell negroes. Between Zawīla and Kuwwār, and in the districts of Zawīla going towards Awjila and Ajdābiya live a group called the Lamṭa who much resemble Berbers. It is they who manufacture the white (antelope/oryx?) shields called Lamṭī shields....'

The presence of the Lamṭa in the Fezzan during the ninth century is confirmed, so is a route for slaves leading into Niger from Libya. There was also an important Oriental Khārijite Ibāḍī influence in a south-westerly direction. (7) Al-Ya'qūbi's passage confirms a persistent Tuareg tradition that the north-east, the Awjila region in particular, was the starting point for their wanderings. The Lamṭa were not the only 'Tuaregs' in this region. They also had elements of the Huwwāra as their neighbours. In the eleventh century when al-Bakrī was to write his *Kitāb al-Masālik wal-Mamālik* the area to the south of Tripoli towards Waddān was inhabited by Huwwāra who lived in hair tents and in camps. Near Qaṣr Ibn Maymūn a statue of Girza (Krza) was raised on a hill, and this deity - the son of the Libyan Ammon - was sacrificed to. His healing powers were sought, and he was asked to bestow material benefits. This paganism was mentioned by the Byzantine Corippus and others. Al-Bakrī was aware that pagan rites continued in his days and confirms the superficial Islamisation of many nomad Berbers at the gate-way to the Fezzan. The Azgar also roamed in the region of Zawīla with their camels.

Thus in the border areas of Libya, Algeria and Niger, elements of the Lamṭa, Huwwāra - Ahaggaren Tuaregs - Targa, and other groups were in contact at an early date, under the spiritual influence of the Khārijites and had open access to routes which led to Air and the Niger buckle. At about the same time the Massūfa joined their company.

The wanderings of the Lamṭa, the Targa and the Massūfa is a remarkable phenomenon in North African history. Somehow along the northern bank of the Niger these confederations were to tread the salt routes in the deserts of Mali and to frequent the major desert entrepots. Everywhere these veiled nomads wandered, they were identifiable by their manufacture of shields, a matrilineal-type social structure, their service as guides or their commerce in salt and slaves.

But amidst this sweeping portrait of the Tuaregs, their true name, the name they use themselves, the *Imashaghen* or *Imohagh* - 'the noble and the free' - does not appear. If it does, at this period, it is to be found in one locality, the Tuareg capital in the Middle Ages, Tadamakkat.

II

Ibn Ḥawqal, writing a century earlier than al-Bakrī, offers the most comprehensive description of the Tuaregs of Tadamakkat. Some tribes he mentions still survive. The facts are brief. Nothing is recorded in detail about their social life. Were they all kinsfolk descended from one 'mother' (*tawshiten*), or patrilineal clans as the Arabic text implies? The rulers of Tadamakkat who may have been part Tuareg, part Sudanese, were probably at least deemed to be *Imashaghen.* Their name, Banū Tānamāk, in all likelihood, has some connection with *Imashegh* or *Imohagh.* There is also the possibility that they may have been a people referred to by Pliny in his *Natural History* (8) as the Libyan Tamiago *natio*, groups of whom may be conjectured, moved into the region known today as the Adrar-n-Ifoghas.

Tadamakkat was an important centre with a multiracial community. It was on a chariot route in Classical times, and it had links with the Ibāḍīs of the Jabal Nufūsa in Tripolitania, with Ouargla (Wārijla) in Algeria and with Gao.

Commerce gave it a cosmopolitan character. There were many slaves, and its rulers were lettered.

There are persistent traditions that Khārijite Islam had an influence in shaping the earliest Islamic beliefs of the Tuaregs. The presence of Basrans and Kufans in Zawīla might well have ensured some contact with the Khārijite urban and beduin Muslims of the Umayyad East. Certain Khārijite customs would not be irreconcilable with some Tuareg customs as we now know them. Women were of high status, they often fought in battle and dressed like men. There were women Imāms. The Kharijites had marital rules unlike other Muslims, and the company of the Qurrā' or 'Qur'ān reciters' and its interpreters were almost a sacerdotal class like the later Tuareg *Ineslemen.* Europeans who knew the Tuaregs traced several (9) similarities between the Ibāḍī Khārijites and the beliefs and customs of the Tuaregs.

During the early medieval period the Tuaregs not only ruled Tadamakkat independently, or under the sovereignty of Mali, they also dominated Azawagh and Air. Several of the traditions of the Air Tuaregs today affirm the early date of their control of the Mali and Niger mountains. The sequence of their migrations into Air and its vicinity is open to conflicting interpretations. Unfortunately none is conclusively confirmed by external documentary evidence.

Lettered Tuaregs believe that the Barkuray or Balkoray were among the earliest Tuareg groups to arrive, though who these people were is far from clear. Perhaps they were Lamṭa. They came from Awjila, together with the Massūfa (Inussufen), the Illisawen and the Imaskikiyen about the eleventh century. They conquered Air. The Itisen followed them in the fourteenth century, and they overcame their predecessors. In the sixteenth century the Barkuray emigrated to the area of (In)Ṭaduq - east of the Adrar-n-Ifoghas - which they eventually controlled. Wars took place between them and the Itisen who were traditionally centred in a 'capital' at Asōday (Assodé) in the Air Massif. Both tribes were by that time under the nominal rule of the Sultan of Air.

The view of these Tuaregs is not dissimilar from the records (10) which survive in the so-called 'Agades Chronicles'. A federation of clans from Awjila is mentioned there. They comprise the Sandal, (which included the Itisen), the Ifadalen, the Ijadaranen, and the Izagharen. To these were joined the Ilisawen, the Barkuray, the Imaskikiyen (var. Imiskikkin) and the Inussufen. The latter seemed to have enjoyed a role which suggests the status of a lettered, commercially privileged Air establishment. It should be noted that it is precisely these latter tribes which allegedly arrived in Air before all others. To the Inussufen may be added the Igdalen, now centred near In Gall.

Other Air groups like the Kel Geres and the Kel Away (Owi) came later, the former perhaps between the twelfth and the fourteenth centuries, the latter perhaps as late as the sixteenth and seventeenth centuries. They, with the Kel Ferwan, pushed the Kel Geres and the Itisen towards the south. Lastly, in the eighteenth century, the Kel Fadey settled near In Gall, and the Kel Tamat, the Ikazkazen, the Ifoghas and the Taitoq came to nomadise in Air itself. All these 'waves' from the first to the last dispossessed the negro Goberawa of Abzen (Air being the Berber name). Reputedly it was the Igdalen, Inussufen and the Barkuray who dispossessed them first of all.

Arabic sources offer little in confirmation or refutation of any or all of the Tuareg claims. Early Tuareg domination of Air would seem to be confirmed by al-Bakrī who mentioned that, 'It is still claimed that Kawkaw (Gao) is a surname, reproduced on the drum by imitative sounds. Likewise for the people of Azwar (Azawagh), Hayr (Air) or of Zawīla, one says that the drums repeat Zawīla-Zawīla.' The Berber Hayr/Air and not Absen/Asben, the most ancient Gobirawa name for the Massif is employed, and communications with Zawīla and Libya stressed. It would be safe to assume that Tadamakkat or independant Tuareg groups had already extended their influence over Air.

Who were these Tuaregs roaming the desert of Tadamakkat, Zawīla and the regions between them and Sijilmāsa? Ibn Ḥawqal confirms that they include the Massūfa (Inussufen), the Tarja (Targa), the Lamṭa, the Lamtūna, the Fadāla (Ifadalen), the Immikiten, and the Izagaren. The last three are among the Kel Innik (11) who were among the Tuaregs to enter Air from the Fezzan. If Ibn Ḥawqal does not state that they were in Air itself, at least they were in its vicinity. The tribe written Kīl Makzen is different. For if they are the Kel Bagzan (Kel Magzan) it would not only confirm that the Itisen - of whom they form a part - were already in Air in the tenth century, but that they had settled in the vicinity of Bagzan mountain, a region which some have argued was known in Classical times and was reached by the Garamantes of Garama (Jerma) in the Fezzan by their wheeled chariots or by horse.

III

The Berber queen and the 'Garamantian Charioteer'.

The phenomenon of a matriarchal, matrilineal or matriocal-type of kinship system forcibly struck Arab Muslims when they first mixed with the Tuaregs. They drew attention to it - invariably with disfavour - and on certain occasions identified an ancestress of a *tawshit*, a tribe or clan who all claimed descent from the same mother, with a queen, or a woman of some supernatural powers or extraordinary physique. These 'queens' of the Tuaregs, or their kinsfolk, were comparable with the Kāhina in Algeria or the empresses of other Berber peoples against whom the Arabs fought. The earliest Arab ideas were a combination of legend and hearsay. In their turn the Tuaregs adopted Arabian ideas. Fable and historical dress were brought together into a theme, countless in its variations. (12)

One legend which may have influenced Oriental ideas about North Africa was that of the Queen of Ethiopia, Candace (Qindāqa), whose domain in some accounts was switched from the Upper Nile to the area of Qayrawān (Samūra) or Qamūda/ Qamūna, the Roman and Byzantine provinces of Sbeitla in Tunisia. With this switch from Ethiopia to Tunisia, other personalities who had any connection with this fabulous Queen were likewise reorientated.

The Copts were good weavers of tales, and their ideas had some influence on the Arabic writers in Egypt. Coptic plots preserved the memory of 'Libyan' inroads into the Nile valley since Pharaonic times. Several ideas emerged. The first of these was a Berber locality named Qamūda or Qamūna vaguely to the west of Egypt. It was inhabited by a Berber queen who was a sorceress and ruled the Berbers to the borders of Egypt. She was the personification of a matriarchy, but she was challenged by a Berber giant who is sometimes called Jālūt (Goliath), at other times Māzīgh b. Kan'ān . He was a rival and foe to Qamūna and its queen.

Something of this myth survives among the Tuareg ancestresses of the Ahaggar nobility. Tin Hinan, according to local belief, dwelt in a fortress at Abalessa. According to some Tuaregs, however, the true builder of the fort was a Christian or a Byzantine named Jalouta (Jālūt) who resisted the Muslims from it when they arrived in the Hoggar mountains and fled from it to As-Sūq (Tadamakkat). Then he returned and died in battle in the Hoggar.

An example of a Coptic story centred in Libya is given in pseudo al-Mas-'ūdī's 'Marvels of Egypt'. (13) In the story an Egyptian ruler called Mālik marched against a Berber people who produced magic vapours, made their bodies invisible or created mirages. They dwelt in a town called Qamūda/Qamūna, and their queen was a sorceress called Asṭā. The town was destroyed by fire.

Who was Queen Asṭā? The Berber queen was a pagan, and her city resembled the temple of Elissa (Dido) at Carthage with its Massyli (Algerian)priestesses, the fire, vapours and the evocation of the dead by magic spells. I suspect that Astā is inspired by Asbyte of Silius Italicus (c. 101 AD) (14), herself patterned upon Camilla in the Aeneid. This Libyan queen was born and grew up among Berbers who, like the Numidians, 'roved at large, a nation that knows not the bridle, for the light switch they ply between its ears turns the horse about in their sport no less effectively than the bit.'

Asbyte was a Garamantian. Both her father and herself were engaged in

Hannibal's wars and died in the events which occurred during the siege of Saguntum in Spain. Hiarbas, her father, was the son of Ammon. He ruled the caves of Medusa, the Macae by the river Cinyes, the Cyreneans, and he was obeyed by the Nasamones of Barce and the Gaetulians who rode without reins. He had built a marriage bed for the nymph Tritonis from whom the princess was born. He dwelt near the Prophetic grove of the Garamantes. His helmet was conspicuous for the horn which curved over his temples and was the insignia of the Siwan oracle of Ammon. Often that oracle had promised a safe return but on this occasion he was slain among the heros of the Carthaginian army.

Asbyte was of the people of 'two tongues' - Egyptian and Libyan - and she came to fight the Romans from the region of Marmorica - the interior of Cyrenaica. Jupiter was her fore-father, and she derived her name from the prophetic grove of Jupiter Ammon (Saturnus). She was a maiden of forests, thickets and groves, yet she urged on steed and lay wild beasts low without mercy. In battle, aided by the Amazons, she rode in a smoking chariot drawn by two horses. Despite the shield on her left arm she was protected from arrows by the self-sacrificing Harpe. When the latter died, furious Asbyte hurled spears at the city of Saguntum, and she wielded her heavy battle axes. However, attacked by Theron, she was slain and decapitated much to the fury of Hannibal. Her remains were cremated by the Numidians on a huge pyre occompanied by a spectacular ritual revenge.

In Asbyte may be found a sorceress of royal blood, mistress of wild creatures and priestess of the grove and temple of Ammon with its warning divinatory idol of gilded copper. The burning of Qamūda/Qamūna is perhaps a reformulation of the episode of her pyre, together with certain other features familiar to Coptic story-tellers who wove them into the fight to the death between Asṭā and Mālik, each the representative of a 'matriarchal' and a 'patriarchal' tradition of rulership and lineage engaged in a struggle for supremacy.

Long after the Arab conquest, in the *Māghāzi* literature, the epics of the early Arab heros, Qamūda/Qamūna, to the south of Qayrawān was the battle ground for Arabian heros and Companions of the Prophet. Subayṭila was conquered in the reign of 'Uthmān b. 'Affān in 657 AD. The defeat of the Byzantines in these parts left an impression on Muslim poets and romancers. Amidst their romances are tales of Byzantine and Berber queens and princesses, tales which were in part based on some truth, in major part Oriental fable. These entered the stream of oral traditions of the peoples of the Maghrib, and into the encyclopaedic *sīra* of the Banū Hilāl which was to be used to explain social and pseudo-historical changes which were to alter the life of Arabs and Berbers alike.

IV

The 'Equestrian Diviner', 'Oqba al-Mustajāb

A Berber 'matrilineal' queen was to be superseded by a 'patrilineal' commander, the 'Equestrian Diviner' who is called by the Sahelians 'Oqba al-Mustajab. He is a composite character uniting two great Muslim commanders, 'Uqba b. 'Āmir, who was a Companion of the Prophet, and 'Uqba b. Nāfi' al-Fihrī. The latter is held in the greater esteem as the founder of the Tunisian city of Qayrawan and as the conqueror of the Maghrib as far as the Atlantic and along the Garamantian routes southwards into the Fezzan. Before turning attention to what is semi-historical in 'Oqba's character, observations ought to be made of the wholly miraculous and socially significant elements in his personality.

Dozy (15) summarized the link between this man and the Berber peoples who idolized him as a 'father-figure' in their ancestry. 'The Berbers have, indeed, never played an important part in the world except when instigated by their religious teachers. The Marabouts laid the foundation of the vast empire of the Almoravides as well as that of the Almohades. In their wars with the Arabs, the Berbers of the mountains were for a long time led by a prophetess whom they believed to possess supernatural powers, but the Arab general, 'Okba ibn Nāfi', who understood better than his colleagues the character of his opponents, speedily realized that to vanquish them he too must work upon their superstition, and appeal to their imagination by the miraculous. He therefore boldly played the part of a sorcerer and a Marabout; he would charm serpents and claim to hear celestial voices and puerile and absurd though such methods may appear to us, they were so successful that a multitude of Berbers, impressed by the miracles which 'Oqba worked, and convinced that it would be vain to resist him, laid down their arms and were converted to Islamism.'

Several symbols indicate the legendary 'Oqba, who was given the honorific title of *al-Mustajāb*, 'he whose prayers have been answered by the Almighty'. In his nature are found represented the attributes of a warrior, martyr, and a water diviner. 'Oqba is accompanied by his horse. He seeks out and uncovers water pools and springs, and he plunges into the depths of the sea in his mission. He is inseparable from his steed. As a superstitious regard for horses was typical of the ancient Libyans, - the Romans found the Berbers to be great horse breeders, and the Numidians were horsemen of repute, - 'Oqba filled requirements of the Berbers to perfection.

'Oqba's ride into the beaconless sea in Morocco or his disclosure of water in the desert at Mafaras - 'the horse's spring' - (Mā'al-faras) - in the Fezzan, Ghadames or elsewhere were episodes which appeared in belief and legend of both Arabs and Berbers. Triumphantly marching to the Sūs in furthest Morocco or the edge of the Sahara,'Oqba mastered the Massūfa, yet he himself was pursued by Kasīla al-Barbarī. Kasila or Kusayla was a Berber prince who had feigned conversion to Islam. Kusayla was paired with his predecessor, the Kāhina, sorceress queen of the Aures. Among certain Berbers the two were fused or closely related. To the Ifoghas Tuaregs, Kusayla was not a man but a woman. One may speak of a 'Kusayla/Kāhina' to offset an 'Oqba who is the personification of Islamic manly heroism.

The power to divine water had aided 'Oqba. Beyond the Fezzan he had divined it at Mafaras and had saved his men from thirst in their fabulous march towards Kuwwār, along the route of the Garamantes. He had founded the city of Qayrawān in a watery valley wherein were many trees and *Arāk* bushes. It was a haunt of wild beasts and reptiles. He expelled them to found his city. By strategem he had reduced the 'Ethiopian troglodytes' of Khuwwār and Jado in Niger. He had punished infidels who had rebelled. Yet after having reached the ocean or sea or river, whose character were to be found in his steed and his own restless nature, he was to meet disaster at the hands of a Berber prince, once a captive whose character was confused with that of a sorceress queen. 'Oqba's cunning had been outmatched by the guiles of God's opponents. Slain by Kusayla 'Oqba died as a martyr and with him also died his steed. Both were transformed into a Muslim Centaur, a Numidian hero, who among a company of hero-martyrs entered an Elysian land - *janna* itself, a Paradise of flowing rivers and gardens.

His progeny, initially his successor - al-'Āqib - continued the ever-recurring role of his father to convert the heathen, to divine water, springs or rain-clouds, to found settlements, to clear the groves of denizens and *jinn*, to keep horses picketed in the *jihād*, to heal and counteract the evils of a Berber foe. The latter was an uncouth traitor, the fleecer of sheep, or a sorceress whose spells brought plague and whose matrilineal dominance was an affront to the *Sunna* of Islam and the divine *Sharī'a*.

In the desert, the nomads found a response to 'Oqba in their hearts. 'Oqba had certain features in common with the Hilālī heros, Abū Zayd and Dhiyāb b. Ghānim whose exploits were already beginning to influence legends and reflect changing social systems. To the forebears of the Tuaregs 'Oqba had an appeal. The Pharusii had been attached by the Byzantines and the Arabs to the Furs or the Persians. But Pharusii was also a name similar to 'horse' or 'mare' (*faras*) in the Arabic tongue. Possibly Mafaras, the water source discovered by 'Oqba in the Fezzan or Ghadames was in some way connected with the Pharusii. The latter, according to Strabo, crossed the desert, fitting water-skins under the bellies of their horses. Sometimes they came to Syrtis through marshy places and lakes. They may have brought gold to Syrtis using the trans-Saharan routes, then less barren than now. For such people 'Oqba would be no stranger.

As ‘Oqba’s exploits evolved into the supreme epic of Muslim Africa, so his companions and patrons were introduced into his mission. Chief among the expeditors was the Caliph himself. In some accounts this Caliph is said to be the Umayyad Caliphs Mu‘awiya or ‘Umar b. ‘Abd al- ‘Azīz. The favourite is ‘Uthmān b. ‘Affān whose Caliphate lasted from 644-656 AD. He gave the command to march. Such is his role in the late *Maghāzī* literature attributed to ‘pseudo’ al-Wāqidī (d. 823 Ad.) (16)

Some general observations on the mythical Saharan and Sahelian scenario of ‘Oqba’s exploits seem appropriate. A cross section of motifs and personalities has been presented. In the later medieval period they had beccme sufficiently correlated or fused to suggest an acceptable calque of a ‘combat myth’ for the ethnic groups who were Muslim or were in the process of Islamisation. (17)

Supreme is a Caliph or Commander in Baghdad or Medina. He has entrusted the conquest of Africa to a prince (*Amīr*) who combines in his person the military valour of the holy warrior (*mujāhid*) and the spiritual power and sanctity of a religious leader (*murābiṭ*). An expedition of Arabs sets out to conquer, build cities, found dynasties or spread the faith. In the process there are physical and human obstacles to overcome as well as wild beasts and *jinn.* These latter may be serpents, dragons, watery groves, the wiles of a sorceress or an enemy equipped with a formidable armoury of enchantments. By supreme effort all goals are achieved.

Then at the height of success the hero of the tale is treacherously slain. His death seems a tragic *dénouement*, but its disaster is mitigated by suggested ways in which the society has been radically helped during the life of the hero so that in the future it is enabled to face and overcome all difficulties and misfortunes which may beset it. The choice is framed within a ‘contrast epic’, the contrast between the human predicament and the assured future of society. The perennial promise of triumph and group survival is assured by the establishment of Islam, the founding of a dynasty, the acceptance of a stable line, the building of a city, the banishment of demonic powers, or access to an inexhaustible water supply. Either singly or as a whole these achievements remain, despite the treachery which brought about the death of the hero. It transcended the grave misfortune which insome way threatened the future of his community.

V

The First Ineslemen, the Kel Es-Suq and the ‘Oqba Saga

Saharan and Sahelian societies have a sacerdotal class. The Tuaregs are no exception. I have explained in my introduction that they are called *Ineslemen* (s. *Anislem*), a word derived from the Arabic words, Islām, Muslim and Muslimīn.

From documentary evidence it is not possible to give a date when this class was first integrated into Tuareg class structure. One needs to possess a far more comprehensive record of the Islamisation of the Tuaregs. The Ṣanhāja of the Western Sahara were certainly extensively Islamised by the eleventh century, and it would appear from Ibn Ḥawqal that Tadamakkat in the tenth century had devout Muslims among its Tuaregs, as well as the Khārijites who controlled most of its commerce.

Some features of the mentality and function of the *Ineslemen* are to be found in the description of the Azgar Tuaregs by al-Idrīsī in his great twelfth century geographical work, *Nuzhat al-Mushtāq* (18):-

'The land of the Zaghāwa is adjacent to the land of the Fezzan. In it are the towns of Jerma and Tassāwa. This latter town is called by the negroes 'the lesser Jarmā'. These two towns are of a close proximity to one another. The distance between them is a day's journey or a little less. They are in size and population on a par. They derive their water from wells. There they have date palms, and they grow millet, barley, and they irrigate them with water controlled and canalised by a device which they call *Injaqa.* (19) In the Maghrib this device is called a *Khaṭṭāra.* In their habitat is a silver (iron?) mine in a mountain called Jabal Jawjis (Jirjīs?., Gurza/Gurzil/Gurzenzis?). It is of little worth, and those who seek (silver) have ceased to mine it and extract it for those who sought it. The distance between Tassāwa and this mine is some three days' journey for those seekers. Tassāwa is some twelve days' west of a Berber tribe. They are called Āzgār. They are nomads, and they have many camels, and their milk is abundant. They are a people of intrepidity, force and courage and invincibility, nonetheless they live in peace with those who keep the peace with them, but they are hostile to those who deceive them with pretences. They spend the spring and the summer round about a mountain called Ṭanṭāna (south of Ghat). On its lower slopes around it are springs and sources which flow with water and many marshy pools where the waters collect. Grass in abundance shoots forth there, and their camels pasture. From it they wander to places where it is their custom to camp permanently . . . . From this mountain, around which the Āzgār wander, to the land of Baghāma is a distance of some twenty days across lands which are empty of humanity, scant in water points and whose climate is hot like a furnace. Its routes are erased, and landmarks obliterated. From the tribe of the Āzgār to Ghadames is eighteen days' journey. From the Āzgār to the town of Shāma is some nine days' journey. In between the two are two uninhabited deserts where waters are infrequent. Sometimes the wind sweeps through them together with the heat of the air, and the water points evaporate so that they no longer exist . . .

According to the reports of the inhabitants of the Maghrib, the Āzgār are the people who are most knowledgable in the science of magic characters which are attributed to the Prophet Daniel. Despite the number of the Berber tribes there is not found among them a tribe so knowledgable in this system of writing than the people of the Āzgār. When one from amongst them, be he an elder or minor, has an animal which has strayed or he loses one of his possessions, he marks out a sign in the sand. Thereby he learns at what place his stray may be found. Then he journeys and finds his property just as he had beheld it in his characters. Sometimes a man among them steals the possession of his companion, and he buries it in the ground, at a distance or nearby. The man who has lost his possession and wishes to know the locality where it is hidden draws a magic line. Face to face with (the place) of the hidden (stolen) object, he draws another character. He recovers his possession, and what is lost. By what he has drawn he also knows who is the man who robbed him of his possession. He assembles the elders of the tribe. They draw similar lines, and thereby they learn who is innocent, and who is the perpetrator. Among the people of the Maghrib this (art) is famous and widely reported. One of them who report such things said that in the city of Sijilmāsa he saw a man of this tribe. A hidden treasure of his was concealed so that he knew not where it was. For the sake of it he drew a magic line, and he went to the place where it was, and he unearthed it. He repeated this action of his three times. He uncovered it on the second and third occasion as he had done on the first. It is a remarkable thing that they are so masterly in this science, despite their gross ignorance and their coarse character.'

These Azgar of the Tassili-n-Ajjer and of Sijilmāsa would seem to be in some way forerunners of the Kel Es-Suq of Tadamakkat in the Adrar-n-Ifoghas. Significant is the name of the Prophet Daniel, who appears later as a name among scholars of the Kel Es-Suq who claim to have come from Sijilmāsa. The knowledge of magic signs, of *Tifinagh* or 'Maraboutic' geomancy have a link with the Tuaregs of today. There was already a latent pacifism in this Azgar group, who seemed predisposed to avoid unnecessary hostility. No mention is made of any lineal descent from Arabian ancestors.

The Kel Es-Suq of Tadamakkat have played such an important part in Tuareg Islam that a fuller assessment of them, and a fuller discussion of their ancestry will be left to later chapters. Their scholars claim to know who their ancestors were, and how they are related lineally to their brethren. But the science of genealogies is an erudite pastime. The nomads among whom these *Ineslemen* were to minister needed some simple statement of 'history' which summarized their past and supplied an *apologia* in a few paragraphs. Paper or writing matter of any kind was scarce in the desert, particularly in the remoter areas of the Adrar and in Azawagh. In Agades, Tadamakkat perhaps, and in Timbuctoo, the material upon which to record history was in more plentiful supply.

In the Sahel scrubland books did not survive long, due to the climate, the white ant or the wear and tear of tribal warfare or seasonal wandering.

The Kel Es-Suq became masters of the Kufic-type, Andalusian Arabic script which was employed in epitaphs, engraved on desert rocks or incised in inscriptions on mosques or steles. They adapted it for their own calligraphy, and a form is still used in manuscripts. It is among the most artistic Arabic scripts of the Sahel. Scanty historical material has survived. One wonders whether the Kel Es-Suq were ever compelled to turn to historical composition but confined the fragments of historical tradition which they wished to preserve for posterity to notes and details included in works of genealogy or of jurisprudence.

The Kel Es-Suq confess their historical ignorance. One of their most versatile scholars of the nineteenth century, Sīdī Mawlay Muḥammad al-Hādī, whose book *Naṣīḥat al-umma fī isti'māl al-rukhṣa* will be quoted, was totally uncertain as to how they came to forsake their home-town of Tadamakkat: 'We do not know whether it was due to the destruction of the town where they dwelt, namely as-Sūq which in ancient times was called Tadamakkat. This destruction came about due to the evil liver and evil doer, the Songhai king, Sunni Ali in the ninth/fifteenth century. The people dispersed in all the countries of the earth. Because of this, what was theirs came to nought. God knows best the reason for their lack of scholarly concern with it all, despite the presence in ancient times and at the present day among them, and among others also of scholars who could pronounce a lawful ruling that they were descended from the Companions of the Prophet (Ṣaḥāba) and that 'Uqba al-Mustajāb b. 'Āmir who raided as far as Morocco in the time of the Caliph 'Uthmān was their ancestor and also the ancestor of the Kunta. They are qualified to know their history of that and of their categories of status, for such is the wont of scholars. I have not seen a history belonging to anyone in Takrūr from the people of as-Sūq, Air or the Kunta regarding what occurred prior to the ninth/fifteenth century.' (20)

The most comprehensive surviving epistle about 'Oqba al-Mustajāb among the Kel Es-Suq was once possessed by Muḥammad Ouginnat of the Kel Es-Suq of Gourma. (21) It may have been written about the same time as the passage of Sīdī Mawlay Muḥammad al-Hādī, but its content comes from an established record - part oral, part documented - which had been handed down among the Kel Es-Suq and other *Ineslemen.*

'In the name of God. This is an account regarding the origin of as-Sūq. It is a famous story among the scholars and the intelligent but not known to him who is little lettered and who is ignorant. When Mu'āwiya b. Abī Sufyān (22) assumed the office of authority and princeship, after the Caliphate of al-Ḥasan b. 'Alī, he sent 'Uqba b. 'Āmir with the army - he being 'Uqba al-Mustajāb - in the year 61/680.'

'Uqba journeyed from al-Qayrawān conquering the cities and villages as far as the furthest Sūs, adjoining the sea (river Nile?) Then he returned through those lands until he came to as-Sūq. It was a mighty city. In it there were many people. At that time it belonged to the infidels. 'Uqba fought them in the *jihād*, and God conquered as-Sūq by his hand. He took their prince whose name was Kusayla. He alleged that he became a Muslim for fear lest 'Uqba should kill him. 'Uqba stayed in as-Sūq for a period, and he built mosques in it.'

'He appointed men to call the people to prayer in the mosques, he established the religion of God, and he made it to thrive there. Then he departed from as-Sūq. In it he left a large company of the Companions of the Prophet - some 'Emigrants' (*Muhājirīn*), others 'Helpers' (*Anṣār*). They are buried in as-Sūq at the present time. The graves of the 'Emigrants' are in one particular place, and the graves of the 'Helpers' in another. On every grave was inscribed the name of its occupant, among them Abū Maḥdhūra, the prayer-caller (Mu'adhdhin) of the Prophet. They were the ancestors of the people of as-Sūq.'

'When 'Uqba departed from as-Sūq, and Kusayla journeyed with him to (I) Walāta(n), Kusayla killed him there, treacherously and by craft, while he was praying the noon-prayer on the day of the sacrifice, the tenth of Dhū 'l-Ḥijja ('Īd al-Aḍḥā). (23) 'Uqba lies buried in (I)Walāta(n) at the present time. It was thus reported by Abū 'l-Haṣan al-Maghribī in his text *Sharḥ al-Barādhi'ī fī kitāb* al-dhabā'iḥ, where he says, 'And the night of the man who strangled his sacrificial victim and sacrificial offering at Mecca by his own hand'.

'The Companions, in place of 'Uqba, appointed as his successor a man of the Banū Balwa (Zuhayr b. Qays al-Balawī). That successor was killed in a most grievous murder. Then the army returned from thence to Medina without passing by as-Sūq. This is the true and authentic account regarding the origin of as-Sūq. All of it was in the time of Mu'āwiya (b. Abī Sufyān) - God be pleased with him.

One of the chief problems in interpreting foundation myths of this type is to date their composition. They are statements of social belief, and not of detailed correspondence to a sequence of minutely recorded facts or events. The latter are expressed in a different format, either orally as in Tuareg year lists, of no great age, or in annual chronicles of which those of the city of Agades are examples. The 'Oqba legend is shared by the Kunta, the Kel-Es-Suq, the Kel Intasar, the Peul and certain scholars of the Algerian Zāb.

The Sahelian 'Oqba myth began to take its final form in the region between 1600 and 1700. It is barely a slice of the reputed exploits of 'Uqba b. Nāfi' handed down in known Arabic historical works by Ibn 'Abd al-Ḥakam (d.c. 871 AD.)

Abū 'l- 'Arab al-Qayrawānī (d. 944 AD), Ibn al-Athīr (d. 1234 AD), and later Maghribi variations of these writers. The story of the Conquest was shorn of essentials. Tales of exploits by 'Oqba al-Mustajāb ignore the alleged march of the Arabs into the Fezzan as far as Kuwwār. Instead emphasis is given to the westward march into Sudanic regions. The sea in Morocco is interpreted as the 'River' - the Sudanic Nile - be it the Senegal or the Niger. The two great protagonists of the tale are historical characters. Kusayla who personifies the indigenous population of North Africa is retained, likewise the hero himself. But here there is some disagreement stemming it would seem from the debates of Abū 'l- 'Arab and others. Was 'Oqba al-Mustajāb the Qurashite 'Uqba b. Nāfi', or was he 'Uqba b. 'Āmir, the hero of the Anṣār and the Yemenite faction in the Arab forces? These uncertainties are exposed by Abū 'l-'Arab. (24)

The confusion was compounded in the popular *Maghāzī* literature of late medieval date since in it 'Uqba b. 'Āmir is always the hero, one of the Companions (*Ṣaḥāba*) of the Prophet. The legendary 'Oqba al-Mustajāb transcended the argument whether he was a son of Nāfi' or a son of 'Āmir.

The version of the story of the Kel Es-Suq records the co-existence of two Sahelian centres, Tadamakkat and Walāta. The tale of 'Oqba's martyrdom is built on a relationship between the two. The former town as we have seen was in existence as early as the tenth century. Walāta came into being four hundred years later. One of the essential features in this Suqi chronicle cannot be earlier than the fourteenth century, although there is a tradition that Ghana and the Lamtūna Almoravids once raided Tadamakkat in a *jihād.*

A late date is indicated by the theme of 'Oqba's death, for the Kel Es-Suq believe that 'Oqba was not slain in battle at Tahūda in Algeria, but was treacherously murdered by Kusayla at Walāta. The latter was a Massufa centre. It was visited by the Moroccan traveller, Ibn Baṭṭūṭa, in 1352. He makes no mention of a tomb or mosque or any other site in the town being associated with the Arab conqueror of Africa. Had there been any associations known, even legendary, he would certainly have mentioned them.

Some accounts - particularly Kunta ones - maintain that it was not 'Oqba who was slain there but his son called al-'Āqib. No son of his of this name is known in the chronicles either in the Maghrib or the Orient, or in reputable histories of the Sahel. The name al-'Āqib is found among the Massūfa at least as early as the fifteenth century and notably during the period when the Songhai ruler Sunni Ali drove many Massūfa from Timbuctoo, harassed them in Walāta, and instigated an exodus of their scholars to Tagedda. In this disturbed period Tadamakkat was also involved, and it could be argued that the treachery of Kusayla in the stories of the Kel Es-Suq owes something to the memory of atrocities committed by Sunni Ali against Ṣanhāja Massūfa scholars in the West, something to the semi-legendary martyrdoms of Ṣanhāja religious leaders by the poisoned arrows of Sudanese pagans in the Almoravid era. Such tales would have been preserved among the Massufa or the Banū Wārith near the Niger. At least one Sahelian book of legends and lineages (circa 1600-1650) claims that these Saharan tribes, as well as the Lamtūna owed their Islamic fervour to the inspiration of 'Oqba al-Mustajāb who was sent by the Prophet to the Maghrib. He bore a letter addressed to al-Lamtūnī b. al-Nu 'mān who was its king. He read the letter to his people, placed it in a silver chest and buried it somewhere in the middle of the Maghrib so that the land would become fertile and its crops flourish due to its *baraka.*

Important differences between the Kunta version of the 'Oqba story and that of the Kel Es-Suq may be noted. For the Kunta it is a lineal manifesto. They are the progeny of 'Uqba b. Nāfi' in a paternal line, and they identify Kusayla with the Tuaregs. The Iwillimeden, the Imedideghen and Bu Ifarwin in particular, are the descendants of Kusayla. Their vendetta with them is a continuation of the conflict between 'Oqba and the Berbers. The Kunta claim that 'Oqba is buried in Qayrawān. It is al-'Āqib who is buried in Walāta. Foul murder took place there but it was during a Friday sermon and not during a feast. To quote the *Risāla al-Ghallāwīya* of the Kunta, 'One day 'Uqba was preparing to deliver the Friday sermon. Kusayla asked him to let him be a neophyte. Kusayla was released. While 'Uqba was in the pulpit, the Berber chief crawled close to him produced a hidden blade and stabbed him while he was facing Mecca. 'Uqba fell face downwards. Kusayla was seized. His flesh was cut up, and it was cast into the fire.'

This dastardly act patterned, it would seem, on the stabbing of the Caliph 'Umar b al-Khaṭṭāb, - was committed at a moment of great sanctity. It ensured 'Oqba a martyr's crown. At the same time there is an element of the cycle of the tales of Abū Zayd al-Hilālī in these happenings. Abū Zayd owed a charmed life to his mother's descent from female *jinn.* This charm made him impervious to iron, whether it be an arrow, sword or spear until the day he testified to the unity of God. At that moment the *jinn* who had protected him from the front and from the rear withdrew their protection from the front, so that he became as other men in that he could be killed from that direction. The whole setting for the murder is the converse of the temptation of Hamlet to kill his uncle.

> Now might I do it pat, now he is praying;
> And now I'll do it: - and so he goes to heaven;
> And so am I revenged; that would be scanned ...

The traditions of the Kel Es-Suq Tuaregs are also concerned with 'Oqba but lineal links are inconsequential. There are only a few family trees which trace a direct line to 'Oqba. Lineages are by preference those of the Prophet's household. Greater stress is laid on some association with 'Emigrants' and 'Helpers'. Furthermore 'Oqba al-Mustajab is 'Uqba b. 'Āmir, not 'Uqba b. Nāfi', and he was murdered during a feast, not while he was in the pulpit. What matters more than lineage is the town of Tadamakkat - as-Sūq, - the cradle of the Tuareg *Ineslemen.* It is the recollection of a glorious era or a Muslim 'Paradise Lost'. The murder of 'Oqba by Kusayla is a tragedy repeated again and again by men of wickedness.

The Equestrian Diviner

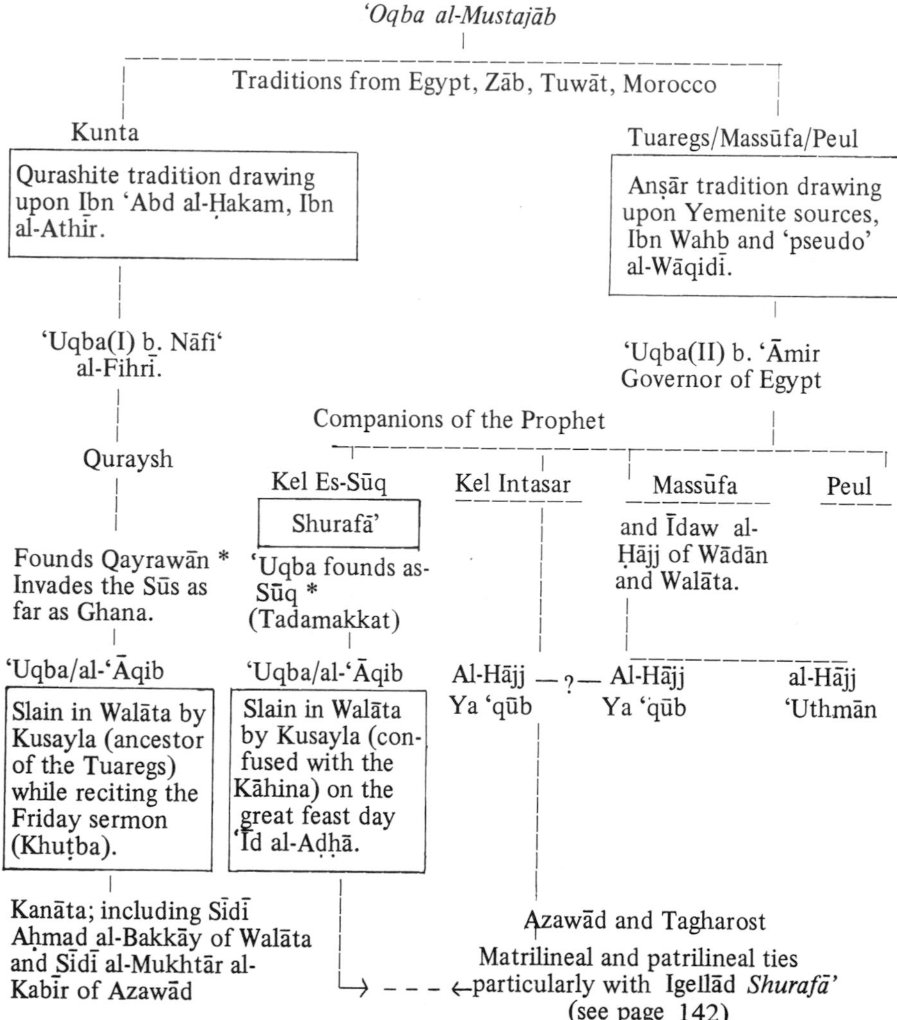

* This theory may contain elements about tales of Qamūda (Sbeitla), elements of the Kuwwār raid, and exploits elsewhere in North Africa.

VI

'Oqba the ideal Anislem

Despite divergence, the accounts of the Kunta and the Kel Es-Suq agree that 'Oqba al-Mustajāb was not slain in battle in Algeria at bewitched Tahūda (Qamūda/تهودة /قمودة), but that he was murdered while engaged in a ritual of the sacerdotal class in the Sahel. Their major duties were to preach the Friday sermon in the name of the Caliph or his *Imām*, or to lead the sacrifice on feast days in the Muslim calendar. Their 'Oqba was a martyr but not on the battle-field. The point is stressed. It may be for didactic purposes or social reasons may have prompted it. The Kunta and the Kel Es-Suq became sacerdotal communities in the Sahelian system. They normally depended on the co-existence of a military class who were princes of the Banū Ḥassān, or the Tuareg aristocracy of the *Imashaghen.*

Some light on this apparent change of emphasis and what constituted the ideal actions of the Muslim saint, is shed by the Lamtūna 'Tuareg' scholar Muḥammad b. Muḥammad b. 'Alī, whose questions addressed to the Egyptian scholar al-Suyūṭī (d. 1505) and the replies he received from him, are among the most valuable source material about Islam in the Sahel in the fifteenth century. (25) The forty first section (*faṣl*) is concerned with a martyr's death:-

'Some persons, if Muslims seek them out to kill them or plunder them, fight until they kill or are killed, having in mind whoever is killed in defense of his property, is a martyr. Some come to battle (and wait) until they are killed without moving, having in mind (the thought), 'I wish you to bear the burden of my own sin and yours so that you shall be a dweller in Hell,' just as Abel and (the Caliph) 'Uthmān did. Which of those two (types of person) is the more exalted?'

In his reply al-Suyūṭī specifically stated that 'He who does not fight is more exalted.'

I shall argue that this Lamtūna scholar was possibly writing from Tadamakkat. At any rate he was writing from an area where the Kel Es-Suq became the principal *Ineslemen.* It is possible that he was one of the Kel Es-Suq. The reply of al-Suyūṭī could have been crucial in forming the pacific ideas of their scholars. If pacifism was morally superior, then it was clearly more fitting for their hero 'Oqba that rather than fight to the last at Tahūda, he should die a martyr in the pulpit, at prayer, or when celebrating a feast. Murder at prayer associated his death with that of the Caliph 'Uthmān, whose reign marked the first conquests in Africa. Murder during a sacrificial act of the utmost sanctity established a loose relationship with the story of Cain and Abel as told in Sūra V in the Qur'ān, more specifically with the person of Abel.

'Uthmān, the third Caliph had been abandoned by the people of Medina. They left him without a protector, besieged in his own house. The insurgents stormed it. He was reading his copy of the Qur'ān. The hand of the assassin fell on him, and his blood stained the page on which was Sūra II v. 131. There his bleeding ceased.

'If they (Jews and Christians) believe in that in which ye believe, then are they guided; but if they turn back, then are they only in a schism, and God will suffice thee against them, for He both hears and knows.'

This passage and the event seem to have had some significance for the Kel Es-Suq, for they seem to be responsible for a painted shrine at Tim-m-Missao (26) on the ancient 'chariot' route between the Hoggar, Abalessa, fortress of Tin Hinan, and Tadamakkat. The well of Tim-m-Missao is sited in a wadi in the Tassili-n-Adrar. It is a canyon with steep cliffs. In hollowed shelters of the cliff, a little upstream from the well, are painted inscriptions, partially effaced, but one of them is of particular interest. It appears to read:-

> 'And God will suffice you against them, for He both hears and knows. Bestow Thy blessing and peace upon Muḥammad, 'The Gentile' (*ummī*) Prophet, the blessed, the rightly-guided, as Thou hast bestowed Thy blessing and peace upon (the prophet) Abraham.'

This whole inscription, not only its beginning, reminds the beholder of Sūra II v. 131.

The style of the lettering is that known in Tadamakkat. (27) The Tim-m-Missao inscriptions cannot be precisely dated but they are almost certainly attributable to the Kel Es-Suq. The Tuaregs know of these writings. A poem of Oua Infen agg Mekiia of the Tegehe-n-Efis at the end of the last century refers to having 'left for the rock - which forms a natural roof - of the Companions of the Prophet Muḥammad' (*essekkabaten*,/Ṣaḥāba). The inscriptions were made by the Kel Es-Suq, they claim. Duveyrier in his book shows that they were there in the middle of the nineteenth century. (28) He refers to them as 'Kufic', and the rock shelter at Tim-m-Missao was reputedly a mosque of the Companions of the Prophet, the men of 'Uqba b. 'Āmir. When these Companions are mentioned the Kel Es-Suq are implied. The route to Tadamakkat suggests a date prior to 1700, but probably not earlier than the fifteenth century, as the date of these inscriptions. Tim-m-Missao is still frequented. The famous text from the *Sūra* 'of the Cow' is regarded as a talisman. It is said that every letter in the heart of the inscription indicates a number of words which have mystical meaning and power, and that small groups of Kel Es-Suq *Ineslemen* will travel to the rock in order to spend some time in meditation.

The reference to Abel in the question of Muḥammad b. Muḥammad b. 'Ali al-Lamtūnī likewise reflects a concept foremost in the minds of the *Ineslemen,* in his day, in the region of the Adrar-n-Ifoghas. The central theme is a sacrifice, as it is in the text of the Kel Es-Suq, and a noonday murder on the day of the greatest sacrifice of all (al-'Īd al-kabīr). 'Oqba al-Mustajāb is cast in the role of Abel *(Hābīl)* while Kusayla is a second Cain (*Qābīl*). According to the Qur'ān Sūra V. vv. 30-35) when the two sons of Adam made their offering to God the sacrifice of Abel was accepted. Fire descended from heaven, and his offering was devoured. Cain was enraged, but he concealed his envy until Adam performed a pilgrimage. The *'Īd al-kabīr* (*aḍḥā*) is the sacrifice at the height of the Meccan pilgrimage. Then Cain said to Abel, 'I will assuredly slay thee.' Abel said, 'Why?' Cain answered, 'Because of the acceptance of thine offering to the exclusion of mine.' Abel replied, 'God only accepteth from the pious. If thou stretch forth to me thy hand to slay me, I will not stretch forth my hand to slay thee; for I fear God, the Lord of the worlds. I desire that thou shouldst bear the sin which thou intendest to commit against me by slaying me, and thy sin which thou hast committed before, and thou will be of the companions of (Hell) fire.' And that is the recompense of the offenders - But his soul suffered him to slay his brother; so he slew him; and he became of the number of those who suffer loss . . . This was to be the argument of the *Ineslemen*, at least the Kel Es-Suq. To fight unbelievers was not their divine duty. That was the prime duty of their *Imashaghen* masters or an *Amīr* whose obligation was to prepare his people for battle.

The story of Cain and Abel also showed up the evil of pre-Islamic customs which were still practised among the Berber nomads, feuds which involved the slaying of a brother by a brother or murder within an extended family. The exploits of the Banū Hilāl and the Tuaregs share many common ideas in this respect. (29) The Islamic sacerdotal class, whether Kunta *Zwāya* or Kel Es-Suq *Ineslemen,* was confronted by moral dilemmas and had to provide Muslim standards to transform society. Hence the importance of behaviour patterns of the Companions of the Prophet, foremost among them 'Oqba al-Mustajāb. He was either a warrior, the embodiment of Muslim chivalry, or a mystical and pacific idealist. The latter was to find favour with the Kel Es-Suq when the Sufi orders penetrated the Sahara and the Sahel.

Medieval Sahelian society was mixed in its beliefs, in its population and in the composition of its urban communities. The medieval Tuaregs either rejected or had been untouched by Islamic civilisation, or some compromise had taken place in their social systems. In certain areas and among certain groups, Middle Eastern and Maghribi Islamic beliefs and institutions took root. Among the non-Sahelian Tuaregs were the Ahaggaren. Ibn Baṭṭuṭa called them 'a rascally lot'.

Yet he conceded that, 'We encountered one of their chiefs, who held up the caravan until they paid him an indemnity of pieces of cloth and other goods. Our arrival in their country fell in the month of Ramāḍan, during which they make no raiding expeditions and do not molest caravans. Even their robbers, if they find goods on the road during Ramāḍan, do not touch them. This is the custom of the Berbers along this route.'

The Hoggar *Imashaghen* maintained their descent from 'Queen' Tin Hinan. They have in principle done so up to the present day. But if this claim is closer examined the borrowing of Islamic ideas from an early date is detectable, whatever these *Imashaghen* may assert. From the tenth century, the Ahaggaren were toying with pseudo-Yemenite ancestry. According to al-Ya'qūbī this habit was common among Berber groups in the Fezzan and areas where major Tuareg migration towards the south-west originally began.

It would seem that the Tuareg rules governing descent, succession and chieftainship were marked by concession to Islamic practise emenating from Islamic centres with which they were in contact at every stage of their history - Libya, the Western Sahara, Tunisia, the Sudan and Egypt. The ebb and flow of Islamic forces left their mark to a greater or lesser degree, depending on the course of events, the movements of nomadic groups and the impact of strong individuals.

Some writers (30) have quoted *Ineslemen* and Kunta sources about the northern Tuaregs which report a medieval royalty, *Imanen,* who were descendants of the Prophet through 'Alī, his son-in-law, or from the Idrisid rulers of Morocco. These *Imanen* formed an endogamous series of 'holy families' who had their own negro guard *'iklan wa-n-tawsit'* and drums (*ṭabl/eṭṭebel*) which were used to summon supporters among their subjects and were chiefly insignia. The *Imanen/ Imenan* (Arabic *Imām* or *Mu'min/Īmān*) rulers maintained their power by fictitious claims to the Prophet's family.

They were warlike and despotic, particularly the last of them Sultan Goma. In order to appease the nobles he divided the land among the noble Tuareg women and distributed it as hereditary fiefs which were to be transmitted to their descendants. In bestowing these fiefs on the women and not on the men Goma wished to avoid their loss to outsiders through the marriage of the men-folk to women in neighbouring tribes. In giving the fiefs to the women he also kept a firm control on the nobles and compelled them to marry within his domain, that is, if they wished to have any right to enjoy these hereditary fiefs.

Goma was allegedly assassinated around 1650 by one of the Azgar nobles, and the medieval dynasty of the *Imanen* was overthrown by Mukhammad agg Tenekeṛbas of the Uraghen of Niger who marched to assist their Azgar relations. Following the downfall of Goma and his religious aristocracy, the system of fiefs continued, but the Ahaggaren and the Azgar split into separate confederations, and anarchy reigned followed by disastrous war. The Ahaggaren had to re-establish some order and were constrained to seek elsewhere for lettered Muslims to help impose it. They found them among the Kunta who were at first anxious to consolidate their power by military means, but, when unsuccessful, exerted a spiritual influence in a subordinate status to the Ahaggaren.

Such accounts were no doubt falsified by the lettered to support the case of one party to the detriment of another. Their history reads like a story explaining how the Kunta came to supplant the religious and secular chiefs who had originated among the Kel Es-Suq or had come to dominate the Ahaggaren from the region of Tadamakkat or from Air. The sequence of events as outlined above seems to imply that the social and political history of the Ahaggaren followed the general pattern of their kinsfolk in other Tuareg lands.

'Queen' Tin Hinan, Tāzakkay 'the lame', Lamtūna and other legendary ancestresses of varied date and location, have been retained in a 'patrilineal' scheme, often without regard to chronological order. One Arabic source records the passage of Tin Hinan through In Salih in Algeria as late as 1611. (37) Some *Ineslemen* of the Hoggar have claimed that Tin Hinan was a man despite prevailing Tuareg traditions which affirm the opposite. These contradictory tales indicate efforts to preserve the memory of certain personalities, ancient queens or heros, Asṭā, Tin Hinan and Lamtūna or 'Oqba al-Mustajāb. They represent the unrecorded past of Saharan and Sahelian antiquity.

In chapters to follow I hope to show how lettered Tuaregs were to pioneer Islamic ideas to the west and to the east, between Azawād and Air. In whatever capacity they spread their message, they were inspired by memories. Supreme among them was 'Oqba and his horse. He was a diviner of water and a martyr, cut down in battle or stabbed by a traitor who symbolized the 'Garamantian', Berber or 'Ethiopian' past which the *Ineslemen* believed they had disowned. Warriors or pacifists, skilled with the pen or the sword, the spear and the oryx shield, the Tuareg Muslim leaders were to leave an indelible mark, for better or for worse on other Tuaregs who roamed or settled on the fringe of the Muslim Sudan. Astride the 'chariot routes' leading to Morocco, Algeria and Egypt both nature and history had determined the tasks they were to accomplish and the location of the towns which they were to found and to rule.

NOTES

1) See Muhammad Bin 'Uthman Al-Hashashi, *Voyage au Pays des Senoussia à travers la Tripolitaine et les Pays Touaregs,* translated by Serres and Lasram, Paris, 1912, pp. 177-184.

2) See De Calassanti - Motylinski, *Le dialecte berbère de R'damès,* Paris, Leroux, 1904, Chapter III.

3) See H' St. J.B. Philby, *Sheba's Daughters* Methuen, 1939, pp. 26-29.

4) Wholly different arguments are put forward by A Bourgeout in 'Le contenu sociologique de l'apellation Tuareg (Kel Ahaggar): Histoire d'un nom, Revue de l'Occident Musulman et de la Méditerranée, Aix en Provence, no. 11, ler Semestre, 1972, pp. 71-83.

5) See *Ya'qūbī les Pays*, tr. by Gaston Weit, Cairo, 1938, pp. 205-7.

6) The region of Jado, Bilma and North-east Niger.

7) See T. Lewicki, *Arabic External Sources from the History of Africa to the South of Sahara,* Wroclaw, Warszawa, Krakow, 1969.

8) See Pliny, *Natural History,* V, vv. 35-37.

9) See E. F. Gautier, *Le Passé de l'Afrique du Nord,* Paris, 1942, pp. 327-328.

10) See pages 49-57.

11) See P.V., pp. 369-370.

12) Introduced and explained in Henri Basset's *Essai sur la littérature des Berbères* and in René Basset's *Loqmân Berbère,* Paris, 1890, and 'La légende de Bent el-Khass, *Revue Asiatique,* vol. XLIX, 1, 1905, pp. 18-34.

13) See 'La Reine Magicienne' in R. Basset's *Mille et un Contes,* Paris, 1924, Vol. i, pp. 231-235. The death of a holy man sent by Abraham to Qamūniya (Qamūna/Qamūda) and the arrival of al-Khaḍir there with Dhū 'l-Qarnayn is found in the *Kitāb al-Tījān* by Wahb b. Munabbih, Hyderabad edition (1347 AH), pp. 81-126.

14) *De Bello Punico,* Loeb Classics, ii, 56-269.

15) R. Dozy, *Spanish Islam,* London, 1913, p. 129.

16) Since St. Louis and the Crusaders appear in the narrative of this work, it is clear that a 'pseudo' al-Wāqidī is the author of the text which survives.

17) With the exception of such works as *Futūḥ Ifrīqiyā,* the legends are far later than the medieval period, and are sometimes recent oral traditions. However, there is little doubt that the 'scenario' itself dates from stories formulated in the fifteenth and sixteenth centuries, possibly earlier. Hence the use of 'late medieval' to describe the temporal aspect of the disparate legends. See P. Marty *Etudes sur l'Islam et les tribus du Soudan,* p. 5.

18) See R. Dozy and M. J. De Goeje, *Description de l'Afrique et d'Espagne,* Brill, 1866, pp. 39-43. I have translated from the 1971 edition of al-Idrīsī's text in *Opus Geographicum,* (Brill), edited by E. Cerulli, F. Gabrieli, G. Levi Della Vida, L. Petech and G. Tucci.

19) Perhaps from *manjanīq* 'ballista'?

20) *N.U.* in the copy preserved in *A.N.,* document no. 94.

21) See *D.G.* collection, Manuscript 133, *Tarikh El-Braziri.*

22) Mu'awiya b. Abī Sufyān reigned between 661 and 680 AD.

23) *'Īd al-Aḍḥā* or *al-'Īd al-kabīr* 'the Great Feast', to celebrate the concluding rites of the Meccan Pilgrimage including the lapidation of three pillars by the pilgrims symbolising the rejection of the Devil and all his works.

24) *Ṭabaqāt 'ulamā' Ifrīqiyā wa Tūnis,* edited by 'Ali b. Shabbi and Na'im Hasan al-Yafi, Tunis, 1968, pp. 58-59.

25) J. Hunwick, *African Perspectives,* C.U.P., 1970, pp. 7-33.

26) See Th. Monod, Sur les inscriptions arabes peintes de Tim-missao, Sahara central, *J. Soc, Africanistes,* 1938, pp. 83-95. Barth in his *Travels,* 1858 edition, Vol. V, Appendix I, p. 458, relates a tradition of a footprint of a horse of Moses in this locality.

27) *ibid.,* where specimen examples of calligraphy are shown. See also the *estampages* of De Gironcourt, and Van Berchem in *Missions de Gironcourt en Afrique Occidentale,* Paris, 1920, pp. 292-353.

28) See H. Duveyrier, *Les Touareg du Nord,* p. 487, and De Foucauld *Poésies touarègues, Dialecte de l'Ahaggar,* Paris, II, 1930, p. 264.

29) See B. Thomas, *Arabia Felix,* Jonathan Cape 1938, pp. 239-242, and **A.** Hanoteau *Essai de Grammaire de la langue Tamashek,* Algiers, 1896, pp. 150-151.

30) See M. Benhazera, *op. cit.,* pp. 99-103.

31) See Temoignages nouveux sur Tin Hinane, *Ancêtre Légendaire des Touareg Ahaggar,* in *Revue de l'Occident Musulman et de la Méditerranée,* Aix-en-Provence, Nos. 13-14, Ier Semestre, 1973, pp. 395-400.

CHAPTER III

TAGEDDA, MASSŪFA SULTANATE OF COPPER AND SALT.

> 'A land whose stones are iron, and out of whose hills thou mayest dig brass.'
> *Deuteronomy,* 8, v. 9.

In my introduction I referred to a second medieval focal point of Tuareg Islamic life. It lay to the east of Tadamakkat and a little to the west of the Air Massif. It was called Tagedda. Its centre may have been in the ruins of Azelik near Tagedda-n-Tesemt.

Greater Tagedda was the home of the Igdalen and the Eastern Massūfa. According to Barth the Igdalen's 'whole appearance, especially their long hair, shows them to be a mixed race of Songhay and Berbers; and there is some reason to suppose that they belonged originally to the Zenága or Senhája.' (1) The Igdalen became men of religion. Their tongue (*Tagdalt*) is markedly similar to *Tasawaq* (2), the language of the sedentary population of In Gall and Tagedda-n-Tesemt. Nowadays they dwell in tents made of mats and not of skins like their neighbours, the Iwillimeden. The Igdalen do not seem to have formed politically autonomous groups. Each fraction became attached to a tribe of the adjacent noble *Imashaghen.*

The Inussufen/Imussūfen (Massūfa), their neighbours showed a greater cohesion and political aptitude. Those of Tagedda were eastern brothers of the Ṣanhāja Massufa who founded towns such as Walāta and Tīshīt in Mauritania and formed an important element in the Almoravid Empire. To this day they preserve memories of western connections. They were drawn to the east by the pilgrimage route to Mecca, and driven by the persecutions of the tyrant Sunni Ali in the fifteenth century, massacres which afflicted those in the vicinity of Timbuctoo. The Kel Sūf are sometimes called 'sons of the jinn,' but more often 'those of the *bādiya,* the open desert and plain', who live the lives of the nomads yet are not truly nomads, men who are urban in their tastes, driven by circumstances to live in open spaces.

The most famous of all descriptions of Massūfa Tagedda in the Middle Ages is that of Ibn Baṭṭūṭa who visited it in 1353. (3) The life of the 'town', its Tuareg ruler and its scholars can be glimpsed, even if the precise locality where he stayed cannot be fixed. The plural nature of the Tagedda settlement can hardly help in the search for the house of the *Qāḍī* who was his host.

Tagedda was cosmopolitan. Caravans of Ghadames merchants passed through it from Gao, and it had its own community of Maghribis. The Tagedda merchants supported an annual caravan to Egypt from whence they imported fine fabrics and other goods and luxuries. Life was easy, and slaves were plentiful and expensive.

Commerce was not only with Ghadames and Egypt but also to the south to Gobir and Bornu. The medium of exchange was locally smelted copper bars. By it Tagedda purchased its meat, fire-wood, millet, butter and corn. Scholars and jurists found it a place where their services were in demand. The Tagedda *Qāḍī*, Abū Ibrāhīm Isḥāq, the host of Ibn Baṭṭūṭa may have come from the Janet oasis in the Tassili-n-Ajjer, but its indigenous Berber population was almost certainly Massūfa, and it is reasonable to assume that its 'Sultan', who was a tent-dweller in the desert, was of the same tribe. All the local traditions and tales which still persist among the Inussufen make them the masters of Tagedda. (4)

The 'Sultan' of Tagedda was called Izār. This was unlikely to have been his proper name. It suggests the Tamashegh word *Imūzar* 'chief' or the roots *izar/ ezzer/yezzaaren* signifying 'first' or 'to come before'. His true name is possibly unknown, and his status was hardly that of an *Amenukal* or chief of a major Tuareg confederation. However, he was a fine example of Tuareg nobility, and he honoured the Muslim devout. He rode a horse without a saddle, a red rug laid on the animal's back in place of it. He was dressed in blue robes and wore a blue turban. With him were his sister's sons. 'It is they who inherit his kingdom.' Ibn Baṭṭūṭa was lodged in one of the tents of the *Yanāṭibūn/Ibetamen?*, servants or coloured tributaries. The 'Sultan' sent him a roast sheep and a bowl of cow's milk. Close by was the tent of his mother and his sister. They came to visit the Tangier traveller and to welcome him. The 'Sultan's' mother sent milk after the evening prayer, for this was the hour of milking. The milk was drunk in the evening and the early morning. 'As for cooked dishes, they neither eat them , nor do they know of them.'

At that time Izār was the receiver of a peace making mission on behalf of a Berber 'Sultan' called al-Takarkurī. The two chiefs were in dispute, and the peace delegation included the *Qāḍī* Abū Ibrāhīm of Tagedda, Muḥammad 'preacher' (of the Friday sermon?), a certain Abū Ḥafṣ, and Shaykh Saiʿīd b. 'Alī al-Gazūlī of the Moroccans.

In the opinion of some lettered Tuaregs, the 'Takarkurī Sultan' was chief of the Tuaregs of the 'Tegare(y)garey' - 'those of the centre', who are now part of the Iwillimeden of Abalagh and Tahoua. Ibn Baṭṭūṭa says nothing of the reason for the dispute and the negotiations. It may have been freedom of transit for the commercial caravans of Tagedda, or it may have been the sharing of feebly saline sources at Azelik in the rainy season. (5)

This same 'Sultan', or another called 'al-Karkarī', was the master of the Air

Massif where herbage abounded, and sheep were bred. It is possible that the centre of this 'Sultanate' was at Agaraguer near Aṣūday (Asōday/Assodē), or the 'Sultan' may have been the chief of the Itisen or the Kel Geres, (6) who by that time had occupied the Massif. It is probably this 'Sultan' to whom al-'Umarī refers and not the 'Sultan' of Tagedda when he recorded that, 'The land of the Sudan also has three independent kings who are 'white' Muslims and who are Berber in race; the Sultans of Air, Damūshūh and Tadamakkat. These three 'white' kings are they who rule to the south of Morocco, between the coast of the Straits, the empire of the Sultan Abū 'l-Ḥasan, and the country of Mali. Each one of these kings is independant. None has authority over the others. The most powerful is the king of Air. They are Berbers, their dress is similar to that of the Moroccans, the shift *(darrā'a)* but rather narrower, and turbans with a flap below the chin. They have no horses and ride camels. The Marinid Sultan wields no authority over them, nor does the Sultan of Mali. Their food is that of the men of the interior: meat and milk. They have few cereals.

'Shaykh Sai'īd al-Dukkālī told me that he crossed the country of these people during one of his journeys, but that he did not stay amongst them and that their resources are meagre.

'Al-Zawawī told me that these Berbers have cultivated mountains where fruits grow in abundance. All are in the hands of these three kings whose empire aspires to half that of the kingdom of Mali, or a little more, but the ruler of the latter has more revenues, on account of the proximity of the lands of the pagans where the gold 'grows'. He dominates these pagans. It is for this reason that his revenue is considerable. Also, it is due to the innumerable items of merchandise which are sold in his country and the profits which accrue to him from raids made against the pagans. The situation is quite different for the Berber states whose country is sterile and who have no means of making gains. Their principal resource comes from beasts of burden'. (7)

Assuming al-'Umarī to be reasonably correct, al-Karkarī, the Sultan of Air, seems more likely to have ruled the mountains than Izār of Tagedda. Even if the rule of Mali never reached Tagedda, there are several differences between al-'Umarī and Ibn Baṭṭūṭa. Izār had a horse, while the Sultan had none. The Sultan of Air had 'cultivated mountains', while Izār had no mountains under his domain, nor did fruits grow in abundance at Tagedda. Al-'Umarī implies that these Berbers had no means of making gains save beasts of burden or livestock, while the copper of Tagedda and its slaves, if Ibn Baṭṭūṭa is correct, gave a wholly different picture of the life of the Massūfa west of Air.

From the fourteenth century onwards Tagedda was a haven for men of learning who enjoyed the patronage of its rulers. There was a need for a class of scholars who could effectively turn a Tuareg *Amghar* or *Izār* into an *Amenukal* or Sultan. There was also an unprecedented influx of lettered Saharans - some from Mauritania, others from Tadamakkat - in the following century. Many of them came from the region of Timbuctoo. Sunni Ali, foeman of the Berber nomads to the north of the Niger, was responsible for this influx. A number of the Walāta Ṣanhāja scholars of Alfa Gungo took refuge in Tagedda (Tikda). Sunni Ali declared that they had gone there to appeal to the Tuaregs to ask them to come and take arms against him. Sunni Ali was later to relax his policy, but 'those persons of Alfa Gungo who had taken refuge in Tagedda remained there and made the town their new country.' (8)

By the end of the fifteenth century a number of Walāta Massūfa had moved east, gaining influence at the expense of the non-Tuareg lettered who had preceded them. They were embittered and were ready to welcome a man of radical and puritanical Islamic ideas. 'Abd al-Karīm al-Maghīlī of Tilimsān (d. circa 1504 or 1532) filled these requirements. Hailed as a 'miracle worker' (9) and as a renewer (*mujaddid*) of the truth, he stayed for some time in Tagedda and Air on his way to Katsina, Kano and Gao. In the latter, the capital of the Songhai Empire, the pious Sultan al-Ḥājj Muḥammad Askia had succeeded Sunni Ali, and there was a revival of Islamic ideas and social institutions in the Central Sahel. Al-Maghīlī left his impact on the religious views of the Tuaregs.

Among them were two Inussufen. The first, a pupil of the Egyptian Imām al-Suyūtī whose name was a byword among Air and Tagedda jurists and mystics, al-'Āqib b. 'Abdullāh came from Anū-Ṣamman in the Tagedda complex. (10) Aḥmad Bābā, the great Massūfa scholar of Timbuctoo, described him as an alert *faqīh* with a sharp tonque. He was a commentator on Khalīl and wrote an epistle about the obligation of the Friday prayer in his town of Anū-Ṣamman. (11) His views were opposed by other scholars in the town. They sent his findings to the learned in Egypt for verification and rectification. Al-'Āqib wrote to the *Qāḍī* Muhammad b. Mahmūd of Timbuctoo, and he replied to questions sent to him by the Songhai ruler al-Ḥājj Muḥammad Askia. He disputed with Makhlūf b. 'Ali b. Salih of the oasis of Tabalbalat about several theological or legal matters.

His successor the Inussufen, al-Najīb b. Muḥammad Shams al-Dīn also came from Anū-Ṣamman. A *faqīh,* he wrote two commentaries on the *Mukhtaṣar of Khalīl*, one large in four volumes, the other half its size. He wrote a commentary on the major miracles of al-Suyūṭī and an 'Appendix' on the *Mu'jizāt* of al-Bakrī. Both these learned Inussufen lived during the sixteenth century.

The shift of scholastic circles to Anu-Samman, today a complex of ruins, (12) is indicative of the growth of adjacent Agades, the future capital of Air, and the decline of Tagedda which on the evidence available seems to have preceded it chronologically. What happened to Tagedda? Was it destroyed by the forces of Agades, as some local legends maintain, (13) or were there economic factors which doomed its alleged copper wealth but made it a major source for salt? It is hard to believe that the scholars' refuge in Tagedda ceased to exist. There are tombstones of jurists, not only at Anū-Ṣamman, but in Tagedda-n-Adrar and at the foot of Bogonuten. Away from the villages Tuareg *Ineslemen* of the Inussufen studied and taught. The Egyptian al-Sakhāwī mentions the name of two of them, father and son. Details are fuller on the latter. (14) 'Abū Yaḥyā b. Yaḥyā b. Muḥammad b. 'Alī al-Takrūrī al-Massūfī al-Nākanatī, (15) whose father was known as Ibn Sugen *al-Faqīh.* He died in the Tagedda desert *(bādiyat Tajiddah)* on Wednesday night, the 19th of Dhū 'l-Ḥijja in the year 948 (19th March 1543).' The precise details underline the knowledge of the Tuareg scholars of Tagedda and Air among the lettered of Cairo and in Mamluk Egypt.

1. Ruins of Tagedda at Azelik

NOTES

1) *T.D.N.C.A.*, p. 205

2) See E. and S. Bernus, *Du Sel et des Dattes,* pp. 12-29.

3) See J. Devisse, *Textes et Documents Relatifs à l'Histoire de l'Afrique,* Dakar, 1968, pp. 72-78.

4) See E. and S. Bernus, *op. cit.,* pp. 107-108.

5) A *cure salée* could have been held, even if Bogonuten salines had not yet been exploited. The views of Henri Lhote that 'copper' (*naḥās*) should read 'salt' (*milḥ*) is untenable. Ibn Baṭṭūṭa's text refers to 'pouring and casting' (*sakaba).* This verb would not be used for salt.

6) Ker Geres (ī) (var. Kel Geres) in the 'Agades Chronicles' is not an impossible reading of Kar Garī (Karkarī).

7) al-Omari, *Masālik al-Abṣār fī Mamālik al-Amṣār,* tr. by Gaudefroy-Demombynes, Paris, 1927, pp. 94-95.

8) T.S., pp. 108-109, Fr. text, pp. 66-67, Ar. text.

9) See *P.V.,* pp. 291-293, and *T.D.C.A.,* pp. 170-171.

10) See *Carte des Régions Sahariennes au République du Niger,* 1/200.000. Feuille, NE 32 VIII, Teguidda in Tagait, marked as *Anésoumén,* 7° 46 E, 17° 10 N.

11) See A.D.H. Bivar and M. Hiskett, 'The Arabic Literature of Nigeria to 1804: a provisional account', *B.S.O.A.S.*, Vol. XXV, Part I, 1962, pp. 111-112.

12) Engraved in script of Tadamakkat /Tagedda type including such names as al-Faqīh Ḥamd b. Mīn, 'Abdullāh b. Muḥammad b. Aḥmad b. A'mar, A'mar b. Yaddar, Muḥammad 'Abd al-Raḥmān b. Muḥammad b. Ḥannah (?) akh (?) al-Faqīh Min.

13) See E. and S. Bernus, *op. cit.*, pp. 107-114.

14) al-Sakhāwī *al-Ḍaw' al-lāmi',* 1354, Vol. X, p. 147.

15) The *nisba* either refers to Janet (Ganet) oasis. Tassili-n-Ajjer, see page 164, or to Ugannat in the Mali Adrar, or to Alrénēt Carte F. NE -32-VII (Teguidda In Tessoum) 6° 39'E by 17° 22'N, or some other locality in the Tuareg Sahara, possibly the Wa-n-Gānet (see page 44) where the genealogy of Abū Yaḥyā may refer to one or other of these persons.

CHAPTER IV

AL-SUYŪṬĪ AND THE TUAREGS

> 'I love you for the sake of God and am greatly longing to meet you. My name is Muḥammad b. Muḥammad b. 'Alī al-Lamtūnī. Do not forget me in your prayers.'

Recent studies of the life of al-Suyūṭī (1445-1505) and his correspondence have brought his influence in the Sahel to the notice of Western scholars. (1) No Muslim people in those lands escaped his influence. He was encyclopaedic and eclectic. His mysticism of vaguely Shādhilī sympathies was liberal enough to bless the Qādiriya , the most popular Sufi *ṭarīqa* among the Tuaregs of Tadamakkat, Tagedda and Air. He was indulgent where it came to many popular practices. He tolerated amulets and magic figures, use of the vernacular and a broad definition of the obligations in the *Sharī'a.* While al-Maghīlī was narrowly legalistic, the Egyptian genius was his opposite. The Tuareg *Ineslemen* could turn to him for a second opinion. They could contact him in Cairo on their way to the Holy Places. His works were popular. They were copied and re-copied, quoted and used for ideas. More than this, al-Suyūṭī took an active part in the political upheavals of 'Takrur', Air and Tagedda. He sent exhortations to rulers, dissuading monarchs from military adventures, and he staged the investiture of Sahelian Sultans by the Caliph in Cairo.

The peak period of the influence of al-Suyuti on Tuareg scholars appears to have been between 1464, after his pilgrimage to Mecca, and 1496. His writings began to circulate in the Sahel in 1477, and in 1484 a Sultan, possibly a Sultan of Bornu, sought the help of al-Suyuti to obtain a diploma of investiture (*taqlīd*) from the Caliph, al-Mutawakkil, so that his rule would be legitimate according to the *Sharī'a.* In the years 1496 and 1497, when the Songhai ruler Muḥammad Askia visited Cairo on his way to and from Mecca, major troubles beset the Egyptian capital, including a plot by the Caliph aimed at the Mamluk Sultan al-Nāṣir Muḥammad b. Qa'itbay, a plot which failed and nearly toppled the Caliph and his judges. In the same year, the Caliph al-Mutawakkil appointed al-Suyuti as supreme judge over the world of Islam. The year which followed was equally eventful. The Caliph died and was succeeded by al-Mustamsik, his son. Al-Suyuti lost his post as superintendant of the Baybars School following students' demonstrations which nearly cost him his life. A fearful epidemic swept Cairo soon after, and 200,000 lost their lives. Eight years later al-Suyūṭī died.

During these upheavals Muḥammad Askia obtained his investiture. Doubts exist as to whether it was at the hands of the *Sharīf* of Mecca, or in an interview with the Cairo Caliph. (2) In either event the personality of al-Suyūṭī, respected as a scholar, ear of the Caliph, dictated the course of politics in cities as distant as Gao, Tadamakkat, Katsina, Kano and Agades.

The Inussufen *Ineslemen* of Tagedda region, and the great scholars of the Kel Es-Suq in Tadamakkat, saw in al-Suyūṭī a sea of wisdom and learning on innumerable matters of Islamic law and practise which they found great difficulty in resolving themselves. Some of them had met him on the pilgrimage or had studied in his circle, reading his works and airing their problems. If there was some matter which needed an expert opinion or upon which al-Maghīlī had not fully answered their problems, then it was to al-Suyūṭī they turned for a definitive decision. He sometimes disappointed them especially near the end of his career, yet they retained a loyal, almost pathetic belief in his infallibility. No wonder 'Abd al-Qādir al-Shādhilī, a biographer of al-Suyūṭī, could write, 'God instilled into the hearts of the Takrūris love of him and faith in him. They had complete faith in him, to the extent that one of them said to me, 'In our country we vow that if a son is born to us we will name him 'Abd al-Raḥmān after him hoping to find blessing through him and through his name.' In their opinion not one of the *'ulamā'* is of his standing or in his class; indeed, for them he is almost like the Imām Mālik, may God be pleased with him, in the way they trust, venerate, and love him and readily accept his learning.' (3)

II

The Daghūghīyīn of Tadamakkat and 'The men of Abū Ruways'.

When Tagedda saw an increase in activity due to its links with Egypt and stimulated by emigré Massūfa from the region of Timbuctoo, Tadamakkat began to decline. Whatever the causes may have been, there seems little doubt that many of its leading scholar families decided to leave. They settled at (In)Ṭaduq in the desert on the fringe of Azawagh, (4) at Tagedda and later in Agades, but especially in hermitages and sanctuaries deep in Air, at Jīkat, Agallal and Tefis. These men were mystics, members of the Qādirīya Sufi order. The lonely mountains and valleys of Air were a perfect setting for their devotions.

Among the most respected were the Ishsherifen who claimed descent from Ibrāhim al-Daghūghī. (5) There had been a long tradition in the Sahara of descent from 'Alī, the Prophet's son-in-law. The branches of his family were numerous and crossed at points. All the *Shurafā'* claimed to be descendants of Mawlay Idrīs, but certain from Sijilmāsa in Morocco claimed descent from his brother Muḥammad. Both branches held that their ancestral home was Yanbu' in the Hijaz. One of the *Shurafā'* of Tāfilālt (Sijilmāsa), named Ibrāhīm went on pilgrimage at the end of the twelfth century and sought the help of the *Shurafā'* in Yanbu' to send one of their descendants to Sijilmāsa to increase the *baraka* of the family and to enhance their prestige. So al-Sayyid Mawlay al-Ḥasan arrived in the company of Ibrāhīm in Morocco. The Daghūghīyīn were powerful and influential until they became involved in a bloody dispute. They fell foul of the Sultan of Fez and were dispersed. The descendants of Ibrāhīm al-Daghūghī found a home among the Azgar and the Tuaregs of Tadamakkat and the Adrar-n-Ifoghas. They adopted the Qādirīya Sufi order and formed a major family of the Kel Es-Suq.

The foremost Sufi group in Tadamakkat were the 'men of Abū Ruways', *Mashā' ikh* of the Qādirīya under Shaykh Abū Ruways. These men included Muhammad b. Yūsuf al-Daghūghī, Shaykh Aḥmad b. Abū Ruways, and one of his novices (*talāmīdh*) al-Ḥājj Abū 'l-Hudā al-Sūqī. The latter was one among the great names of Tuareg Islam in the fifteenth and sixteenth centuries. According to Mawlay Muhammad al-Hādī (6) Abū 'l-Hudā was 'the author of two sets of questions addressed to al-Suyūṭī and al-Maghīlī.' He made the pilgrimage to Mecca, and while in Cairo he encountered the Egyptian scholar. According to the Tuaregs the two became good friends. Abū 'l-Hudā who owed his nickname 'Father of true guidance' to al-Suyūtī did not return to Tadamakkat, but went to (In) Ṭaduq where he died about 1500. Ṭaduq was a satellite town of Tadamakkat, and its mosque was founded by the saint 'Uthmān al-Mawhūb b. Iflawas. It was to enjoy some fame for nearly two centuries. Abū 'l-Hudā was buried there, and his tomb iststill to be found in the ruins of Ṭaduq. (7) Those who have visited it report the survival of an inscription with words to the effect, 'Muḥammad b. Muḥammad - who was surnamed Abū 'l-Hudā - the 'brother' of al-Suyūṭī and who wrote a commentary on the Qur'ān.'

Another noted saint of this group was Muḥammad b. 'Alī. He is reported to have 'disclosed to the people of Tadamakkat some of those things he had perceived by psychic vision regarding the city's ruin and a disaster which would come upon them. They paid no need to that, so he went forth on his own to Tindahagga where his tomb is situated.' (8) Muḥammad b. Aghanfas, another scholar, was an ancestor of the mystics collectively referred to as Itman. They were a clan of eight scholars, all of them brothers.

Many Sufis of Tadamakkat left the Adrar-n-Ifoghas and Ṭaduq altogether. The most famous of them were Abū Ruways who died at Sanbali in Air, and Shaykh Aḥmad b. Muhammad Wan Tefis b. Muḥammad al-Rabbānī who reputedly founded the great mosque at Agallal, near Iferouane, in 1480. It was to become one of the holiest, if not the most famous, sanctuary in Air. Shaykh Aḥmad al-Rabbānī, was one of the sons of Shaykh Muḥammad b. Muḥammad b. Ibrahīm, named Wa-n-Tefis who was a *Sharīf* from Tadamakkat and one of the Daghūghīyīn who founded the Tefis mosque. (9) It is named 'the elder, most senior or mother' of the mosques of Air. It preceded those of Takriza, Agallal, Afis, Tefgum and Asoday (Assodé). Muḥammad Wa-n-Tefis was the ancestor of the Kel Tefis. According to the legends of Air he came from Tadamakkat on an elephant. The latter then transported his relations and the great beams for the construction of the Tefis mosque.

This family is related in the following manner:-

Ibrāhīm

Muḥammad (Mukhammad)

left Tadamakkat . . . . . *Sharīf Muḥammad (Mukhammad) Wa-n-Tefis*

Hārūn

Uways Wa-n-Barwa

Fāṭimata (m)Muḥammad Wa-n-Tagedda b. Ag Khamma Wa-n-Gānet

Mūsā Wa-n-Agallal

Sidi Mālik Wa-n-Takriza *

Muḥammad Wa-n Tinābser.

Hārūn Wa-n-Jīkat (slain by Barkuray) . . . . *'Abd al-Qādir* milk brother. (Kel Geres)

Aḥmad al-Rabbānī. Founder of Agallal, c. 1480. (d. 1520?)

Abū Yaḥyā

'Abd al-Qādir

* He came from Kidal in the Adrār-n-Ifōghas following a magic cooking pot of copper.

The move of Qādirīya Sufis from Tadamakkat was of major importance in the Islamisation of the inner Massif. It also led to settlement in the Air valleys. Returning pilgrims brought with them seeds of Oriental fruits and vegetables and agricultural techniques such as the *Takarkarat* (10) pulley for raising well-water and guiding it into irrigation channels. Date groves grew from shoots brought from Medina and from North Africa by the Ishsherifen, and the cultivatable valleys became estates. The emigration of the lettered from Walāta to the Inussufen of Tagedda, and the Sufis of Tadamakkat to the centre of Air hastened the integration of Tuareg institutions in both these districts. Petty Sultanates became increasingly impractical. More and more factors encouraged centralization of the Air region. A definitive site for a capital had to be found. It was eventually to be Agades.

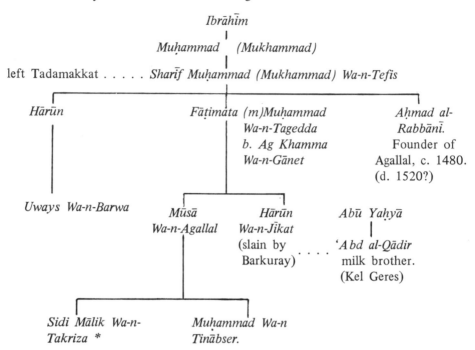

III

The Questions of Muḥammad al-Lamtūnī to al-Suyūṭī

Reference has been made to this Sahelian text of the fifteenth century, a comprehensive series of fifty-seven questions which indicate the crudities of Islamic practise against which thinking *Ineslemen* were in conflict, and on which they sought the advice of al-Maghīlī and al-Suyūṭī to combat. (11) These questions make sad reading. Professor Hunwick has demonstrated the nature of the communities concerned. Some were undoubtedly Berber, probably Tuaregs. The custom of inheritance passing to the sister's son, a practise which Muḥammad al-Lamtūnī feared was non-Islamic and reprehensible, recalls the urban Massūfa of Walāta and the *milieu* of Izār at Tagedda. Unveiled women, their use of magic and playing of the flute, lute and tambourine were also found among the Massufa. *Jinn* possession was known among the Tuaregs and in the Hausa *bori* cult. Other customs recall the Fulbe. Muhammad al-Lamtūnī condemns the scholars of his age who neglected the Qur'ān and the *Sunna* and relied heavily on legal texts. Bribery was rife, some claimed to be *Shurafā'* to gain selfish advantage. Talismans were much in use.

The rulers had absolute control of the land. Then they apportioned it to chiefs and their favourites. They appointed their own nominees to collect taxes. The post of *Qāḍī* was obtained through bribery. Idol worship was still tolerated in this Islamic community. Qur'ānic learning was of a superficial kind. 'Some teach boys recitation of the Qur'ān. When one completes the whole, or a half or a third, they carry him on a shield on their heads or on a horse or camel, and the Qu'rān reciters gather round him and parade him around the whole town, reciting over him verses (of the Qur'ān) which pray for success, and (poems) in praise of the Prophet, may God bless him and grant him peace. Then people give them food and drink and sheep and clothes, and they (the reciters) leave (the offerings) with the *faqīh.'* (12)

This custom, like many others attacked, recalls Ibn Baṭṭūṭa's description. In Timbuctoo he observed such a custom, not upon the recitation of holy-writ but in the appointment of a chief of the Massūfa. 'The majority of its inhabitants are Massūfa who wear the face muffler (*lithām)* and whose governor is called Farba Mūsā. One day I found myself in his presence when he had named one of the Massūfa as *Amīr* of a troop of men. He clothed him in a new robe, a turban, and a pair of trousers, all of them dyed a bright colour, and he had him seated upon a (Lamṭī) shield. The chief men of the tribe carried him aloft above their heads.' (13)

Muḥammad al-Lamtūnī was an opponent of literalism in religion. He wished to interpret the *Sharī'a* soundly, yet he was uncertain on several issues. (14) Written in the 1490's, these questions predated the pilgrimage of Muḥammad Askia and al-Suyūṭī's fall from office. They may have been despatched in the year of the death of Sunni Ali, or in the following year 1493, when we know that the epistle reached Cairo. Muḥammad al-Lamtūnī had not yet met al-Suyūṭī. It had been his hope to leave the Sahel to pay his respects to the scholars in Cairo on his way to Mecca.

The exact place from which Muḥammad al-Lamtūnī wrote is hard to locate. His questions give the impression of a wide and varied terrain. As a semi-nomad he may have been familiar with many places and peoples. His oblique references to the salt-trade, to fan-palms and to manna, and to town gates through which travellers and market folk passed, have a meeting point in the city of Agades, which I hope to show in my next chapter had been extensively built in 1493. Tagedda never seems to have been walled, and the nearby villages have fortifications of no great size. Agades and Kano were walled on a large scale but the former is to be preferred since Muḥammad al-Lamtūnī describes a place a little distance from the *Bilād al-Sūdān,* not in the heart of it.

Tuaregs who are familiar with this document point out that some of the customs are atypical of Air society. (15) The existence of the salt-trade from Bogonuten or Bilma through Agades to Hausaland was not certain in 1493, fan-palms are found throughout, and the proximity of manna to Agades, though mentioned by Leo Africanus, is not confirmed by other travellers. (16) In the year Muḥammad al-Lamtūnī wrote, al-Suyūṭī wrote a letter addressed to the 'kings of Takrūr, in particular to Muḥammad (b.) Ṣaṭṭafan, the ruler of Agades, his brothers Muḥammad, 'Umar, and Ibn Aktham (?), Muḥammad b. 'Abd al-Raḥmān and to Ibrāhīm, the ruler of Katsina. The letter exhorted them to be just to their subjects and to observe the *Sharī'a.* The Agades rulers are referred to in the Agades Chronicle. (Ibrāhīm) Muḥammad Ṣaṭṭafan, the chief figure of the four brothers ruled between 1487 and 1494/1496, when al-Suyuti composed his letter. Muḥammad al-Kabīr had already retired from office, while Muḥammad b. 'Abd al-Raḥmān, the son of the sister (Aktham?) of Muḥammad Saṭṭafan had not yet come to power. (17) Al-Suyūṭī seemed to know the rulers well, by name if not personally, and if Muḥammad al-Lamtūnī had Agades explicitly in mind it seems likely that al-Suyūṭī would have discerned the source of his writings. His replies are impersonal and reiterate points of law.

Air and Azawagh *Ineslemen* who are versed in history favour Tadamakkat as the 'Vanity Fair' portrayed by Muḥammad al-Lamtūnī. The region of the Adrar was being abandoned by Sufi Shaykhs and the pious; its ancient semi-Songhai settlements and commercial centres seem to mirror the kind of localities Muḥammad al-Lamtūnī portrays. Tadamakkat was not exactly 'a walled town' but it was, and had been for centuries, a centre for trade and commerce of all kinds and a long established meeting place for the lettered. There were Ṣanhāja Lamtūna in the city. In modern times a noted scholar of Azawagh was named Muḥammad Lana b. 'Abdullāh al-Sūqī al-Lamtūnī, known as 'Balkhu'. (18)

Tadamakkat had access to salt. From the age of al-Bakrī onwards it came from a place called Tawtek through Tadamakkat to Gao and beyond. Possibly sited at Erebeb north-west of the Adrar-n-Ifoghas, these underground mines might have been located near (In)Ṭaduq (Tawtek?), which could explain why this locality became an outlier of Tadamakkat, despite its isolation. Detailed exploration could confirm or deny the former presence of underground salt in the locality. If salt passed through Tadamakkat and other items to its markets, then a system of taxation at its 'gates' in the 'Isle' in the valley would seem logical. (19)

My friend Muḥammad Ibrāhīm al-Aghlālī of Abalagh in Niger has several hypotheses. To him, Muḥammad b. Muḥammad b. 'Alī al-Lamtūnī was one of the scholars of Tadamakkat, who left it and made a new home in Ṭaduq or in Air. Two possible scholars come to his mind among the circle of Abū Ruways. There was Muḥammad b. 'Alī whose predictions of the doom of Tadamakkat may allude to the inditements in the questions addressed to al-Suyūṭī, or there is Muḥammad b. Muhammad, later Abū 'l-Hudā, 'the author of two sets of questions, addressed to al-Suyūṭī and al-Maghīlī.' Perhaps these were the questions to al-Suyūṭī?

Abū 'l-Hudā could have gone on pilgrimage after 1493, met al-Suyūtī and studied with him. Possibly Muḥammad al-Lamtūnī was a pupil of Abū 'l-Hudā who phrased the questions on his teacher's behalf. He may not have been a *Lamtūnī* at all, but as Shaykh Muḥammad Ibrahīm has also suggested, one of the Itman - eight brother mystics - and that *Itmanī* was misread as *Lamtūnī* by an Egyptian copyist to whom the latter name was familiar? In any event, either through the questions or in person on his pilgrimage Muḥammad b. Muḥammad Abū 'l-Hudā met al-Suyūtī. He joined the growing company of Tuareg scholars who owed much to the teachings of al-Maghīlī on the one hand and to the advice and counsel of al-Suyūṭī on the other.

NOTES

1) See the valuable article of E.M. Sartain 'Jalāl al-Dīn al-Suyūṭī's relations with the people of Takrūr' in *Journal of Semitic Studies,* Vol. XVI, No. 2, 1971, pp. 193-198.

2) *ibid.,* pp. 195-196.

3) *ibid.,* p. 197.

4) Michelin map 153, *Afrique* (Nord et Ouest), In Tadok, 5° E, 18° N. Some

Tuaregs maintain that another Ṭaduq exists to the west of the Mali/Niger border in the same region.

5) See pages 141-143.

6) *N.U.* in the text preserved in *A.N.,* Niamey.

7) I have not yet had the opportunity to visit Ṭaduq (Niger). The ruins are well known and reported by Shaykh Muḥammad Ibrāhīm of Abalagh.

8) Tindahagga, is an unidentified locality in Air or the Adrar-n-Ifoghas.

9) See F. Nicolas, *Contribution à l'Etude de l'Aïr,* pp. 482-487.

10) On garden cultivation in Air, see *P.V.,* pp. 132-133. Many names of vegetables and fruits in Air are directly borrowed from Arabic, for example *rummān, tuffāḥ, Khawkh* and *zabīb* which have entered the area from Libya and Algeria or from the Middle East.

11) See E.M. Sartain, *op. cit.,* in various passages of her article.

12) *N.T.,* p. 20, Section 35.

13) See J. Devisse, *op. cit.,* pp. 69-70.

14) See *N.T.,* where mystical tendencies are apparent, in sections 50, 51, 53.

15) *Sic* Ghubayd agg Alojaly and Shaykh Muḥammad Ibrāhīm.

16) See Leo Africanus, *Description de l'Afrique,* p. 452, note 166 by H. Lhote.

17) See page 56.

18) See page 188.

19) See Cortier, *D'une rive à l'autre du Sahara,* pp. 203-212.

CHAPTER V

THE AGADES SULTANATE AND THE MYSTICS OF AIR

> 'The king of Agades supports an important guard and has a palace in the middle of the town. But his army is composed of men of the country and the deserts. In fact, he is in origin from these peoples of Libya, and sometimes these latter banish him and replace him by one of his relations. But they do not kill him, and it is the one who gives the most satisfaction to the people of the desert who is named king of Agades.'
>
> Leo Africanus

While doubt remains about the homeland of Muḥammad al-Lamtūnī, there is no doubt whatsoever about the source of another question about herbage, sent to al-Suyūṭī. It is to be found in the same collection of his answers, *al-Hāwī lil-fatāwī.* (1) It bears no date nor name, but it is likely to be earlier than the questions of Muḥammad al-Lamtūnī, and the letter of al-Suyūṭī to Muḥammad Ṣaṭṭafan, the ruler of Agadeṡ.

'Matter in question - In the land of Air is the city of Agades. It is a land of Islam, only Muslims are in it. Each tribe amongst them has a territory wherein they camp and settle. In it there is neither tilled nor cultivated land, nor crops by which benefit may be gained. Such is the prevailing situation. The plants which are lawful, and which are of benefit there, are predominantly the plants and fruits of trees open to every one, such as the fruit of the fan (*dōm*) palm, the lote tree (*sidr*) and others besides these two, trees and bushes which grow without human effort, and similar grains and berries from herbs which grown without tilling and sowing and toil and belong to the earth. He who comes and gathers acquires something of worth and value.'

'The land referred to is owned by its people who have been mentioned. They do so by the permission of the trustee of the country, the client-lord *(mawlā)*, (2) appointed by the permission of (the Caliph), the Commander of the Faithful. The said prince of the country has divided it into fiefs for its people who dwell there, in his interests and those of the Muslims in their assignment of it as feudal tenure. So, can he who is there sell its herbage,and anything from its trees? Can they forbid and prevent others from pasturing there or benefiting from and making use of anything therein?'

'The origin of the land aforementioned is unknown. None knows whether it is land conquered (for Islam) by force, or in peace. Since ancient times (*min qadīm al-zamān*) it has been only in the hand of the chief *(muqaddam)* of the country who divides it into fiefs for those whom he wishes. They have followed this tradition as their custom from forebear to successor. The bulk of their benefits, interests and welfare are connected with that. If you were to say, 'They can sell its herbage and even forbid others from (using) it,' then what is the import of the Prophetic tradition regarding the forbidding of the sale of surplus water, so forbidding herbage with it.? What is the import of the Prophetic tradition to the effect that, 'Among that which is reported there are four things which are not forbidden nor denied - among such mentioned are water and fresh herbage.' Give us a legal ruling (*fatwā*) as those who are rewarded. May God Almighty bestow on you the exact knowledge of the truth. Peace be upon you.'

The answer: - 'Praise be to God and peace be upon His servants whom he has chosen. The scholars agree that fresh herbage, when its plants be clipped, cut and obtained by removal and by transfer, then its gatherer has the right to ownership. The sale of it is his due, and there is no obligation upon him to surrender it. As for the fresh herbage which exists in its uncut or unclipped state as a plant, if it be growing on 'dead' (uncultivated waste) land, then the people who are in it are all alike. The case is applicable to water which is lawful for everybody.'

'This is the intention conveyed in the comments of the Prophetic tradition in respect of its denial and prohibition. However, if it be growing on land which is owned then it is the property of the lord of the land. He has no obligation to give it away, and it is lawful for him to sell it. One category remains, namely fresh herbage which grows in land which the Sultan has assigned to people in estates. Here there is a distinction. If that land be 'dead', then its assignment as fiefs is unlawful. It is so because it is a *ḥimā* - forbidden and sacrosanct territory - according to the saying of the Prophet, 'There is no *ḥimā* but it belongs to God and to His Messenger.' Solely lawful is the division into fiefs of 'dead' land which is free and utterly devoid of herbage and plant. If that land is not 'dead', and it belongs to the lands of the Public Treasury *(bayt al-māl)* which the Sultan currently divides into estates and fiefs among the Egyptian provinces, then its division into fiefs is sound and correct. The liege lord has the exclusive possession of the fresh herbage therein. He makes use of it, and he sells it because it is part of the wealth of the *bayt al-māl.* The Sultan permits the exploitation of it to this explicit liege lord. It would appear that the land of Agades is in a similar category as regards its division into feudal estate and its exploitation. God knows best.'

Aside from the intrinsic interest of the question of right to pasturage, the above passage sheds some historical light on the Air Sultanate in the middle of the fifteenth century. Agades was the administrative centre for Air by that date. Its ruler is not referred to as a 'Sultan' but as an *Amīr* whose title had been conferred on him because he was a *mawlā* of the Caliph who, it may be assumed, had given him his title by some form of investiture (*taqlīd*) comparable to those arranged by al-Suyūṭī. Yet the implications seem to be that the investiture here had occurred at an appreciably earlier date than some others. The Air writer implies a history of rulership dating back to an indeterminate period, implicitly supporting the claim of Ibn Baṭṭūṭa that a 'Sultan' was ruling Air in the mid-fourteenth century, perhaps earlier than the investiture of Yūnus, the first recorded 'Sultan' in the 'Agades Chronicle'.

Air was emerging from a past of relative disunity, and the jurists were anxious to establish fiefs which corresponded to *Sharī'a* principles. The administrative system of Mamluk Egypt could furnish a model where appropriate. The influence of the Mamluks may have been one factor in the origins of the popular story of a 'Slave Sultan' of Air and Agades who had arrived from Istanbul or from Turkish or Ottoman domain. Nothing is said of such an improbable origin in this text. There is nothing to suggest that the *Amīr* was other than a Tuareg like the rest of the people who grazed in Air. Some Mamluk administrators cannot be excluded. Agades and Air were becoming increasingly known in Cairo owing to the growth of commerce. 'Greater Takrūr' was a refuge for Mamluks. (3)

II

The Five Tribes and the Sultan

The local Air history of the origin of its Sultanate is a scanty record. It is derived from a text, now lost, written by one of the Shaykhs of the Air village of Jīkat, al-Mukhtār b. 'Abd al-Qādir al-Jīkatī. His history is not particularly old. Urvoy dates the bulk of its content to the seventeenth century, incorporating matter from other sources perhaps a century earlier. (4) The records as a whole are not a history of the Sultanate of Agades but a romance of the Tuareg tribes. Nothing is said about a prince from Istanbul, nor of descent from Mamluks or Turks let alone Byzantine princes. The omission shows that this tale of Levantine origin was little known or unknown, prior to 1600.

The popular history of the Air Tuaregs who established the Agades Sultanate begins with four tribes who came from the oasis of Awjila in Cyrenaica, the ancient home of the Classical Nasamones. Who these four tribes were is not entirely clear, nor is it wholly clear how the number later came to be five instead of four. The tribes were known as the Kel Innik, 'those who came from the East', the tribes of the King.

Muḥammad Bello in his *Infāq al-Maysūr* names the five tribes as the Imikitan,

Tamgak, Sandal (Sandar), Igdalen and Ijadnarnin (Ijaranen). His list by no means squares with the text of al-Mukhtār b. ‘Abd al-Qādir al-Jīkatī, where the four names seem to be the Itisen (a), the Ijdanarnen (b), the Izagharen (c), and the Ifadalen (d). These four were said to be the patrons of the Sultanate of Air.

‘They went forth from Awjila, and they drove the tribes of the ‘blacks’ from the country of Air, and they dwelt in Air for a long time without a Sultan appointed and established. Their state resembled that of the Arab nomads, because the latter had only their Shaykhs to arbitrate between them. Such was the state of these four tribes. Only their Shaykhs arbitrated between them. Then, after that, there arose confusions and troubles amongst them and those similar to them began to impoverish their families and those who were poor and weak amongst them. This impelled them to seek for a Sultan. Then the five tribes of the Kel Sandal arose and sought for a Sultan, and they found him in the country of Ighram Ṣaṭṭafan. They carried him to the town of Tādilīẓa, and they installed him there.’

The sequence of events led to the selection of a Sultan and his establishment at Tadeliza, a village some sixteen miles to the north of Agades. The four tribes, then five, were called by a collective name, the Kel Sandal. Elsewhere in the Agades records they have a short text devoted to their origins and branches which meet in an ancestress named Bashan who had three daughters:-

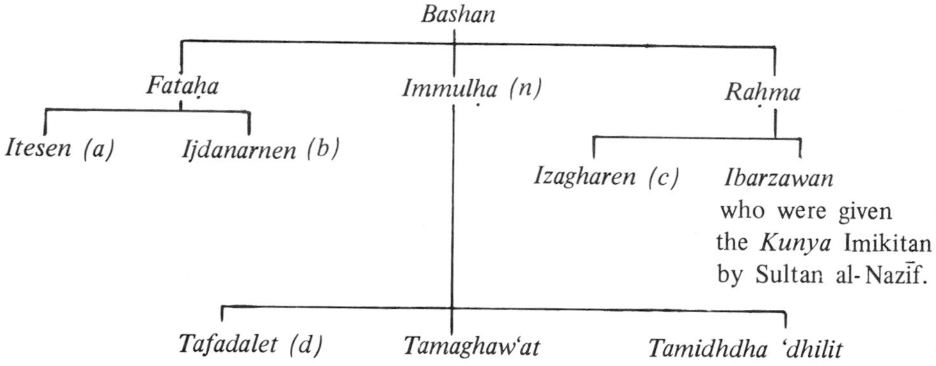

From this lineage it would seem that the Kel Sandal included the ‘four tribes’ of Air together with the Imikitan who are central in the Tuareg Bornu epics. They were presumably brought into the histories at a later date for reasons of tribal prestige. Certain of these tribes are now little known in Air. They have moved elsewhere or have become absorbed by others, and an exact identification is difficult. (5)

The whereabouts of the country of Ighram Ṣaṭṭafan has led to debate. The first Tamashegh word indicates a place of sedentaries, villages where cultivation is carried on in gardens and small plantations, while the second word denotes the colour 'black', It has been presumed that the place where the Sultan was discovered signified some Sudanic region, or possibly the Fezzan. The district of Murzuk has been proposed. (6) Muḥammad Bello makes it clear that the Sultan came from the 'people of Ṣaṭṭafan', the Kel Ṣaṭṭafan. Not only does this name appear in genealogies of the Kel Away, but it is also the name of the Sultan of Agades Muḥammad Ṣaṭṭafan who received counsel from al-Suyuti and who according to the Agades Chronicles ruled Agades between 1487 and 1494. The same name occurs among the Kel Es-Suq. One of their leading scholars was called Aḥmad b. Muḥammad b. Wa-n-Sattafan ('the one from the village of Ṣaṭṭafan'). The locality is known in the Adrar-n-Ifoghas, and the Sultans of Agades who were of this family returned to it after the upheavals in the Sultanate in the later sixteenth century, during the reign of the Sultan Aḥmad b. Tilẓa. The Suqi scholar Mawlay Muḥammad al-Hādī specifically states that following the martyrdom of the saint Sīdī Maḥmud al-Baghdādī - whose life in Air will shortly be described - the people of the dynasty of the Kel Inṣaṭafan, were driven from office and 'they returned to their land of Takarannat' in the Adrar-n-Ifoghas, their homeland and their village. (7) If this is correct, then the first Sultans were Ishsherifen. Their investiture would follow a common Tuareg precedent for rulership, and it is supported by the oral tradition in Agades that the Ishsherifen were the first who settled in the city. (8) The Agades records preserve oral traditions of the establishment of Agades as the capital of Air.

'After that they saw that it was unsuitable for the Sultan to dwell in Tādelīẓa, because the cattle which carried millet to Air were harmed and troubled. So they transported him to Tin-Shaman (Tasha-Aman), and they built a palace for him. He had no companions save those who were members of the 'four tribes' which built the house of the Sultanate. They built the Sultan's residence, and each of them had a share and part in its building. Such were the tribe of Lisawen, the Balkarray (Barkuray), the Imiskikkin and the Imussūfen. They were the owners of this land from Barghut (Bargot) to Tagedda and Adarbisinet. They built the houses in front of the mosque of Friday assembly in Agades. Then, after that the Sultan's sons stayed in those houses up to the present time. The 'five tribes' became those who controlled the power and authority, the power either to 'loose' or to 'bind'. This capacity they share with none other of the tribes.'

'When they were in mutual contentment with their Sultan, and there was agreement and harmony between them, then all the world was at peace. The whole land prospered and thrived. But when a difference between the Sultan and those who were in authority occurred, then the whole world was corrupt, evil and a wasteland. The land was in tumult, also the uninhabited localities, and the life of the people and their livelihood was meagre, hard and difficult.'

'Two matters, (9) obvious to themselves - but hidden from those who were not of their circle, who were unaware of the cause and who only knew that which was in their own age, not of the deeds of past times - were the cause of the difference and dispute. This then is the origin of the Sultanate of Air. It happened in the past and has been so to the present time. Whosoever seeks to distort it, or to alter it, seeks to change the origin or to distort the origin. He seeks the impossible. He will grow weary to no advantage, and he will repent when repentance will avail him nought. As for the 'five tribes' which carried Ilaswen (Alisaw) and appointed him to be Sultan and who built a palace for him in their land, it was their pleasure to do so, because their Sultan ruled them neither by force nor by compulsion. On their part they conquered by force the tribes of the negroes. Because of that they became men of power and authority. They had the power to 'loose' and to 'bind'. They treat their Sultan with favour and respect. Because of this he exalts them and shows them honour over all the tribes who enjoy no share in the ruling and government of the Sultanate of Air. Those tribes which seek to be their equal and are a confusion and embarrassment to them in their royal seat do them an injustice and wrong them, since they desire something to which none of the tribes has prior claim.'

The above passage sets out to explain how the Sultan first had his seat, not in the heart of modern Agades but at Tin-Shaman, the wells which lie near the site of the present fort less than two miles from the city centre. Air villagers in Tadeliza point to a rock from which they say the Sultan cast his spear in the Agades direction. It landed at Tin-Shaman, and it was there that he eventually resided. Later the Sultan's palace and the house of the *Qāḍī* and his other officials were built in the walled town, in the Katanga quarter. The builders were urbanised Iswaghen-speakers, the Inussufen, the Barkuray, the Imiskikkin and the Lisawen, whose territory is defined as the area from Bargot to Tagedda and Adarbisinet. These are old centres of the Tagedda Sultanate in the south and west. Adarbisinet is some distance to the south of Agades, Beurkot or Bargot some distance to the east. So Tagedda and the ancient routes and centres near Marandat were the Sultan's domain. The choice of Agades had fixed a point which lay astride all the routes, particularly those which led south to Hausaland and to Bornu.

After emphasising the dependence of the Sultans on the favours and whims of Air tribes, the text of al-Mukhtār b. 'Abd al-Qādir al-Jīkatī proceeds to discuss other matters, more particularly the dues and taxations which were the right of the 'five tribes' as protectors of the commercial routes between Timbuctoo and Egypt. A specific reference to a series of questions sent to Cairo would seem to refer to letters sent to al-Suyūṭī, or allude to further correspondence at some later date, on points of the legality of actions within the *Sharī'a* as interpreted by the Cairo *'ulamā'*.

'As for the gift of horses to them (by the Sultan), this is in no way a favour bestowed, since the 'poll-tax' (*kharāj)* paid in horses from the caravan (commerce) came about because of them and because of their activities. This is so because, at the time when they transported Ila swen (Alisaw) and seated him upon their throne, Ilaswen sent an elder of the tribe of the Imashshawen to the land of Islam. He (the Sultan) had it reported to the *'ulamā'* that 'I, Ilaswen, have been carried by the company of the Tuaregs who have taken the land of Air by force and by conquest. They have appointed me to be their leader, they have built a palace for me and have made me their Sultan. It is their custom to take the 'poll-tax' (*jizya*) in horses from those who are engaged in the commerce which traverses their mountains and deserts. I have accordingly sought, before God, and by your counsel, is this tax lawful or unlawful?' The *'ulamā'* answered him and said, '(Regarding) the men who preserve the road which passes between their mountains and who have preserved it from thieves, freebooters and highwaymen, it is for you to take the horses and the cloth from the caravan (traffic) and those engaged in commerce. You should give it to the men who guard the road which is situated between Egypt and Timbuctoo because it is a major route, used by all (engaged) in the transport of Egyptian cloth and the gold from Timbuctoo. These men are your power and strength. By them you control the land with power and with might.' Such are the people of the Air Sultan from ancient times until the present day.'

The reference to Timbuctoo is a later and distorted picture of the gold trade of Songhai which was so important for Agades. At one time the city had its own standard weight for the metal. Long after its disappearance it continued to regulate the circulating medium of exchange. Later it gave way to the salt. The Agades text gives no picture of the true situation. Far from being subject to the whims of the 'five tribes' the Sultan of Agades had much mightier masters. The period when the Sultans of Air enjoyed real independence was relatively short, nor can it be said that the city attained its greatest wealth when it was independent of its neighbours. The Massif in the days of Ibn Baṭṭūṭa ran its own affairs. There was a period far later in the seventeenth century when Agades was vaguely expansionist. The letters sent to al-Suyūṭī cover a brief span in the fifteenth century. Then, and only then, is it reasonable to assume that a Sultan of Agades, like Muḥammad 'the great' or Muḥammad Ṣaṭṭafan, was capable of solely controlling affairs. The Sultan was principally a Tuareg chief, arbitrator of the Tuaregs in Agades. The latter was in the views of Barth, a settlement 'made for the purpose of serving as a great commercial *entrepôt* for the commerce with another country.' (10)

One point where these Agades romancers seem obscure is the reference to the stage by stage shift of the Air capital. A move from the Massif to Tadeliza, to Tin-Shaman and finally Agades is presented. But is this historically sound? According to Marmol, Agades was built towards 1460, and this date probably accurately reflects what happened. The Agades list of Sultans records the reign of al-Ḥājj Ilaswen who was brought to Agades, as spanning the years 1430 to 1449 / 1450, when he was assassinated. Agades was well established when al-Suyūṭī wrote to Muḥammad Ṣaṭṭafan about 1492/3. If the questions of Muhammad al-Lamtūnī concern the affairs of Agades, and not Tadamakkat, then many of the social institutions of the city were by that time functioning, however misguidedly in his eyes. There remains the anonymous query about the right to herbage in the desert areas of Air also addressed to al-Suyūṭī. Here Agades is specifically mentioned, but with the implication that the administration was in a less evolved state, and hinting at a somewhat earlier date than the other correspondence with al-Suyūṭī. The reputation of the latter began to penetrate Air just after 1470, and his fame was well known in that region by 1484, when an unnamed Sultan of the Sahel was granted investiture. Now this was after the reign of al-Ḥājj Ilaswen, and perhaps during the ten year rule of Muḥammad al-Kabīr. In the light of all the above evidence an approximate date of 1460 is eminently probable.

The Songhai ruler Muḥammad Askia passed through Agades on his way to and on his way back from Cairo and Mecca between 1495 and 1497. He did so escorted by at least eight hundred armed men, possibly one thousand five hundred. (11) His return not only brought with it an enhancing of his religious prestige but also of his political status by virtue of his investiture (*taqlīd*) through the good offices of al-Suyūṭī. This date heralded the doom of any independant future for the Agades Sultanate. Its occupier, Muḥammad b. 'Abd al-Raḥmān, could have been only too pleased to see the Songhai monarch depart again for Gao.

Despite the growth of Agades city older haunts of the Air chiefs in its proximity were not abandoned. In the idyllic setting of Tadeliza amidst boulders, green glades, tiny fields of vegetables and corn, there stands to this day the ruins of a small castle and lordly residence made of stone blocks. From its spur on a terrace overlooking the valley of the Eghazar Wa-n-Agadez a fine view, suitable for defense, greets the eye. (12) Perhaps Tadeliza was already a centre for the semi-nomad ruler of Air at the time of Ibn Baṭṭūṭa's journeys.

Muḥammad Askia returned to Air, the Chronicles tell of the 'calamity of the Askia'. Towards 1500 he mounted an expedition against Tadeliza. (13) He compelled it to submit to his authority, for the Air Sultan was then in residence there. The copper Songhai trumpets echoed in victory along the valley where the little castle stood. The infant Agades Sultanate was compelled to pay tribute to Gao, 150,000 ducats to quote Leo Africanus.

In or just after this Tadeliza expedition, the Sultanate was ruled by two brothers, Muḥammad al-ʻAdil (Ghudāla) and Muḥammad Ḥumad. Perhaps one resided in Tadeliza and the other in Agades? Their joint rule was one of troubles. These brothers, sons of Faṭā 'the white', may have ordered the construction of the walls of Agades. In 1512 and 1513 Muḥammad Askia attacked Katsina. Between 1514 and 1515 he launched a campaign against al-ʻAdil (Ghudāla), Sultan of Agades who was one of the brothers. He had refused to pay the tribute hitherto imposed. Both brothers were unseated, and in the following year Muḥammad b. Taladha (var. Taluza) was appointed.

It may be asked whether Songhai dominance markedly changed the course which the Agades Sultanate would otherwise have followed. This seems unlikely. The city of Agades, its commerce and much of its life thrived and flourished as a satellite of Gao, nor is it clear that the Songhai yoke was exceptionallysevere. It was to become increasingly nominal. Rodd is inclined to the view that 'Agades was perhaps at the height of its prosperity before and immediately after the conquest of Muhammad Askia.' (14)

III

Tuareg epics of Bornu and Kanem

So much attention has been given to the dependence of Agades on Gao, that the influence of the earlier Sultanates of Bornu on the affairs of the Air Tuaregs has often been overlooked. Some lettered Tuaregs of Air place greater weight on the Bornu connection than on that with Gao. While the west of Air shows the culture of Tadamakkat in its customs and architecture, the eastern part of Air has been influenced from Bornu. These influences met in Agades. It has even been suggested that Bornu had a considerable say in shaping the original Air pre-Agades Sultanate, before it fell under the influence of the Songhai Empire. (15)

Bornu was a state which prior to the eleventh century owed much to the might of Tuareg tribal chiefs as well as to the Tubu. Apart from the entrance into Air from the north-east, other Tuaregs entered it from the south-east, from the region of Chad. The fortunes of Bornu had much to do with Tuareg settlement in the Massif.

Rodd held the view that, 'I shall simply regard the Tuareg of Bornu as part of the Lemta of the Fezzan which we may assume from various sources they were. In consequence, however slender the evidence, it becomes difficult to avoid the conclusion that the Tuareg reached Bornu from the north along the Bilma road in the course of the Arab invasions of the eighth century. They remained as rulers of the country until they were driven from there also, in consequence of increasing Arab pressure in the Fezzan and in Equatoria itself, for in the middle of the eleventh century the Hillal and Soleim Arabs are found extending their conquests as far as Central Africa. Their fighting under Abu Zeid al-Hillali against the Alamt (Lemta) Tuareg in the Fezzan is still remembered in the traditions of the Equatorial Arab tribes.

'All we can say with any degree of certainty is that somewhere between the eighth and eleventh centuries the Lemta Tuareg eventually emigrated from the Chad countries.'

From these emigrants arose the 'five tribes' who mastered the Massif. In later centuries relations between the Air Tuaregs and the rulers of Bornu were to be of considerable importance and to lead to fierce wars outside the walls of Agades and in the mountains.

The Tuareg stories in Air attempt to assign to themselves a major role in the foundation of the Sultanates of Kanem and Bornu. Far from seeing their status there as one supplanted by others for centuries, the texts of al-Mukhtār b. 'Abd al-Qādir al-Jīkatī credit the Tuaregs with the military power which put the Sultanates on their feet. They founded Air and Agades, their descendants founded a Sultanate in Adar. Why should not Bornu and Kanem likewise be embraced by their achievements, despite the reliable sources which credit Turkish musketeers with the military successes of the Bornu ruler Mai Idrīs b. 'Alī (Alooma) in the sixteenth century? Yet there were reports, quoted by the Egyptian al-Sakhāwī and others, that the rulers of Bornu were of the 'people of the veil' (*mulaththamūn*) and those lettered among the Tuaregs who knew of their tradition, would not be unwilling to take advantage of it.

'As for the origin of the Sultanate of Bornu, it came about that at the time when the Sultan Ilaswen (Alisaw) was brought, and when he was installed in the town of Agades by the tribe of the Aghunbulutan (supreme chief of the Itisen), they, the Imikitan (Sandal) did not accept him, and he fought with them to compel them to follow him. They refused to do so, until a Sultan who was called al-Nazīf (?) conquered them. His tomb is in the village of Tafazat.'

'They fought with him over a long period until he gave them the agnomen (*kunya*) of Imikitan. Then he mastered them and chased them in Air. He expelled most of them from Air until they reached a country called Tin Wadan. There they found tribes of the negroes. They were many, but they pursued them to their mountains, and they occupied their land which they had conquered by force. They were in dire straits because they had no Sultan in their land, because a land is neither settled nor prosperous without a Sultanate. It has been said that religion and kingship are a twin-pair. 'Religion is a basis and foundation while the Sultan is the guardian who keeps watch.' That which has no basis is destroyed and perishes. That which has no guardian to keep watch is lost and is a wilderness. The absence of any Sultan harmed them so they moved to Kanem.'

'When they came to the Sultan of Kanem, the tribe of the Sawṭāṭen (var. Sawṭan) was to be found there. - Nowadays they are behind Birni Bornu, and every year in the 'winter' the Sultan of Bornu makes a raid on them. Feuding broke out between them. So one of the tribe of the Sawṭāṭen went to the Sultan of Kanem and said to him that if he gave him a specific sum as recompense, he would show him a land amidst the waters, for the latter surrounded that country. So he gave him the reward. The Sultan said to the tribe of the Imikitan, 'You have come to me from the direction of the west, and it is only you who can carry me there.' So the tribes of the Imikitan bore him to the land of Bornu which is between the rivers, and there they dug a large trench, a fortress (Birni) for him, and they named it Birni Bornu. Then the Imikitan, when they had installed the Sultan of Bornu in the place where his power and authority rested, and when he ruled the whole of the land of Bornu, sought his permission and said to him, 'At the time when we left the land of Air we were rulers and conquerors of the land of the negroes. Air is better than the land of the negroes and better than the land of Bornu. We ask your permission to return to it.' So he granted them their wish. He said to them, 'Return to your country."

'When the tribes of the Imikitan returned to their territory - Tin Wadan - which they ruled by force and might - and dwelt therein for a time, then it was that the tribes were too many in number for it. Their circumstances compelled them to reflect on the choice of a Sultan. It was as if they consumed their offspring and those among them who were weak and feeble. They reflected, and they deliberated, and they said, one to another, 'Negro Sultans we cannot endure. Let us return to Air wherein dwell our brethren the 'five tribes', including the Sandal, who have promoted the Sultan over them. Let us set aside wealth for (him - the Sultan?) on our own part. Every chief of ours will provide a two year old camel and four cows.' So they concurred in that (var. their view deviated over this). But their chiefs unanimously approved what their course of action should be. They said, 'We are people of the *Sharī'a* law. It can only be enforced through a Sultan and by a just king and by a learned *faqīh* who is an authority in the branches of the *Sharī'a.'* When they had fulfilled these conditions they made a promise to their Sultan (in Bornu) that they would guard the country of Bornu from Tuareg raids, because they were the ones who had established the Sultan in Bornu.'

'When the Sultan of Bornu made an agreement with the tribes of the Imikitan, and they were satisfied among themselves and their intentions accorded with a desire for peace and well-being, the land of Bornu being wide and their daily life peaceful, then it was that a difference occurred between the Sultan and the tribes of the Imikitan. (16) The fire of war was set alight and dissension (*fitna*) raged in the land of Bornu in its entirety. When God desires peace, God makes a Sultan agreeable to the hearts of the 'five tribes', including the Sandal because they are the people in authority who 'loosed' and 'bound' in ancient times, and they do so until the present day. Because it is they who ruled the land of Air by force, seizing it from the infidel negroes. They appointed their Sultan to rule over them in accordance with their wishes.'

This curious piece of Tuareg national sentiment, must, if Urvoy is correct, (17) refer to the foundation of N'gazargamu, the capital of Bornu, by 'Alī (Ghāzī) b. Dunama (1476-1503) who set up a stable administration and in 1484 founded N'gazargamu (Birni Bornu) on the river Yo. During his reign the chief *Imām* 'Umar Masbarma (d. 1512) tried to ensure that the ruling class at least observed the minimum requirements of the *Sharī'a.* That this ruler is the one referred to would appear to be confirmed by the fact that he was a near contemporary of Ilaswen (1430-1450) who was involved with the expulsion of dissident Imikitan from Air. The interest of the Air text is that it claims that these Tuaregs were active helpers, if not key warriors, in the establishment of this Bornu ruler in N'gazargamu. While this is not in itself impossible, if these Imikitan were mercenaries, the latter part of the tale, which contrasts or confuses their allegiance to the Sultan of Air and the Sultan of Bornu, is dismissed by Urvoy as a *pastiche absurde,* (18) It is possibly a whim of the copyist, for there is no certainty that the manuscript ends in this fashion in the original book of al-Mukhtār b. 'Abd al-Qādir al-Jīkatī, although the copyist specifically claims to have quoted the original.

The tale may not be wholly devoid of fact. If the Sahelian Sultan who came to Cairo in 889/1484 (19) and by al-Suyūṭī's mediation was invested by the Caliph al-Muta wakkil, was this Sultan of Bornu, this might explain why errant Imikitan undertook to guard the Bornu Sultanate and to accept its Islamic legitimacy on a par with that of Ilaswen of Agades. As for dissensions which raged in Bornu and involved the Imikitan there can be no historical certainty. (20)

This Tuareg tale of the Imikitan and the Sultan of Bornu cannot be dismissed wholly as a fiction of *Ineslemen* 'royalists'. There was an interelationship between the way the Sultanate evolved in Agades and other Sultanates in the same region. Perhaps this is the true message hidden in the Tuareg Bornu romance.

IV

Sufi Orders in Air

One of the remarkable contributions of the saints of Air to the spread of Islam was the welcome they gave to the Khalwatīya *ṭarīqa.* If their records are correct this order reached Air in the sixteenth century. Several Sufi orders found a refuge in the Massif. The Qādirīya first arrived with the Kel Es-Suq. But the Khalwatīya came with one man. He was martyred in a lonely spot called Aghalangha. He became the holiest saint of Air. He taught others who passed on his teachings. The impact of Egyptian and Oriental ideas among the Tuaregs is nowhere more remarkable than in the diffusion of the Khalwatīya.

When the sanctuary at Agallal was founded about 1480, the men of Abū Ruways were affiliated to the Qādirīya order which had reached the Adrar-n-Ifoghas. The Qādirīya had been founded by 'Abd al-Qādir al-Jīlānī (1077-1166), a Persian who established his centre in Baghdad. It became the parent order and was established in Morocco at least as early as 1450, and in North Africa as a whole at least two centuries earlier. From the Maghrib it spread to Tadamakkat and from thence to Air. How it came to be dominated by the Kunta is still unknown. There are only very late and biased sources which inflate the part played by their Shaykhs in its diffusion. (21)

As far as Hausaland is concerned its Sufism owed much to Tagedda and to Air. According to oral tradition the oldest branch of the Qādirīya was established in Kano by Abdullahi Suka (Thiqa), a famous Kano scholar who had received the *ṭarīqa* from the Fezzan. Thiqa lived in the seventeenth century. He was a pupil of Shaykh al-Bakrī who was still alive in 1597. The latter was a pupil of Shams al-Dīn al-Najīb b. Muḥammad of Anū-Ṣamman and Tagedda, so it is possible that the Qādirīya came to Kano direct from Tuareg lodges in Air. 'Uthmān dan Fodio is reputed to have received his 'litany' (*wird*) from Jibrīl b. 'Umar, who was resident in Agades. The Khalwatīya came to Air from the East, from Egypt and ultimately from Turkey. It stands apart from the spread of the Qādirīya.

A *khalwa* in Arabic denotes both a method of isolation from the world for mystic purposes, and a cell in which these mystic rites are carried out. In its origin and throughout much of its history the Khalwatīya was an urban order. Its half-legendary founder, 'Umar al-Khalwatī (d. circa 1397) was probably so in a very restricted sense. His piety did not embrace talents in the organisation of an institution or a system. This task was undertaken by the second *pir* Shaykh Yaḥyā Shīrwānī (d. 1463) from Shamakhi in the Caucasus. The order took root in Azarbaijan and the Caucasus. About 1460 Shaykh Yaḥyā Shīrwānī moved to Baku. He sent his *khalīfas* to all parts of the region, and after his death his followers moved to Amasya in north central Anatolia.

The thirty year reign of Sufi Bāyazīd (1481-1511) was the heyday of the Khalwatīya in Ottoman Turkey, and it was during this period that the headquarters were moved to Istanbul. The Khalwatīya began to make its mark in urban Egypt a little before 1500. It was supported by officials, soldiers and civil servants but it also took root among the common populace. It had noted personalities. The first Khalwatis to arrive in Egypt were three Turks from Tabriz; Shams al-Dīn Muḥammad Demerdash (d. 1526), Shāhīn b. 'Abdullāh al-Jarkasī (d. 1547) and Ibrāhīm b. Muḥammad Gülshenī (d. 1534). They seem to have come during the reign of the Mamluk Sultan Qānsawh al-Ghawrī about 1500.

Demerdash integrated himself in Egyptian society and built a Zāwiya in Cairo. He had a remarkable Egyptian follower, Karīm al-Dīn (1485-1578), a man of *baraka,* a singer and a magician-astrologer who became a master of science of magic squares, (*'ilm al-awfāq*) and horoscopes using letters and concentric circles (*zā' iraja*). The use of magic squares, charms and talismans helped the popular spread of the order. In the early sixteenth century the Khalwatīya order was established in Cairo under Mamluk patronage. If the Air traditions are correct, an adherent of this order called Sīdī Maḥmūd (Makhmūd) al-Baghdādī came to Agades and Air during the rule of the Sultan Aḥmad b. Taluẓa (1542-1556).

There is some confusion in Air between Sīdī Maḥmūd al-Baghdādī and al-Maghīlī of Tilimsan. There are Tuaregs who maintain that the Qādirīya, and not the Khalwatīya, was brought to Air by a saint from Baghdad. The case for mistaken identity is not strong. Al-Maghīlī did not stay long in Air. He preferred Tagedda and Gao. Furthermore, whatever Sufi sentiments he possessed, they were not uppermost in his teaching. Agades, its scholars and saints, owed more to al-Suyūṭī than to al-Maghīlī who died before Sīdī Maḥmūd al-Baghdādī reached Air. The Qādirīya had established lodges at Agallal and elsewhere as early as 1480. It was embraced by the Kel Es-Suq who had moved east to Air before or after the reign of Sunni Ali at the end of the fifteenth century. It is unlikely that the Qādirīya would have come to Air from Egypt, particularly at a time when the Khalwatīya was in favour with the Mamluks.

Muḥammad Bello had no doubts that Sīdī Maḥmūd al-Baghdādī came after al-Maghīlī and the Massūfa scholars of Tagedda. To quote his *Infāq al-Maysūr,* 'Among them is the Shaykh and *Imām* al-Rabbānī Sīdī Maḥmūd al-Baghdādī, who performed rare deeds of piety and remarkable miracles. He was the unique 'pearl of his age'. He was a *Quṭb,* revivifier of the *Sunna* and suppressor of innovation, caller to the truth. He spoke with the speech of saints, lord of the *ṭarīqa,* proof of the *Sharī'a,* who spent all his time in worship and devotion and in the reciting of litanies. He entered the land of Air enlighting and guiding. Men hastened to him to partake of his light and his guidance, men who saw their need and their necessity for one who would save them from error and lead into true guidance, and who would save them from wickedness by the light, from ignorant uncouthness by the light; and from heedlessness would lead them to wakefulness, and from pre-occupation with other than God to pre-occupation with God, from whim and fancy to piety. God have mercy on all such and grant them His pardon.

His companions studied with him, and many persons became Shaykhs on account of him. Many Shaykhs partook of his light, and the effects of his blessing and their blessings and the *baraka* which was bestowed remained. His companions exalted and highly esteemed him to the extent that they gave him the title of the *Mahdī* who was awaited. About him they recounted *ḥadīths* and traditions, how near they were to reality only God knows best. Nonetheless, he was a lordly scholar and eternal succour. The saints of God declared him before he appeared. When he became famous in the country, the jurists of his age took exception to him, and they incited the Sultan against him so that warfare took place between them until they slew him at Aghalangha. May God Almighty be pleased with him and withhold it from those who slew him.' (22)

Muḥammad Bello drew on Air sources which outlined the life of Sīdī Maḥmūd. These sources were similar to the text of the manuscripts about his life and his miracles which still exist and which are recent version of older manuscripts. (23) The figure portrayed by Muḥammad Bello is unmistakably Sufi. Sīdī Maḥmud is also described as the 'lord of the '*ṭarīqa'*, though which Sufi order is unspecified. Muhammad Bello and 'Uthmān dan Fodio, his father, were both affiliated to the Qādirīya. The Khalwatīya had mainly come to his knowledge as the parent order of the Tijānīya. But it would be hasty to see this reference to 'the *ṭarīqa'* as only implying the Qādirīya. 'Uthman dan Fodio admired the Tijānīya and had received the *silsila* - the mystic genealogy of Shaykhs - of the Khalwatīya among those passed on to him by Shaykh Jibrīl of Agades. Muḥammad Bello meant to emphasize the highly Sufi character of the teachings of Sīdī Maḥmūd and to lay stress on 'illumination' and recital of litanies, both of which reveal how very different this Oriental preacher was from al-Maghīlī.

The claim of 'Mahdihood' to Sīdī Maḥmūd is of interest, particularly its possible occurrence in the middle of the sixteenth century. It may have been a ploy used by the advisers of Sultan Aḥmad b. Taluẓa to engineer the death of this 'false' Sharīf at the hands of semi-pagan Kel Away. Had Egypt an interest in his religious activities? Much depends on the date 1556, if the Agades list of Sultans is reliable.There are some Tuaregs who would dispute this date. They attribute the martyrdom of the saint to a Barkuray fanatic, Ḥadāḥadā, who was active in the area of Ṭaduq at the end of the century and the early part of the next. Ghubayd agg Alojaly of Agades is an advocate of a late date. In a note sent some years ago to me he remarked, 'Sīdī Maḥmūd al Baghdādī came to Air after 'Abd al-Karīm al-Maghīlī. He brought the religious fraternity called the Khalwatīya order. He gained following in the tribes of the Kel Away and the Itisen but he was rejected by the tribe of the Ibarkurayan (Barkuray) who were dwelling at that time at Ṭaduq and in its vicinity. This was the reason for the kindling of war between these tribes. The Ibarkurayan carried out a raid on the area of the Kel Away until they reached Aghalangha (mountain) where Shaykh Maḥmūd al-Baghdādī was, and the tribes of the Kel Away which followed him. The warriors of the Ibar-kurayan were under the leadership of Ḥadāḥadā (var. Khadăkhadă). A decisive battle took place between them. It ended in the defeat of the tribes of the Kel Away and the martyrdom of their Shaykh Mahmūd al-Baghdādī. His tomb is to be found there, and it is visited.'

The chronological gap between the reign of Aḥmad b. Taluẓa and that of the Sultan al-Tafrija, a contemporary of Ḥadāḥadā, is a century and is irreconcilable. Either both traditions are partly incorrect, or one or other must be mistaken. Scholars of the Kel Es-Suq, like Mawlay Muḥammad al-Hādī, attribute the fall of the house of Ṣaṭṭafan to the martyrdom of Sīdī Maḥmūd, and there are several texts which favour the reign of Aḥmad b. Taluẓa in particular. The principal Air book about Sīdī Maḥmūd, *Ṣifat al-Wird,* attributed in part to a recent compiler, Mūsā Abatul, is entirely about the Khalwatīya and the sixteenth century.

Ṣifat al-Wird is full of non-historical hagiography. When the coming of Sīdī Maḥmūd drew nigh, the Air saints rejoiced. Among them 'Abd al-Karīm al-Maghīlī. A *faqīh* of Agades named Awgar secretly disclosed the portents. They were overheard by his son Aḥmad al-Muqaddam who recited the Qur'ān before his father. 'Abd al-Karīm al-Maghīlī confirmed his father's words, for Awgar smelt the hand of the former which was filled with fragrance. The reformer from Tuwat had raised his hand skywards and had absorbed the scented *baraka* of the Baghdad mystic who was to come. Aḥmad al-Muqaddam was one of the first followers of Sīdī Maḥmūd. Other saints defended the latter against his critics among the Agades *'ulamā'.* They included famous names such as Abū 'l-Hudā al-Sūqī and 'Abd al-Raḥmān b. Tkrs (?). Al-Najīb (al-Anūṣammanī?) Muḥammad, who was nicknamed al-Sayf (the sword) told the Sultan of Agades Aḥmad b. Taluẓa, that Sidi Mahmud 'the Mahdi' was one of God's servants. When Abū 'l-Hudā replied to denigrators he is alleged to have said, 'Those who doubt that he is the Mahdī, have no doubt that he is a saint, and those who doubt his sanctity, have no doubt that he is a scholar. Those who doubt that he is a scholar, have no doubt that he is pious. Those who doubt his piety, have no doubt that he is a true believer, and whosoever claims he is other than this is bereft of his reason, and no medicine will cure him.'

Muḥammad al-Faqīh b. Muḥammad b. Ibrāhīm of Tefis (24) said, when he was asked about Shaykh Maḥmūd, 'he is a scholar and a saint.' Tefis was an active centre of the Shaykh's activities.

Who were these holy men who were advocates of the newcomer? They were Qādirīya who were willing, in the main, to adopt the litany (*wird)* of Sīdī Maḥmūd, so it would appear that the latter was undemanding in regard to affiliation to his order. Tuaregs maintain that there was no hard and fast distinction then between the Qādirīya and the Khalwatīya. Sidi Maḥmūd drew his support from ex-students of al-Maghīlī, of al-Suyūṭī, or of Abū Ruways of Tadamakkat. Certain novices were students of Shaykh Aḥmad al-Zarrūq (d. 1493), the commentator of Ibn 'Aṭā' allāh of the Shādhilīya order. A few were pupils of a local mystic, 'Uthmān al-Mawhūb b. Iflawas, the founder of the mosque at Ṭaduq.

The support given to Sīdī Maḥmūd was almost universal among the Qādirīya mystics of Tadamakkat. Abū Ruways, until his death at Sanbali was one of his novices. Another was Muḥammad al-Amīn who journeyed to the Orient and studied there until he was allowed by his Shaykhs to return to Air. He was buried at Tawāz at the foot of Mount Bagzan. Another disciple was Shaykh Muḥammad b. al-Walī Inirgaray. He was among the company of Shaykhs who was blest with a vision of al-Khiḍr (25) and Elias. Aḥmad b. al-Faqīh Raḥmat Allāh of Agallal said, 'I came to my Shaykh, and he told me that he had been visited by the Prophet of God, Elias, and the latter had shown him the mat which he had made for him.' The Shaykh sat upon it and chatted for a little while. Shaykh Aḥmad said, 'Then he moved in yearning and longing to meet the Prophet Muḥammad, and the mat moved before him, due to the action of the Prophet.' The saint used to say to his disciples, that whosoever sat with him for forty days under his tree at Agallal would have his needs supplied if God so willed. Sīdī Maḥmud had other followers. They included Muḥammad al-Ḥājj Jīkat and Muḥammad b. Yūsuf al-Sūqī al-Daghūghī who adopted his *wird,* and this led, it is said, to a dispute between him and Muḥammad b. 'Alī of As-Suq until the latter repented of his views.

To Sīdī Maḥmud al Baghdādī are attributed litanies in Tamashegh and a peculiar *dhikr* or form of religious chanting to induce a state of spiritual ecstasy (*wajd).* In his *wird* there were lengthy prayers combined with Qur'ānic readings. How the exclusive principles of the Qādirīya were accommodated with those of the Khalwatīya are not disclosed. In a heady 'charismatic movement', in which the holy men of Air were adoring devotees, the Baghdad *faqīh* cast a spell over the mountains to the dismay of the Sultan of Agades and his jurists who viewed the unbridled Sufism of Agallal, Tefis, Jīkat and their lodges with suspicion or distate.

Whatever the date of these mystical adventures, the Tuaregs of Air maintain that it ended in the martyrdom of Sīdī Maḥmud. The centre of the tragedy was at Agallal, and later at Aghalangha. The slayers of Sīdī Maḥmud were either the Kel Away or the Barkuray. If they were tribesmen of the first then a date prior to the establishment of the Kel Away in Agades in the seventeenth century is a near certainty. If tribesmen of the latter, then the seventeenth century is to be preferred since it was an age of violence by fanatical Barkuray against the Sufi lodges of Air.

Agallal was and still is the major Islamic shrine in Air. Founded as a Qādirī retreat it was for twelve years the haunt of Sīdī Maḥmūd al-Baghdādī. According to the early tradition the pagan Kel Away compelled him to withdraw to Aghalangha, a wild place of rocks and crags. He was a militant mystic and had defended Agallal as long as he could with his magic lance. He fell into a trap and was killed treacherously, but his body miraculously disappeared. His blood stained the stone, and his clothes hung suspended on the branches of a jujube tree in the valley. His son, Shaykh Mūsā, survived him, and he was married at Agallal. Both Agallal and Aghalangha became places of pilgrimage. In days past the rocks of the latter re-echoed to the prayers of believers who camped amidst the forest of jujube trees, the 'Christ-thorn' lotes (*sidr*), tree of the Seventh Heaven. There in the thorn is the empty tomb of Sīdī Maḥmūd al-Baghdādī. The pilgrims devoutly used to insert a stick into a hollow at the spot where it was believed his head once rested, to acquire his *baraka.*

A sceptic will view with extreme suspicion these Sufi traditions and suspect all as a survival of pre-Islamic beliefs or local superstition. Irreconcilable dates, the confusion of al-Maghīlī, who allegedly founded a mosque at Abatul, with Sīdī Maḥmūd and rival claims of Sufi affiliation suggest the existence of a 'synthetic saint', a prototype figure around whom were built tales of Qādirīya sanctity to be borrowed at a later date by the Khalwatīya.

In 1550 the Kel Away were not 'people of the king'. They had no say in the Sultanate, like the Itisen, but by 1650 during the reign of al-Tafrīja their power in Agades was steadily growing. It would have been politic to find another band of culprits who had slain the 'holy man,' The Barkuray were their foes at that time. Thus, two consecutive theories emerged in which the common martyr was Sīdī Maḥmūd.

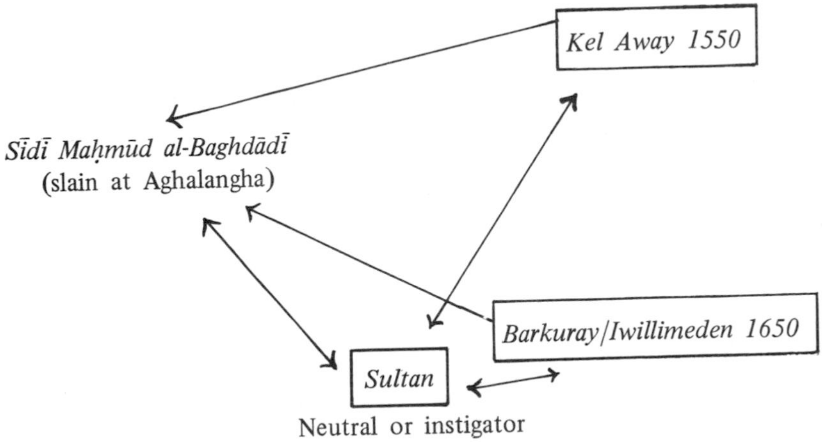

Despite chronological and theological confusion, there seems to be some truth which defies the sceptic, hinting that about 1550 a martyrdom did occur. The arrival of the Khalwatīya via the Sudan in the mid-seventeenth or early eighteenth century seems too late, too close to the age of Muḥammad Bello not to escape his notice, (26) nor is the Kel Es-Suq Qādirīya likely to have entered Air via Bilma and Libya, the route taken by Sīdī Maḥmūd al-Baghdādī. Despite confusion as to whether he was slain by the Kel Away or the Barkuray, the people in Air consistently attach him to the arrival of the Khalwatīya. If this be fact and not fancy, then Mamluk Egypt in the sixteenth century would have been the obvious centre from whence Sīdī Maḥmūd began his mission. The mystery is unsolved. An empty tomb, a magic lance and torn raiment in a wild mountain valley in the land of the Tuaregs is the sole visible evidence of this militant Sufi who fought in Air amidst a grove of jujube trees. (27)

NOTES

1) *Al-Ḥāwī lil fatāwī*, Cairo, 1933, pp. 148-149, and *E.C.P.T.*, p. 180.

2) *mawlā* - Any Muslim who was not a full member by descent of an Arab tribe. However, the title has many other senses including *trustee, patron* and *freed slave.* See *Encyclopedia of Islam* under *mawlā.*

3) This may be seen in a passage of Muḥammad b. Aḥmad b. 'Iyās al-Ḥanafī, describing events in Egypt in *Dhū 'l-Ḥijja*, 909/1503. 'In *Dhū 'l-Ḥijja* it was rumoured among the people that 'Anbar, the chief (*muqaddam)* of the Mamluks had fled and had gone in the direction of the land of Takrūr. The reason for that was that the Sultan asked him for money which he did not possess, so he fled. He thought that his affair had become a thing of the past. Then, after four days had elapsed they arrested him, and they brought him before the Sultan who decreed his imprisonment in the *'Arqāna* ('sweat house'). It was said that when he was arrested, and he stood before the Sultan he verbally rebuked him and said to him, 'Why did you flee, when you were still *Muqaddam* of the Mamluks, officer (*Amīr*) over ten?' 'Anbar replied, 'It is the habit of negro slaves to flee.' The Sultan, thought well of his reply.'
If 'Anbar never reached Takrūr it seems unlikely that he was the first Mamluk or the last to attempt to do so. The arrival of Mamluks in Air, Agades, Bornu, Tagedda, and the whole of this region may go some way to explain how local traditions evolved and how local institutions began to look decidedly Egyptian, Turkish or Circassian.
Badā'i' al-zuhūr fī waqā' i' al-duhūr, Istanbul, 1931, pp. 63-64.

4) See *C.A.*, by Urvoy pp. 146-147.

5) See *P.V.*, pp. 393-400.

6) See H. Lhote, *Notes Africaines,* No. 137, p. 9, Jan. 1973.

7) See page 142.

8) See S. Bernus, *Henri Barth chez les Touaregs de l'Aïr,* p. 174.

9) Obscure passage in the text.

10) See *T.D.N.C.A.*, p. 206.

11) See Bovill '*The Golden Trade of the Moors*', chapter IX, and S. Bernus, *op. cit.*, pp. 176-179.

12) H. Lhote, *ibid,* pp. 10-12.

13) *ibid,* pp. 12-15.

14) See *P.V.*, p. 411.

15) *Sic,* al-Ḥājj 'Abdu Malam Mūsā.

16) The text either implies a conditional situation on the lines of the state of affairs in Air or suggests that a dissension actually occurred.

17) See *C.A.*, by Urvoy, pp. 157-158.

18) Urvoy argues an adumbration of the Air Sultanate text in the final sentences of the tale of Bornu. The texts are not identical. Even if his interpretation of a 'conditional situation' be accepted, there is a clear difference between tumult, and hard life, in Air, and 'the fire of war' and dissension (*fitna)* in Bornu. Dissension specifically occurs in the Bornu text, and there is marked difference in vocabulary.

19) See E.M. Sartain, *op. cit.*, p. 195.

20) *ibid,* p. 197.

21) See C.C. and E.K. Stewart, *Islam and Social Order in Mauritania,* pp. 36-44.

22) *I.M.*, ed. Whitting, p. 16.

23) See texts in collections *A.* and *A.N.*

24) See *P.V.*, pp. 256, 258, 418.

25) On this character, al-Khaḍir or al-Khiḍr, cf. *Encyclopedia of Islam* under *al-Khaḍir.*

26) 'Abdullāh b. Fūdī wrote a book on the Khalwatīya called *Bāyan al-arkān wal-shurūṭ lil-ṭarīqa al-ṣūfīya al-Khalwatīya.*

27) Regarding the arrival of Sīdī Maḥmūd, see similar episodes in Hausa literature, for example, in 'The song of the Shaihus miracles, a Hausa hagiography from Sokoto' by M. Hiskett, *African Language Studies,* XII, 1971, p. 81.

A Note on a Young Massūfa Mystic who visited towns of the Turks.

The constant journeyings of scholars from Tagedda, Agades, Tadamakkat, Timbuctoo and Walāta, whether on pilgrimage or for reasons of study and commerce, meant that a number of their descendants grew up in Arabia and the Middle East. Some of them lost touch with the Tuareg lands, others may have maintained loose links with relations. Al-Sakhāwī (1) mentions one of the Massūfa whose religious pursuits took him into remote regions, far removed from Air or the Adrar. Muḥammad b. Muḥammad b. ʻAbdullāh b. Ibrāhīm al-Shams b. al-Shams was one of the Massūfa by birth, Mālikī in his *Madhhab*. He lived much of his brief life in the holy city of Medina. He was born at the beginning of *Dhū 'l-Qaʻda* in the year 859/1454 in Medina, and there he memorized the Qur'an, the *Risāla al-Farʻīya* and the *(A)jurrumīya* and the *Alfīya* of Ibn Mālik on Arabic Grammar and other texts. He did well in his studies, and he composed Arabic verse. Then he travelled to Damascus and to Aleppo, Māridīn and Ruhā (Edessa). The two cities were north-west of Mosul in the province of Diyār Bakr. Māridīn was assigned in 1108 to Il-Ghazi by the Saljuq ruler of Baghdad. The descendants of Il-Ghazi, the Ortuqids, ruled until after the death of Tamerlane, and they were benefactors of dervishes and mystics.

Muḥammad al-Massūfī returned to Medina. He died there in *Jumādā I* in the year 885/1480/1, during the life time of his father. The latter wrote down the poetry of his son, and he recited it before al-Sakhāwī who furnishes an example of it in his book, verses quoted among the men of Medina:-

> I beseech the Almighty's intercession, by the title of the Prophet, the
> Chosen One, in that which I desire and hope for.
> I make for the 'door' of the Hashemite, Muḥammad. In all my needs
> and wants I depend upon him.
> I have alighted in the hallowed ground (*ḥimā*). Those who stay as
> guests in it are not oppressed. As long as I live I shall not move to another.
> When oppression touches me sore, I praise and magnify his name.
> He averts that evil from me, and it is taken away.
> I say, my beloved, oh, Muḥammad, my lord, my refuge and
> my shelter, by him I make my supplication.
> O, Lord of Creation, perhaps by a fragrant breeze I
> will be rightly guided. By my straying I am one impeded.

This entry by al-Sakhāwī, portraying as it does a young Massūfa scholar of promise who died young, illustrates the remoter regions of Sufism the Tuaregs of the Sahel were to visit in their mystic quests.

1) al-Sākhawī (d. 1497), *op. cit.*, Vol. 9, p. 115.

CHAPTER VI

AGADES AT THE APOGEE OF ITS SULTANATE AND IN THE AGE OF ITS DECADENCE

> 'Among their vile customs is the deposition of the Sultan without pretext or cause based on the *Sharī'a.* It has led to the enfeebling of their Sultanate, and the widespread war in their country to the extent that their affairs are hardly under control or under any restraint at all. There are other customs besides, too many to be counted.'
>
> *Infāq al-Maysūr*
> Shaykh Muḥammad Bello

I have mentioned the widespread tale in Air that its first Sultan came from Istanbul. Tuaregs today, familiar with Islamic history, acknowledge the contradiction in the arrival of a Muslim ruler from Constantinople still in Byzantine hands. They dismiss the tradition as fanciful. In the past, it was sometimes accepted by the lettered of Agades and by the Kel Es-Suq, and it is mentioned in their manuscripts. The tale is of no antiquity. No reference to it occurs in correspondance with al-Suyūṭī.

The quest to find a Sultan is elaborated in oral traditions. One account describes the departure of a group of Tuareg chiefs to request the Ottoman Caliph to nominate a neutral ruler for the inhabitants of Air. They bore a letter with them to this effect. They reached Istanbul and waited to meet the Caliph. They tarried three years and were reduced to penury. They were compelled to sell their camels and possessions to the Caliph's servants. The Tuaregs sought the help of an artisan who was a friend of one of the Caliph's griots. The latter advised the Tuaregs to wait until the Friday prayer. Then, when in the great mosque they heard the sound of drums and muskets they were advised to shout. The Caliph would ask his griots the reason for the shouting. The Tuaregs did as they were counselled, and they repeated their action on a subsequent Friday. By this time the attention of the Caliph had been drawn to them, and he heard their request.

They asked him for a noble wife, whose son was of noble blood. The Caliph refused, but a wife of his who was of slave birth and had been liberated consented to go, together with her brother and her son. The status of the latter ensured that the Sultan of Agades would be the son of a freed woman until the end of time. He could never be of noble *Imashaghen* status. An entourage set forth for Agades. The desert route led via Bilma and Borku to Air. The ex-wife of the

Caliph died at Aghalghawen on the edge of Air. Her son arrived in Tadeliza. From Tadeliza he moved to Agades.

Another version of the tale can be found in a local manuscript. The Kel Innik were ruled by a chief (*ṭabl*) who bore the title of Agumbulum. (1) There was much discord. It was decided to send a deputation to Istanbul to ask for an impartial chief. No one could be found to accept the office of emissary until an old woman who was called Tāghirit offered to send her three grand-children, Aghwalla Māfīnat, Aghwalla Shiṣidirak and Aghwalla Kel-Taghā. They arrived in the Ottoman capital, and they asked the Caliph for one of his sons. The Caliph consulted his wives, but all his legal wives refused. Eventually one of his concubines allowed her son to depart. He was brought to Air escorted by the Itisen. The latter presented him to the Kel Away who gave him an ox and a couch for his throne. For many years the Sultan lived the life of a semi-nomad escorted by the Itisen. At length a palace was built for him in Tadeliza. Later he moved to Aghghayaghi. The negro Gobirawa still ruled Agades with the Barkuray as their religious advisers. The Itisen settled the Sultan in Agades and built him a residence at a cost of 1,000 dinars. Finally the Itisen expelled the Gobirawa to Hausaland and the Barkuray to the land of the Iwillimiden.

This version is very late. It is no earlier than the period when the Kel Away and the Itisen jointly controlled and dominated the affairs of the Sultan of Agades. It cannot be earlier than the late seventeenth century, by which time the Kel Away were a power in the Air capital.

Such stories cannot be unconnected with the 'take over' of the Sultanate by the Kel Away who had intermarried with negroes. (2) Their dominance began about 1640 during the reign of the Sultan Muḥammad al-Tafrīja b. Yūsuf, who was in descent part Kel Away. Initially ousted by the Itisen he reasserted his claim to authority and ruled for some thirty-one years. The Kel Geres and the Itisen were eventually divested of their supreme authority in the affairs of the Sultanate. (3)

The reign of Muhammad al-Tafrīja saw wars of expansion in Adar and Gobir and confrontation with Bornu. The long reigns of Muḥammad al-Tafrīja, Muḥammad al-Mubārak, his brother, and the latter's son Muḥammad Agg-Abba, marked as never before an era of prolonged stability in the history of the Sultanate, covering the latter half of the seventeenth and the earlier years of the eighteenth century. No time could have been better to tie the threads of legends of emissaries to the Orient together, and to declare the Sultan to be the local representative of the Ottoman Caliph. (4)

The mission to the Caliph of Istanbul is a tale based on the earliest contacts with Cairo and the Mamluks, the arrival of Egyptian and other Oriental scholars

2. The Assembly Mosque of Agades

in Tagedda and Agades, fragments from Mamluk romances, and the renown of the Caliphs and the Ottomans. It was easy for a story to evolve that the Sultanate was a transplant from the Orient.

The Sultanate became a major institution in Air with its own rights and duties though painfully aware of its own limitations. Frequently deposed, militarily weak, among the Sultans whose names survive in the records, there were a few who reigned long and made Agades a political force in the Sahel.

II

Little is known of the Islamic life of Agades between the sixteenth and late eighteenth centuries. The best record is to be found in two or three contemporary or near-contemporary Arabic texts, (5) and in the architecture of its mosques which have been rebuilt or heavily restored. Among the most spectacular of its buildings is the great mosque, the *Sarari-n-mesallaje.* Its spiky minaret today dominates the city and the whole plain around Agades.

According to the traditions of the lettered in Agades the great mosque was first built about a century after the first houses in the city. This would date it to the early part of the sixteenth century. The builder was a holy man who came from Baghdad. He was called Shaykh Zakarīyā' b. 'Abdullāh, and he came to Agades during the reign of the Sultan Muḥammad al-'Adil (6) or possibly his successor of the same name, (10) who came to the throne in the middle of the sixteenth century. Zakarīyā', upon his arrival, settled unobtrusively in a house on the edge of the city at Inabambaghi. There he used to call the populace to prayer. The Sultan heard of his piety. He went on horseback and greeted the saint who told him that he had come from Baghdad. After discussion the Sultan gave him permission to construct a mosque. The saint stipulated that the locality and the materials supplied must be freely given, but in the event the Sultan did not follow his instructions.

The work began. None saw it since it took place at night. To complete the work, dōm-palm beams and great mats were used. But when the building was almost complete it collapsed. The first attempt - the ruins of which still survive adjacent to the present building - was a failure. The saint, Zakarīyā', asked the Sultan whether he had commanded the workers unwillingly to spare their time or donate their materials. The Sultan confessed that he had commanded them. 'That is the reason for the collapse of the mosque,' said the saint. He began to build the mosque a second time, but this time he only made use of materials freely offered by the population who were true believers. His effort succeeded, and the task was finished about 1531 or towards 1550.

The low-naved building which stands today was built much later, though probably, it copies the general appearance of its predecessor, 'the old Sofo'. Most of it was completed in 1844, but the minaret, its most spectacular feature, was rebuilt by the Sultan 'Abd al-Qādir (33) on the 24th of *Sha'bān* (8th August) 1847. It rises to some ninety feet and tapers in the manner of certain Ibāḍī minarets, like the one at Ghardaia in the Algerian Mzab. The projecting transverse rafters remind one of the mosques in Timbuctoo. The mud and dōm-palm edifice is typical of 'Sudanese' mosques in the regions bordering the Sahel. Agades was a city of many other mosques, several of which appear to date in their foundation from the sixteenth century. There are other tales of mosques which collapsed in the Katanga quarter. One figure quoted records the founding of seventy mosques in or near the city, and ten were in use in the days of Barth.

Local traditions tend to give priority in date to the building of these mosques, but they can hardly be much later or earlier than other edifices or city quarters of an administrative or commercial kind which were an integral part of the later Sultanate and its functioning. Agades, as its name indicates, is a place where visitors abounded - *Takadest* - and where they congregated. Its people were of very mixed origin, even excluding Arab, Fezzani and Maghribi merchants. In the heart of the city dwelt the Emgadeshi, the alleged descendants of those who were the companions of the first Sultan. They represented all social classes. Among its families were chosen the principal dignitaries of the court. In religious matters, the oldest element of the city population were the Ishsherifen, in whose family the title of *Alkhali (Qāḍī)* was invested. This family monopoly was much criticized. The whole family and class of the Ishsherifen were linked to the Kel Es-Suq of the Adrar-n-Ifoghas and ultimately to the *Shurafā'* of Fez. The Itisen claim to have first acted to establish the Sultan, and it is they who, up to the present time, designated the *Alkhali.*

The Tuaregs were part resident, part non-resident. The *Anastafidet* or administrative leader of the Kel Away at one time dwelt in Asoday. He established another residence in the city of Agades. The *Imashaghen* owned urban properties, and certain quarters of the city were particularly associated with individual Tuareg groups. According to oral tradition each of the *Imashaghen* tribes had a quarter. The Itisen and the Kel Geres were centred in Fune Hime. The Kel Away were centred in Akunfaya and Amarawet, the Igdalen Kel Amdit in the Amdit quarter, the Ilaswen in Amarawet, the Imikitan in Amaglan Agaja, the Kel Ferwan in Imurden-n-Afalla, and the Imakawghen in (H)oguberi.

The houses were occupied by slaves. Their masters lived in the desert or journeyed with their caravans. The slaves as city dwellers were subject to the Sultan's authority. Their masters could keep at a distance and pursue their affairs and their quarrels without fear of his interference. The Sultan was held in esteem and owned much wealth. He had the right to levy a tax on goods passing through Agades and also to exact dues from the Bilma salt trade. He held direct authority over the negroid populations of Agades and later the villages of In Gall and Tagedda-n-Tesemt. They gave him annual payments. For those who were under his command the Sultan became the arbitrator and supreme judge, and he could try to settle disagreements between the *Imashaghen.* The clever Sultan was the one who could play on the rivalries between the *Imashaghen,* rally their tri bal or religious patriotism, ensure good commerce, regular rain, or by his personality impose some stable order from his palace.

The *Ineslemen* had ritual duties to perform at the coronation of the Sultans. It was they who recited the *Fatekhen (fātiḥa),* the prayer for divine favour upon his person and his subjects. In the absence of the Sultan the Kel Ferwan 'drum-chief' administered his affairs. The Serki-n-Turawa governed the foreign community in Agades and settled questions of trade. The Serki-n-Kaswa collected market dues and controlled the price of commodities. The magazia, the Sultan's sister, was concerned with the Sultan's wives and the womenfolk of the city. She played a key role in many matters and lived in a house next to her ruling brother.

The Sultan was expected to uphold the faith. He was a Muslim ruler and Imām. He had to organise a *jihād* if required, even though he rarely went into battle, but sent his sons as his commanders. He had to pray for rain, and if there was a drought he was liable to be deposed. He controlled the public treasury (*bayt al-māl*), and it was his duty, with the aid of the *Qāḍī* and his *Ineslemen* to practise and enforce the Islamic religion.

In view of the many trials and afflictions which beset it, it is remarkable that the Sultanate survived for so long and on occasions became a power of some consequence. (6)

III

The triumph of Muḥammad al-Mubārak and his son Muḥammad Agg-Abba (1653-1720).

In a long list of feeble rulers, a few Sultans achieved greatness. Among their number were two at the very end of the seventeenth century. During their reigns Agades was independant. Its chief rival, the Sultanate of Bornu, which had sometimes held Agades to ransom, was repulsed. A series of attacks and sieges rallied the population of Air to the Sultanate. The Tuaregs fell back on the mountain fortresses of Tarawaji and Bagzan, and their fierce resistance to the forces of Bornu is preserved in many legends.

For over half a century the Sultanate pushed south into Adar. The first march in this direction was led by the son of Muhammad al-Mubārak, Muḥammad Agg-Abba, together with his brothers. The event is recorded in the Agades texts which allude to the origin of the Sultanate of Adar. (7)

'As for the origin of the Sultanate of Adar it was that (the Sultan) Muḥammad al-Mubārak at the time when the household of Kebbi took the land of Adar and annexed it to their possessions, gave it to his son, the Sultan Muḥammad Agg-Abba. He sent him from Azbin (Absen) to Adar, and he left with the tribe of Lisawen (Ilaswen), the tribe of the Imattukiyas, the tribe of the Amattadha, the tribe of the Ilamatay (var. Alamtan), and the tribe of the Tawantakat. He sent his son, the Sultan Muḥammad Agg-Abba with the chiefs of these tribes to the land of Adar. These tribes were his appointers and his supporters. They were his power and his might, his governors, the people of his counsel and those of his who had the authority to 'loose and to bind' . . . . . ' The real conquest began in 1674. The king of Gabbi (Kebbi) was vanquished and slain, and Muhammad Agg-Abba returned to Agades with his booty. Some time was to elapse before Muḥammad Agg-Abba was to return south again.

The Tuareg domination of Adar began during this key period in the history of the Sultanate. The Lisawen (Ilaswen), and later the Itisen, were to consolidate it. The Sultanate also pushed its forces due south towards Gobir and Bornu, attacking the capital of the latter, and in 1689 launching a decisive reprisal raid on the former. A caravan of Kel Air, led by Ṣāliḥ, brother of Muḥammad Agg-Abba, returning from Kebbi to Agades was attacked at night in Gobir near present day Madoua, and the Tuaregs were compelled to flee to Adar. Muḥammad Agg-Abba carried fire and sword into Gobir.

Despite successes there were also set-backs, both political and economic. In 1667 the Sultan Muḥammad al-Mubārak had to flee to In Gall because of Tuareg tribal disputes. He then moved to Dabak in 1679 in order to launch a raid on Bornu. In 1683 he had to act as an arbitrator at In-Taboraq in order to make peace between the Itisen and the Kel Away. In 1687 a great epidemic ravaged the city of Agades, and the Sultan was among its victims. His son Muḥamma Agg-Abba had to leave the city in 1694 and take refuge in Dabak. Two years later in 1696 fights between the Kel Away and the Itisen in the 'War of Hunger' brought anarchy into the heart of the Sultanate. Routes were cut, the commerce to the city interrupted, and this situation was to worsen in 1697 when one of the grimmest droughts in the Sahel hit the city. In 1699 a torrential fall of rain broke the drought, but nearly drowned the city and wrecked its buildings.

The latter years of the reign of Muḥammad Agg-Abba saw a decline. In 1721 he was dethroned by his brother al-Amīn. He took refuge in Adar which thirty-seven years before he had set out to conquer. Among the Itisen pushed south by the Kel Away he ruled a state which was to rival Agades. He founded its capital Birni-n-Adar and died there in 1738. Adar was to play an important part in future Tuareg history.

IV

The diary of Abū Bakar b. al-Ṭāhir Tāshī

Among the Arabic 'Agades Chronicles' the diary of Abū Bakar b. al-Ṭāhir Tāshī is unique. Unlike year lists *(ḥawlīyāt)* or names and dates of Sultans it is the record of an Agades *faqīh* during the reigns of Muḥammad al-Mubārak and Muḥammad Agg-Abba. The author reveals himself as a young scholar, familiar with the Sultans and their sons. To whom was his writing addressed, and is it complete? Perhaps it was addressed to a Shaykh, or it may be an example of family archives which were once plentiful in the city. The copy in the possession of the present Sultan, Ibrāhīm b. 'Umaru, is disjointed and does not seem to be identical with the copy previously translated. (8) Here and there incorrect dates are given. Yet, there is no mistaking its originality. An exciting period in the history of Agades is disclosed.

Abū Bakar was born in 1657. He grew up in Agades when it was under the rule of the Sultan Muḥammad al-Mubārak. His mother died when he was twelve. He 'donned the turban' when he was eighteen years old. It is not clear what ceremony is meant. A number of his contemporaries performed it at the same time.

Abū Bakar was certainly Tuareg in his family background. The women's names he mentions, Tāshī, Fanna and Asiya are Tuareg names, and his matrimonial life shows that he followed Tuareg customs. He first married when he was twenty-seven years old. It was not a success. His wife 'Aysha came from a respectable and well-off *Ineslemen* family, or from an aristocratic household in the city. She bore him two daughters, with a gap of two years between them, the elder called Fanna, the younger Asiya, both family names. He divorced 'Aysha shortly afterwards in 1688. They had been married for four years. In 1689 he married again, this time Nana 'Aysha who was the daughter of a man of religious standing, possibly a merchant from the Fezzan.

Abū Bakar travelled in the region of Adar, which was then in the process of being occupied by the Sultanate through the campaigns of Muhammad Agg-Abba. He met Ṣāliḥ, the son of the Sultan Muḥammad al-Mubārak who had suffered a reverse at the hands of the Gobirawa. One of Abū Bakar's relations was travelling in the Tuareg army which later was to launch a punitive expedition against the Gobirawa.

Abū Bakar paints a grim picture of the drought of 1697. In 1698 it was followed by violent rains. However, 'None suffered loss nor destruction in the house of my wife Nana ‘Aysha, the daughter of al-Hājj ‘Awnallāh.’

To conclude the part of the diary which has survived he gives a vivid portrait of what appears to be a solar eclipse, an event which cast terror into the hearts of the population. Here the dates are very confused.

One small detail of interest is the use of the word *Tawārik* spelt in the manner which employs the Arabic root ‘to abandon’. Abu Bakar regularly introduces it. In his eyes it could hardly have had a pejorative sense since in one passage he specifically states that in the war against the Zanfara in 1685, ‘God aided the Tuaregs (*Tawārik)* against them.’

***

‘In the Name of God, the Compassionate, the Merciful, the blessing and peace of God be upon our lord Muḥammad. Praise be to God who has created the whole creation and who has created man and who has brought him forth from nothingness into existence and who has returned him to nothingness. Man is prone to be forgetful and to sin.

I wish to establish firmly the dates and events of happenings which took place during the time when I lived among men who were born and who died. Glory to the Everlasting Almighty who never dies. He knows what happened, what did not happen, and He knows what will be, even as though it had already taken place. His blessing rest upon the Prophet, who were it not for him, the world would not have come into existence.

I am Abū Bakar, the son of al-Ṭāhir. (My father) was named after his mother, Tāshī, and I was born on the 13th (or the 17th) for I have forgotten what my father said to me - which was a Wednesday in the year 1067/1657. This was after the Sultan, Muḥammad al-Mubārak b. al-Sulṭān Yūsuf had grasped the reigns of authority. He had done so on the first night of the month of *Ramaḍān* in the year 1064/1654. He had ruled for three whole years. I, Abū Bakar, was born after the Sultan had entered his fourth year at the very beginning of *Ramaḍān*.

On Monday night, the 24th of *Ṣafar* fire broke out in the house of the Sultan, Muḥammad al-Mubārak, before the moon came out. In that year 1067/1657, there were several important deaths. The *faqīh* and learned Shaykh, the commentator on Khalīl b. Isḥāq, ‘Alī al-Ajhūrī, died, likewise Ḥaydāra b. Fāṭima. In the month of *Sha‘bān* , on Saturday the 20th of that month, during the night or day, the Sultan Agg-Abba was born (died) His birth (decease) (9) preceded the decease of Ḥaydāra b. Fāṭima. The Shaykh al-Ṭāhir also died, but he predeceased Ḥaydāra and died before (the birth of) Sultan Agg-Abba - may God have mercy upon the forebear and bestow His blessing on His creation. All this I heard from my father, Muḥammad al-Ṭāhir Tāshī. It is reported among the tally of the years. God knows best. I have written this to confirm it.

My mother Asiya, who was nicknamed Warna, - May God have mercy upon her - died in the month of *Dhū 'l-Ḥijja.* It was the night of 'Arafat, the 9th a Friday night at the end of the year 1079/1669. I was twelve years old. May God illumine her sepulchre and cause her to dwell in Paradise in ample gardens together with the spouses of the prophets.

Then, after my mother died, my grandmother, Tāshī, my father's mother, died. It was on a Wednesday. Khadīja, the daughter of the 'caller to prayer' (*mu'adhdhin*) died that same wednesday. So did the Shaykh and scholarly *faqīh* Muḥammad al-Daylamī. They died one after the other, but I have forgotten which one of them predeceased the other. It was in the year 1082/1672.

After the death of my grandmother, her daughter, Fanna bint Tāshī died. She was the sister of al-Tāhir, her blood kinsman by both her father and her mother. The event took place on the 8th of the month of *Ramaḍān* at the end of the year 1084/1673. May God cause her to dwell in the garden of Paradise.

In that year the Sultan Muḥammad al-Mubārak - may God have mercy upon him - sent forth his army. Its commander (*Amīr*) was his son Muḥammad Agg-Abba, the eldest of his sons, and his brothers al-Ḥājj Aknafaya, Ṣāliḥ and Akhmad. They were sent to Kufkana and the Sultan of Kebbi. Agg-Abba left with his troops in the month of *Dhū 'l-Qa 'da* at the end of the year 1084/1674. Then Muḥammad Agg-Abba, the son of the Sultan Muḥammad al-Mubārak, returned with his army from Kebbi to their city of Agades - may God guard it. He had given them victory over their foe and had crushed the land of Kebbi. Kufkana had died, and the power of Kebbi was brought to nought, to ruin and to waste for ever after. After their return al-Ḥājj Aknafaya, the son of the Sultan Muḥammad al-Mubārak, went on the pilgrimage in the month of *Rajab,* in the year 1085/1675. It was his second pilgrimage.

In that same year, I, Abū Bakar b. al-Ṭāhir Tāshī, donned the 'turban'; so did 'Abdullāh b. Yamūrī and a goodly number of some forty or fifty men. It was in the month of *Rabī' I,* the 18th day of it. A company of the people of Agades joined with al-Ḥājj Akanfaya to perform the pilgrimage. Among them were the Shaykh and *faqīh,* the scholar and Ḥājj Aḥmad b. Taraqtī, the *faqīh* Ayyūb (var. Ya'qūb), his brother 'Abd al-Raḥmān, the *faqīh* Wa-Dderfen and the Ḥājj Agg-arada b. Dādā, the son of the *faqīh* Ilazman. It was his first pilgrimage. They were a large company. In that year died Amma b. Aḥmadu and Bakr, the father of Muḥammad Yaḥyā.

The date when the Sultan Muḥammad al-Mubārak went forth and entered In Gall, because of men who fought, was in the month of *Shawwāl* in the year 1088/1677. Two years and nine months elapsed between the campaign of Kufkana and In Gall. In that year the following sons of the Sultan Muḥammad al-Mubārak donned the 'turban' - Ṣāliḥ did so, likewise his brother Al-Amīn,. (al-Shābu al-Mubāriwi?), the *faqīh* 'Abd al-Raḥman Wa-Talẓiya, and al-Ṭāhir.

The date when the Sultan, Muḥammad al-Mubārak, left for Dabak and entered it was the 15th of the month *Sha'bān* in the year 1090/1679. He stayed there, and he sent his army to Bornu. The commander (*Amīr*) of his army was Muḥammad b al-Ḥājj Ibrāhīm who was surnamed Amma Fāṭim. He was with the Kel Away Tuaregs, and they attacked Bornu and shattered it. They seized children, herds and possessions, then the Sultan returned homewards. The period which elapsed between the time the Sultan entered In Gall and his entry of Dabak was one whole year and nine months.

In the year 1092/1681, al-Ḥājj Akanfay, the son of the Sultan Muḥammad al-Mubārak made his third pilgrimage. He performed it with a company of the people of Agades and its *fuqahā'* and tribes of the Kel Away. Among them was the *faqīh* and scholar Shaykh al-Ḥājj Ahmad b. Taraqtī, the scholar and *faqīh,* the joy of his age, the unique pearl of his time Ad-Dirfan b. al-*faqīh* al-Imām Muḥammad al-Bukhārī (son of the Imām Aḥmad, his son Muḥammad), and the saint Muḥammad b. 'Abd al-Raḥmān, 'Abdullāh al-Fattāḥ, the son of the Sultan Muḥammad al-Mubārak, Tadti b. Ḥaldayt and the *faqīh* Muḥammad Abū 'l-Hudā, al-Ḥājj 'Alī b. al-Ḥājj 'Awn Allāh, Yamūrī al-Mabrūk and his son 'Abdullāh, a large number of people, and Abū Bakr and his group from the Kel Away.

There were those who died among them, including Muḥammad b. al-Imām al-Bukhārī, 'Abdullāh, his father Yamūrī and the *faqīh* Muḥammad b. 'Abd al-Raḥmān. They died on their return journey, after they had made the pilgrimage, between Egypt and the Fezzan. They came back in the year 1093/1682. Among those people who went on ahead were 'Abd al-Fattāḥ, son of the Sultan Muḥammad al-Mubārak, and his companions from among the Tuaregs. They came on Wednesday, at forenoon, on the 15th of the month of God Almighty *Sha'bān,* in the year 1093/1682.

The history of how the Sultan Muḥammad al-Mubārak went forth to In-Ṭaboraq. He did so in order to make peace between the Kel Away Tuaregs and the Itisen on account of the feuding and warfare which had occurred between them. He went forth in the month of *Dhū 'l-Qa'da* and he stayed in In-Taboraq and prayed during the *'Id al-aḍḥā* there at the end of the months of the year 1094/1683. In that year died al-Ḥājj Bibakr b. Ḥāmid, his successor was Baba Dayd, - and 'Abdullāh b. Taghaklaf died in the month of *Shawwāl.* The Sultan left after the death of these two during *Dhū 'l-Qa'da*.

Now for the date when I, Abū Bakar b. al-Ṭāhir Tāshī - the author of this record - married. It was in the year 1095/1684. The first whom I married was

'Aysha al-'Āfiya, the daughter of Muḥammad al-Ḥājj, the brother of Bibakr b. Ḥāmid. I built a lodging in the month of *Rabī' II.* It was after the departure of the Sultan Muḥammad al-Mubārak for In-Taboraq. He returned to his house in the year 1095/1684. Here is the date wherein was born the eldest of all my children, my daughter Fanna. It was the first day of the crescent moon of the month of *Ṣafar,* on Wednesday, in the forenoon, at the beginning of the year 1096/1685

In that same year they slew the chief of the Zanfara Kel Away in the country of Katsina. Some seven hundred men of theirs were killed. The Sultan Muḥammad al-Mubārak rose up, and war blazed. He did so with all his armies and his troops, and all of the Tuareg tribes. He sent his armies, and their commander (*Amīr)* was Muḥammad b. al-Ḥajj Ibrāhīm whose surname was Amma Fāṭim, and all his sons and his brothers and sisters' sons. Among his sons were Ṣāliḥ and his brother Akhmad, and 'Abd al-Fattāḥ and 'Abdullāh and al-'Adil and Ṣāḥib and al-Amīn and the *faqīh* 'Abd al-Raḥmān and 'Umar and Muḥammad Ḥumad and the sons of Muḥammad al-Munfar and all the tribes of the Kel Away and their *Amīr* Abū Bakar and the Itisen. The Sultan Muḥammad al-Mubārak sent them to Zanfara.

They left at the beginning of the month of *Rabī' II,* and fighting took place between them and the people of Zanfara on Thursday at the onset of noon on the last day of *Rabī' II.* In the fighting died Muḥammad Ḥumad, the son of the Sultan Wakaludīma Askiya. They smashed the people of Zanfara. They fled in defeat, and their best men died. More than 1,000 men of the Zanfara died there, God gave victory to the Tuaregs over their enemies. Then they returned and came to Agades with the aid of God Almighty. All of this took place in the year 1096/1685.

Now for the history of the sending of the army of the Sultan Muḥammad al-Mubārak to Zanfara on a second raid. The commander (*Amīr)* was Yūsuf, who was nicknamed Addabāb. All of the Sultan's sons were present, as in the first raid, and all the Tuaregs. It was in the month of *Rābi' I.* Fighting took place between them and the people of Zanfara. The latter were broken in pieces, and their armies were defeated. God aided the Tuaregs against them. In that battle they killed all the chief men of Zanfara and their heros, their courageous men and all their elders and their chief *fuqahā',* until there alone remained in Zanfara those who were poor and weak, the lame, the blind and the women-folk. The destruction of their select men in that battle was a fact of permanent effect. Among the Tuaregs who died were the sons of Abū Bakar, the sons of Al-Amīn and some of the chiefs among the Tuaregs. Most of the people of Zanfara died. All this occurred in the month of *Rabī' I* in the year 1096/1685.

They then returned to Agades. After their return plague broke out, and there was a great death in Agades. - We s eek God's protection from that. Among those who died were al-Fāḍil, the Sultan's son, Maghghir b. Ibrāhīm, al-Ṭāhir, the Sultan's son, Muḥammad al-Tafrīja b. Maghghir, the *faqīh* Ibn Aghāli b. al-Barka, al-Ṭāhir b. Ammat and people who can neither be numbered nor counted. Among those who died was Uhūkin, slave maid of the mother of Abū Bakar, the author of this document, the mother of 'Uthmān and Atta and Khadīja. It was in the month of *Dhū 'l-Ḥijja* on Friday, the 14th day of it, at the end of the year 1097/1686.

Here is the history of the death of the 'Commander of the Faithful', the Sultan Muḥammad al-Mubārak - may God expand the girth of his sepulchre and cause him to dwell in the gardens of Paradise with the Prophets, the veracious, the martyrs, and the pious, and this by His favour and His generosity together with our loved ones. So be it.

The Sultan Muḥammad al-Mubārak died in the month of *Jumādā II* on the night of the seventh of it, a Sunday night. They concealed (the news) of his death. He died between sunset and the *'Ishā'* prayer. They concealed it, and they did not announce it publicly until after the *'Ishā'* prayer, before the moon was absent, near to it. It was in the year *Dafaṣ,* the year 1098/1687. He had held office for 34 years. Then he died - May God Almighty have mercy upon him. His son assumed his authority. He was his eldest Muḥammad Agg-Abba. He did so during that night before daybreak. There was no dispute nor argument. The people were in full agreement. Then also died al-Hājj 'Ummār b. Muḥammad Ilalil and al-Dabāb Alali Wābni (?) in rhe month of *Jumādā I,* on Sunday night, the 22nd of it before the moon came out, but the Sultan Muḥammad al-Mubārak predeceased them in that year 1098/1687. In that year too died the *faqīh* 'Ummār of Timbuctoo. He died in Agades on the night of Tuesday, the 16th of the month *Jumādā II.* In that month died the *faqīh* Ibrāhīm b. Iddāfan, the *faqīh* of the Kel Away. In that year died the *faqīh* Muḥammad Agg Tatal of the Barkuray and the *faqīh* Muḥammad Akwal al-Kabīr. At the end of this year, 1098/1687, died the *faqīh* and scholar Shaykh al-Ḥājj Aḥmad b. Taraqtī. He died in the month of *Dhū 'l-Ḥijja* on the day of 'Arafat, on Friday the ninth of *Dhū 'l-Ḥijja.* That plague and pestilence continued in Agades for two whole years. Then God Almighty relieved the Muslims by His mercy. - We ask God for salvation and safety, for peace and well-being in the two abodes.

The date of the birth of my daughter Asiya was on the Monday night, after the sunset prayer and before the sun went down, the 21st of the month *Ṣafar,* at the beginning of the year 1098/1687. Two years elapsed between the birth of Fanna and her sister Asiya. The mother of them both was 'Aysha al-'Āfiya, the daughter of Muḥammad al-Hājj. Their father, I, Abū Bakar b. al-Ṭāhir and his wife 'Aysha al-'Afiya were divorced. I put her aside and left her with effect from the month of *Dhū 'l-Qa'da* at the end of the year 1099/1688.

I shall now tell of what took place during the reign of the Sultan Muḥammad

Agg-Abba, who ruled after his father the Sultan Muḥammad al-Mubārak. The first misfortune which occurred in his reign was in the year 1100/1689. This was the assault of al-Gobiri against Ṣāliḥ, the son of the Sultan Muḥammad al-Mubārak, and his brothers who were with him, his *wazīr* and the people of Air. With the Gobir, he (the Gobir Sultan?) assaulted them and raided them. They took all their herds, and they left them with nothing save their lives and the horses and camels they rode upon. They attacked them and their dwellings at night in the month of *Jumādā II.* So they came (back) to the land of Adar called Kabar. Ṣāliḥ camped there together with his company, and none knew where his commander went. They came one by one until they had assembled together in Kabar. Only those who had gone forth on their own, supplied by themselves, had anything. Some of them died of thirst and fatigue. This disastrous episode occurred in the month of *Jumādā II* in the year 1100/1689.

I had some experience of it in Adar. I had journeyed there, and I came at that time to Ṣāliḥ, and I gave him my greetings. I gave to him what I had with me of dates and other provisions. Among their company was my brother al-Ḥājj Baba Allil, the son of my father's sister. I left them, and I travelled with the Tuaregs who had fled before the Kebbi (Kabu?). They had taken their camels, donkeys and cows, and they had slain many men of them.

After that I came to Agades, and after my arrival came Ṣāliḥ, the Sultan's son and his brothers and his *wazīr.* His brother, the Sultan Muḥammad Agg-Abba arose then and there, and they made a raid on Gobir on account of that deed which they had committed against his brother (Ṣāliḥ) and his officials (Bellas?). He left two days after the beginning of the month of *Ramaḍān.* It was a Monday and at the onset of the forenoon. He stopped at Anu Imawlay. Then he recommenced his march towards Gobir. He came upon the people of Gobir on a Tuesday. He had heard no news of them until he camped in their midst on Tuesday, the 24th day of *Ramaḍān.* Fighting took place between them on that day, and God aided Agg-Abba (and his men) against their enemies, and they won a mighty victory. They smote the sons of Gobir, whom they defeated, and they looted all their possessions. They captured their herds, their children and their wives. No son nor wife was left. They took captive every servant (Bella) and pack beast, at the command of their Sultan Agg-Abba. He dealt with them in a way far more grievous than that which they had inflicted upon his brother Ṣāliḥ. The Sultan Agg-Abba sent some of their sons and their wives to the country of Tuwāt and others to the Fezzān. Some of them he kept. This event took place in the year 1100/1689.

Then, after that (the Sultan) al-Gobiri complained, and he sought peace from the Sultan Agg-Abba - may God aid him. So peace was made between them, and pardon and security (*Amāna*) guaranteed. In that fighting there died Talza b. Tadyat bint Maggir and Jalallahu b. Muḥammad Fāṭim. They died in the rank of the fighting men (*ṣaff al-qitāl*). (10) The Sultan Agg-Abba returned victorious, and his men were safe and loaded with booty. God be praised. The firm date when thi happened - the Sultan Agg-Abba returned victorious on the date when I, Abū Bakar b. al-Ṭāhir married Nana'Aysha bint al-Ḥājj 'Awnallāh al-Fazzānī. She was my second wife. This was in the year 1100/1689. The marriage was contracted betwee the two . . . . I was travelling in the country of Adar, after there had occurred certain (sad) events, before noon, on the 17th of the month of *al-Muḥarram,* the first month in the year 1103/1691. There were six months between the death of Fāṭima and her grandfather. In that year, on the day when Fāṭima died, died also Māma, daughter of the *faqīh* Mu'allam, the sister of Abū 'l-Qāsim. After the death of Fāṭima, I travelled to Adar, where Ṣāliḥ, the son of the Sultan, was to be found in the month of *Ṣafar.*

The history of the departure of the Sultan Agg-Abba for Dabak. He did so because of the fighting of men there. He left on Saturday the 21st of the month *Rabī' II.* He stopped in Dabak. He stayed there for fifty days. Then he returned to Agades and arrived on Saturday the 11th of *Jumādā II* in the year 1105/1694.

In the year 1107/1696 dissension and fighting broke out between the Kel Away and the Itisen. Then God sent down on men the slayer of the slain, dire calamity, famines, wars, fighting and lack of rain and highway robbery. None came, and none departed. Thus it continued for an entire year. Another year followed it, but it was worse than the first. It spread over all the lands of the Tuaregs. The year was 1108/1697. Disaster hit the city of Agades and the Kel Away and the Itisen. Wars afflicted them, so did famines, mighty calamities, fear, violence and afflictions which were worse than what had gone before. This was in the year 1108/1697. It was as Almighty God said in His book, "We shall indeed afflict you and try you with something fearful," up to, "good news for those who are steadfast." (11) During that year many of the people of Agades died, so also the Kel Away and the Itisen and their governors among the people of the desert places, until their houses and tents became deserted. Men ate carrion. Men measured out millet and thorns of the *tagrouft* and *ashek (wajjak)* at ten *mudds* for a *mithqāl* of gold. They even measured out six *mudds* for a *mithqāl* of gold. People even ate their own herds and animals. (12) They sold all the books and used the price obtained for them. The people were left with nothing, yet they were expectant of hopeful of God's mercy. Then after that God brought relief to the Muslims. He sent His mercy upon them in the year 1108/1697. Peace was made between the Kel Away and and Itisen. The Sultan Agg-Abba sent the *faqīh* Ayyūb b. Muḥammad Baba and the *faqīh* Ad-Dirfan and Ibn al-Azman and Abū 'l-Qāsim b. Mu'allam and 'Abd al-Karīm (b?) Taluwa. They went to the Tuaregs, and they made peace between the two tribes. Peace was ratified between them on the 12th day of the month *Rabī' I* at Jabal Ta'waji ~~(Tarouaji)~~.

In that year 1108/1697 Ṣāliḥ, the son of the Sultan Muḥammad al-Mubārak died, in the month of *Rabī‘ I* in the country of Adar. His brother Muḥammad Gumā also died, likewise Abū Bakar, the Sultan of the Kel Away and Amihin, their best men and their 'freemen'. None was left after them save the men of evil - we ask God for peace and security for ever and ever until the day of judgement.

In the year 1110/1698, God sent rain and dark clouds. Rain fell on the city of Agades in particular, and it poured down in torrents like seas of water. It was on Wednesday the 14th of the month of *al-Muḥarram.* Then after that we had rain again. It also was on a Wednesday - the 21st of *al-Muḥarram.* (July/August) Rain fell on us from noon until after the late afternoon (*'aṣr*) prayer. It was as though the whole air and atmosphere was filled with smoke. Then it rained a second time between the *'aṣr* until the 'pale light' (*iṣfirār*), and we had rain for a third time on the 29th day of *al-Muḥarram*, and for a fourth time on Thursday, on the 24th day of *Ṣafar.* There was no more rain after that due to God's will. The first and second downpours destroyed large houses in the Imurdan quarter as far as the great market. Rain filled the houses and ruined much property in their interiors. Such cannot be accounted for nor assessed. It included salt and millet, rice and wheat, honey and cooking butter and sundry wares. I heard some of the scholars (*Ṭalaba*) say that three hundred houses were destroyed, if not more. I heard some of the elders say that nothing like this had ever occurred before in Agades nor had such ever been heard of. Yet God delivered us. None suffered loss nor destruction in the house of my wife Nana 'Aysha, the daughter of al-Ḥājj 'Awnallah. In those downpours we beheld wonders which were the power of God, the Mighty, the all-Powerful. One whole day passed in a torrential sea. Then afterwards, it destroyed and wrecked. It destroyed the house of the *faqīh* Zayd, and a wall fell on a cat. It remained beneath the ruins for three days. The mud was removed and taken away, and the cat came out safe and sound. Then the house of Sālim Shushufī was ruined. Its wall fell on top of a hen with its eggs. After three days the clay and adobe brick were removed. The hen came out together with its eggs, safe and sound. Not one was broken. Then a wall fell on top of a bird - a small sparrow. It remained beneath the wall for several days. Then it came out alive and whole. This is what I have heard from the most trustworthy of folk and some of the *Ṭalaba* - Glory to God the Mighty and all-Powerful who determines what He wishes to do in His kingdom.

The wonders of creation manifested themselves to us in the city of Agades - may God Almighty guard it - so be it - and all the world of Islam on Friday the 13th of the month of *Dhu 'l-Qa'da* in the year of the termination 1100/1689 (var. 1110/1698). It preceded the rain which has just been mentioned. It was that a cow gave birth to a calf with two heads, two humps and four legs in the body and shape of a single cow - Glory be to the Almighty King. It was during the reign of the Sultan Agg-Abba - may God aid him. Then there also appeared to us at the end of the year 1105/1694 (1108/1697?) in the month of *Dhū 'l-Ḥijja,* a marvel and a wonder. Black clouds rose over us. There was no lightning, nor rain, nor thunder. It was quite contrary to what we were accustomed to in Agades. It dimmed the light of the sun and cast a deep shadow and darkness until - it was said - one saw stars from a certain direction, near the time of the *'aṣr* prayer. The people were gripped by fear and terror. Some of them began to pray, and people hastened to the mosques. Furthermore, a wind like a sombre hurricane came upon us. It seemed to assume colours of a varied hue - black, white, red and yellow. When the atmosphere was calm but oppressive, we were covered by an intense darkness and blackness so that no-one could see his own finger. It remained lik,e this for a while. Then it cleared away in accordance with the will and power of the Mighty and all-Powerful God. That was in the year 1108/1697 (13) on a Saturday in the month of *Dhū 'l-Ḥijja,* well after the *'aṣr* on the 23rd of that month. (Saturday, 13th of July.) O, God, give us pardon and bestow Thy mercy upon us. Amen.'

V

The Sultanate in decadence

By the middle of the nineteenth century the Agades Sultanate had been sapped of its earlier vitality. A majority of its Sultans reigned for very short periods. There were a few exceptions. The political chaos of the Iwillimeden Tuaregs to the west of Air, and the eventual decline of the Saharan commerce upon which Agades depended increased instability and tribal conflicts. Yet, the fact that so much of the former life of the city still survived underlines the solid foundations of its institutions. Mosques were restored, and expeditions, some successful, were launched to the southlands. Scholars of note lived in the city, and its teachers were often sought by the lettered of Kano and Sokoto. It would be unwise to see in the entry and exit of its potentates, a wholly accurate portrait of the overall life of Agades which kept something of its vigour despite adversities. (14) Asoday in the interior of Air was also of importance for the export of senna.

When Barth passed through Air between July and December 1850, in the heart of the Massif the Kel Away *Ineslemen* held considerable power. From their centre at Tintagh-Odé they exerted a wide influence along the key route to north and south. To quote Barth, 'under the authority of these learned and devout men, commerce is carried on with a security which is really surprising.' (15)

At the same time of Barth's journey in Air the nominal chief of the Kel Away *tawshit* was the *Amenukal (Anastafidet)* residing in Asoday. The head of the far greater confederation formed by the Kel Away, Kel Geres and the Itisen and lesser tribes was the *Amenukal* (Sultan) in Agades. He was 'Abd al-Qādir, son of the Sultan Muḥammad al-Bāqirī. He impressed Barth as 'a man of great worth though devoid of energy. All the people assured me that he was the best of the family to which the Sultan of Agades belongs. He had already been Sultan before, (16) but a few years ago, was deposed, in order to make way for Hámed e. Rufäy, whom he again succeeded, but in 1853, while I was in Sókoto, he was once more compelled to resign in favour of the former.' (17) Barth adds elsewhere that the *Amīr* of Sokoto had a say in the choice of Sultan. (18)

Barth was struck by the multilingual population of the city. Arabic, Tamashegh, Hausa and Songhai were all used individually or were mixed. The architecture impressed him, not only the palace of the Sultan and the house of the Alkhali near the great mosque, but also those of merchants and rich citizens. Some were roofless but displayed ornamented niches, ruins of baths and other features of fine workmanship.

It would have been surprising if the great mosque had not fascinated Barth the most among the ancient structures of Agades. He had wanted to enter it but was forced to wait until the departure of the Sultan from the city in order to do so. Amid the crumbled mansions he viewed with interest 'this simple but curious building,' which markedly reminded him of the 'tower above the sepulchre of Hajj Muhammad Askia' at Gao. The minaret was not only used to call the faithful to prayer but also served as a watch-tower. Within the mosque Barth found its naves and 'gloomy halls . . . . . . buried in a mournful silence, interrupted only by the voice of a solitary man, seated on a dirty mat at the western wall of the tower, and reading diligently the torn leaves of a manuscript.' It was the *Qāḍī*. He paid Barth scant attention. The mosque, then only six years after its restoration, seemed to be something in the nature of a monument rather than an active centre of Islamic learning.

NOTES

1) Did Agumbulum suggest 'Son of Umbul (Stambul?) ?
On the title see *P.V.*, pp. 369-397.

2) See *T.D.N.C.A.*, p. 130 and

3) *Ibid,* pp. 392-393.

4) *Ibid,* pp. 144-146.

5) See pages 77-86 and 122-134.

6) See *P.V.*, pp. 115-116

7) Translated from *A.C.* texts in the possession of the Sultan.

8) See *C.A.*, by Urvoy.

9) A reasonable assumption of Urvoy and essential if it is to make sense in the dates for the Sultans in other Agades records.

10) See *C.A.*, by Urvoy. Manuscript J., pp. 168-177.

11) *Qur'ān, Sūra II,* 'the Heifer', v. 150 ff.

12) The plants eaten during the drought, the Tamashegh names of which appear in the text are:- *tagrouft* (var. *tagheruft), Tribulus tenester* and *ashek (*var. *wajjak/wujjeg), Cenchrus catharticus.* A *mudd (*var. *muda)*contains one kilo of cereals.

13) It is possible that the date of *Dhū 'l-Ḥijja* 1105/1694 is more correct. According to P.S. Laurie of the Solar Department, Science Research Council, Royal Greenwich Observatory, 'the nearest total solar eclipse in time and geographical location occurred on December 10th, 1695. The belt of totality ran through South Turkey, Syria, Iran, Persian Gulf, India (Karachi) etc.'

14) See Richardson, *Travels in the Great Desert of Sahara,* Vol. II, pp. 139-145.

15) See *T.D.N.C.A.,* p. 145.

16) See page 93.

17) *Ibid,* p. 178.

18) Ibid, pp. 206-207.

The Sultanate of Agades

	1)	Yūnus b. Taggagi Tahnazayta (var. Tahannazayyat) - who was the sister of Ahinaṣ. Yūnus came to power in 807/1405 (var. 809/1407). He reigned for 20 years.
The House of Aghghayaghi	2)	Aqqassān (var. Aghindas), *son of the sister of Yūnus* (Taggagi Takarawt?). He took power in 827/1424 (var. 829/1426). Six years of rule were shared.
	3)	(al-Ḥājj) Alisaw b. Taggagi - their youngest brother took power in 833/1430. He held it for 20 years, and he died assassinated in office.
	4)	Amatī (var. Aminī), his brother took power in 853/1449/50. He held it for 4 years, and he died assassinated in office.

The Dynasty collapsed under the pressure of the *House of Tasannaghat* who held power from 2-4 months under Ibn Takūma.

The House of Taghazrat Dhigrat.	1)	Ibrāhīm b. Haylas (var. Hīlāz) took power in 857/1453. He reigned for 9 years.
	2)	Yūsuf b. Ghāshatan (var. 'Ayshatan), *his sister's son* took power in 866/1462. He reigned for 16 years.
'Abd al-Karīm al-Maghīlī and Jalāl al-Dīn al-Suyūṭī.	3)	Muḥammad al-Kabīr took power in 882/1478. He reigned for 10 years.
	4)	(Ibrāhīm) Muḥammad Ṣaṭṭafan, his brother, took power in 892/1487. He reigned for 7 (var. 9) years.
	5)	Muhammad b. 'Abd al-Raḥmān whose *kunya* was Ṭalzi Ṭanaṭ, his *sister's son,* took power in 899/1494. He reigned for 9 years, and following conflicts with maternal uncles and dister's son he died, assassinated, while in office.

Power in the hands the sons of Faṭā Mūllat. Muḥammad Askia.

6) Muḥammad al-ʻAdil (var. Ghudāla) and Muḥammad Ḥumad took power jointly in 908/1502, and they held power for 14 years. The Askia 'misfortune.'

7) Muḥammad b. Talādha (var. Taluẓa) appointed Sultan in 922/1516. He ruled for 2 years and died in office.

Confused era. Murder of Sīdī Maḥmūd al-Baghdādī?.

8) Ibrāhīm b. Muḥammad Ṣaṭṭafan took office in 924/1518 and ruled for 24 or 25 years.

9) Aḥmad b. Ṭalyat (var. Aḥmad b. Taluẓa), *his sister's son,* took office in 948/1541 and ruled for 14 or 15 years. He left office *'as a judgement from God and in obedience, not by reason of any-one.'*

10) Muḥammad al-Ghudāla b. al-Ḥājj al-ʻĀqib, his brother took power in 964/1556 (var. 961/1554). He ruled for 39 or 40 years.

11) Akanfaya, his brother, succeeded him in 1002/1594. He reigned for 2 years and 6 months and died in office.

12) Yūsuf (var. b. al-Ḥājj Aḥmad b. al-Ḥājj Abashan), his *sister's son,* assumed power in 1005/1597. He reigned for 28 years.

Dispute

The son of his maternal uncle Muḥammad b. al-Mubārak b. al-Ghudāla took power from Yūsuf. He remained in office for 4 months. Yūsuf planned a counter attempt to regain power with his Tuareg and Kebbi allies. He camped at Sansay. He stayed between Alʻasis and Tin Shaman for 3 months. Then Yūsuf took Tin Shaman and entered and took Agades. Ibn al-Mubārak left for Katsina and Kano. He returned to Air, and the two men met at Anū Ṣamman. Ibn al-Mubārak defeated Yūsuf, and he entered Agades. He stayed there for 15 days. Next he marched to Asawday (Assodé) but did not reach it, and he returned to Agades.

He stayed in it for 20 days, then marched to Gamram. Yūsuf returned to Kebbi. He gathered an army and pursued Ibn al-Mubārak to Gamram. He then fled to Kazway in Bornu. Yūsuf entered Agades. Encounters continued until Yūsuf captured Ibn al-Mubārak in the land of Taghāma at In-Yugar. He tied him up and imprisoned him. He died in prison. The whole period of Yūsuf's Sultanate was

28 to 29 years.

13) Muḥammad al-Tafrīja b. Yūsuf was of the tribe of the Kel Away. His mother was the daughter of Ibn al-Ghudāla. He held power for 2 years. The Itisen deposed him. Awgar b. Ṭalyat succeeded him. Then Muḥammad al-Tafrīja returned and ruled for 31 years. He died in Sha'bān 1064/1654.

Ḥadāḥadā and Karidenna

14) Muḥammad al-Mubārak, his brother, succeeded him. He reigned 34 years less 2 months. He died on the 7th of *Jumādā* II at Deffes. 1098/1687.

15) His son Muḥammad Agg-Abba took power in 1098/1687. He reigned for 35 (var. 33/34) years and died in Jumādā II 1132/1721.

16) Muḥammad al-Amīn, his brother, took power in Jumādā II. He ruled for 9 months.

Era of Drought and Instability.

17) His brother al-Walī, replaced him and reigned for 14 months.

18) The Sultan Muḥammad al-Amīn reigned for 9 months. Died in Rabī' I.

19) Muḥammad al-Mūmin reigned for 9 months. (1721)

20) His son 'Uthmān took power, reigned for 3 years then died?

21) Muḥammad Agg-Aggaysh (Agg 'Aysha), son of the Sultan Muḥammad Agg-Abba (15) ruled for some 11 years? (circa 1722?)

22) His brother Muḥammad Ḥumad, son of the Sultan Muḥammad al-Mubārak (14)? ruled for 6 years (var. 5 years and 5 months) Circa 1147/1734.

23) Power taken by Muḥammad Gumā b. al-'Adil (Ghudāla). He ruled for 5 years (var. 4 years 7 months).

24) Power taken by Muḥammad Ḥumad (22) once again. He ruled for 15 years and 4 months. He abdicated in Shawwāl.

25) Ousted by Muḥammad Gumā b. al-Sulṭān 'Uthmān b. Muḥammad al-Mubārak. He ruled for 3 years and 8 months (var. 4 years 6 months.)

26) Ousted by Muḥammad Ḥumad (22) in Rajab 1176/1763. He ruled for 5 years and 6 months and died in 1181/1767/1768.

27) Succeeded by his son Muḥammad al-'Adil (Ghudāla) who reigned for 25 years (?) until 1225/1810(?) He fought the Amīr of Gobir.

28) Muḥammad (var. Aḥmad) al-Dāni ruled for 5 years and 4 months (var. 7 months). He was deposed in 1212/1797. Air, it is said, had no Amīr for 7 years and was ruled by scholars who sent to the Itisen for an Amīr.

29) Al-Bāqirī came to power in 1212/1797 and ruled for some 19 years. He died in 1230/1231 circa 1815.

30) Muḥammad Gumā reigned for 5 years and 1 month, was then dethroned.

31) Succeeded by his brother Ibrāhīm who ruled for 7 years and was dethroned in 1244/1827/1828.

32) Muḥammad Gumā reinstated. He died a 'martyr', assassinated in 1251/1835.

33) 'Abd al-Qādir ruled for some 20 years and then abdicated circa 1270/1853. (var. 1273/1857).

34) Aḥmad al-Raffā' b. Gumā, then deposed.

35) Muḥammad al-Bāqirī nicknamed Sūfū, 'the old', then deposed.

36) Aḥmad al-Raffa' b. Gumā, reinstated, then deposed after 12 years.

37) Muḥammad al-Bāqirī, reinstated, then deposed.

38) Power seized by Ibrāhīm al-Dusūqī (who held power three times).

39) Muḥammad al-Bāqirī, ruled for 32 years ?

40) 'Uthmān b. 'Abd al-Qādir, ruled for 4 years (5 months), then died in office. (Var. 4 years and was dethroned).

41) Ibrāhīm al-Dusūqī b. Aḥmad al-Raffā' reinstated about 1322/1904 and ruled for 4 years.

42) Taghāma b. Muḥammad al-Bāqirī., his nephew, came to power in 1326/1908/1909. He ruled for 9 years and 6 months. Participated in Kawsen's revolt and was deposed by the French and died in prison in 1920.

43) Ibrāhīm al-Dusūqī recalled as *de facto* Sultan for 4 years and then retired to Adar.

44) 'Umaru definitively installed as Sultan in 1920.

45) Ibrāhīm b. 'Umaru, the reigning Sultan.

In drawing up this list of rulers I have used copies of texts from the private library of the Sultan, Ibrāhīm b. 'Umaru, and the private library of Shaykh Muḥammad Ibrāhīm al-Aghlālī at Abalagh. I am also indebted to John Lavers of the Department of History, Abdullahi Bayero College, Kano, for access to variant lists in the Collection of Sir Richard Palmer, several of which are to be preferred in the clarity of spelling of proper names and in certain details. In the main, however, I have used the Sultan of Agades's copies. For the French version readers are referred to Urvoy in the Bibliography.

A short chronicle of events in Air and the region of Agades between 1683 (1094 AH) and 1888 (1305 AH).
(See Sultans (14) - (39)).

1683	1094	The war of Ta'uj (var. ta'awaj/Taghuji - Taruwaji?).
1685	1096	The war of Bornu and the departure of (the Sultan) Agg-Abba (for Adar).
1691	1102	The pilgrimage of Muḥammad b. 'Aysha to Mecca. Probably Sultan (21).
1696	1107	The 'war of famine and hunger', followed by the battle of Agaraw (Agwan?) at the end of the year.
1701/2	1113	The battles of Shin-Widhin (var. Shuwudhin) and Al-Ṣāṭir.
1702/3	1114	More fighting with no specific battle named.
1705	1117	The Sultan Muḥammad Agg-Abba went to war and entered In Gall (War of Tazmak?).
1707	1119	Muḥammad b. Aghālī went on pilgrimage at the end of the year.
1709/10	1121	Muḥammad al-Tafrīja b. al-Ḥājj Muḥammad b. 'Aysha performed the pilgrimage.
1710	1122	Al-Ḥājj Muḥammad b. al-Tafrīja died. The battle of Tagargar/Takarkar and the peace of Inumma 'zar (var. Almigizu and Anummaren).
1711	1123	Fighting at Jīkat.
1712	1124/5	The battle of In Gall.
1713	1125	The battle of Aṣōday. (Assodé).
1714	1126	The battle and peace of Amdid (Amjid?).
1721	1133	Raid by the Sultan al-'Adil (al-Ghudāla) on Gobir.
1722	1134	War with Kel Geres. Muḥammad Ḥumad, nicknamed Ḥaddi, and Muḥammad b. Kulwatu performed the pilgrimage.
1726	1138	The campaign led by the Sultan of Agades, Muḥammad b. 'Aysha against Gobir.
1729	1141	War between Kel Away and Kel Geres in Imurdan after the '*Aṣr* prayer, Friday, 8th Jumādā I.
1730/1	1143	The Sultan's conquest of Aṣōday. In the battle Ibn Būbu and al-Ḥārith as well as others perished.

1731/2	1144	The battle of Gamram took place in the month of Ṣafar. This was a battle between two bands of Kel Sandal and Kel Away. The Kel Sandal fled on foot.
1733/4	1146	A battle in which al-Sha'alan died. The Sultan Muḥammad Ḥumad took power in the same year.
1739	1152	The battle (?) of Amdigra/Imdaggar took place.
1740	1153	Muḥammad Gumā b. al- 'Adil (al-Ghudāla) b. Muḥammad al-Mubārak came to the throne. Travellers went to the Sudan and the warriors of the Kel Away came in month after the coronation of Muḥammad Gumā (Dhū 'l-Ḥijja). They pillaged Agades as far as the palace and the mosque. The Sultan sent to them to discuss peace. They massacred numbers among a crowd sent out by the Sultan who was with them in person.
1741	1154	Conquest of Aṣōday and battle of Sharsala.
1748	1161	The peace of Irsan and Kulan (?).
1749	1162	The war involving the troops of Agalal. The battles of Tasawa and Intalam with the troops of Zanfara. Three months later the battle of Talayya took place in which the Tagāma Iwillimeden were broken.
1750	1163	A clash between the Kel Sandal and the Zanfara in the city of Katsina.
1751	1164	The peace of Shintaburaw.
1754	1167	The Sultan Muḥammad Ḥumad marched to Katsina.
1758	1171	The battle in which perished many of the Ikaradan.
1759	1172	The battle of Saghalmas (var. Saggalmas), also known as Iruzem. Muḥammad b. Ammaki (var. Makkat) was killed there.
1760	1173	The battle of Bilma. The Tagāma were beaten by the Kel Geres at Tagedda.
1762	1175	The Kel Away marched to Kano. Fighting between the Kel Geres and Iwillimeden occurred at Indish. The former routed the latter on the 5th day of Dhū 'l-Qa'da.
1764	1177	Shaykh Ayya b. al-Shaykh Aḥmad al-Sadiq died on the 5th day of Dhū 'l-Qa'da. The battle of Farak took place at the year's end. Fiyul and his brother Abū Bakr were killed in battle.

1767	1181	The death of the *faqīh* and Shaykh Mūḥ, at sunset, on Friday the 17th of Dhū 'l-Qa'da.
1768	1181	'A company of the (Kel) Sandal and the (Kel) Innik and the (Kel) Maghzan went on pilgrimage with Shaykh al-Baṣarī b. Ilyās. The Shaykh and Ḥājj al-Baṣarī arose, with some of his companions, and they looted the Ikuradan (Igururan?) of their herds in the land of Agaywas. God saved Shaykh al-Baṣarī bestowing his blessing upon him in the year 1769/1182.' The Sultan Muḥammad al-'Adil (al-Ghudāla), son of the Sultan Muḥammad Ḥumad succeeded his father.
1770	1184	Death of Dangudi.
1775	1189	The battle of Inissilakum at Imshilwan.
1778	1192	The battle of Dirfus.
1779	1193	The alliance of the Itisen and Kel Geres against the troops of Air.
1781	1195	Heavy rain in Agades at sun-rise lasting until noon. Many houses were destroyed, and water swamped most of the city. Much property was damaged.
1788	1202	Battle of Tagedda.
1807	1222	Victory of 'Uthmān dan Fodio in Bornu.
1809	1224	Battle of Danlahadi in Bornu. In it died the Amīr al-Bāqirī b. al-Ghudāla.
1810	1225	Fighting between the Kel Air and the Kel Ahaggar when Yūnus b. Sayyid raided in force.
1813	1228	Battles with Muḥammad al-Jaylānī. He slaughtered many Kel Geres and Itisen. The death of Aḥmad al-Ṣādiq b. al-Shaykh 'Umar.
1814/5	1229/30	The death of 'Uthmān dan Fodio. At the end of 1814 the Sultan Muḥammad Gumā killed Abū Bakr, lord of Iduday (var. Adday). For this reason battles, took place between the Kel Away until some joined the Itisen and al-Jaylānī who attacked Air at the end of the year.
1816 - 1817	1231 - 1232	Muḥammad Gumā (Tabdali) came with an army of Itisen and Kel Geres and Kel Tigermat to attack al-Rianat (?) (Riaina?). They took Abū Bakr known as Akaduday and Ḥammād b. Aḥmad. There was pillaging of the Balkuray in the region of Tilaq in 1817.

1818	1233	The Sultan Muḥammad Gumā abdicated and was replaced by his brother.
1826	1241	The battles of Ibrāhīm b. al-Shaykh Aḥmad. He looted Imasakash of his herds by order of the Sultan Muḥammad Ibrāhīm b. al-Mūmin. Ibrāhīm surrounded the Amīr's palace but his attempt failed.
1827	1243	Death of Imasakash at the beginning of the year.
1828/9	1244	Return to power of the Sultan Muḥammad Gumā.
1829/30	1245	Battle of Qubqub.
1831	1246	Death of Shaykh Ḥāmid on Tuesday the 23rd of Rajab.
1836	1252	Death of Muḥammad Bello.
1849	1265	Many Air camels looted at Bilma at the end of the year.
1850	1266	Raid by the (Kel) Air on the sons of 'Abd al-Jalīl and his people the Mini Mini (?) (var. Minyaman).
1854	1271	In Muḥarram the battle of Fagiya in Agades district.
1857	1273	Raid of the (Bilma) Mini Mini into Air. They killed many of its chief men including al-Nūr b. Iduday and al-Ḥājj al-Nūr of the Kel Ṭaduq.
1865	1281	Battle of Tasikilawat. Many Kel Air died.
1868/9	1285	The battle of Ta'a'at (Taghaut), wherin died al-Ḥājj Muḥammad al-Nūr b. Alafu and those with him.
1873	1290	Ferocious war between the Kel Air and Iwillimeden, between Balkhu and their Sultan Mūsā until the latter's death. War between Air and Kuwar. Al-Ḥājj Balkhu rallied his troops but did not join them. To lead them he appointed Igidi b. Tammāna, then A'jir, then his son Lusu. They marched to Kuwar and wished to conquer it and reduce it to ashes. The march failed 'according to the Almighty's decree' in *1888* (1305).

Compiled from Chronicles in the possession of Ibrāhīm b. 'Umaru. These correspond to Manuscripts E, F, H, and I in Urvoy's translation. For even fuller details, see H. R. Palmer, 'Some Asben Records' (The Agadez Chronicle) in the Journal of the Royal African Society, No. XXXVI, Vol. IX, 1910.

CHAPTER VII

KARIDENNA AND THE IWILLIMEDEN

> The *elfeqqi* replied to them, 'They are my children; they are in the process of learning. .... It is for this reason that they bear the name of Iwillimeden.'
>
> Digga Agg Khammad Ekhya.

The Sahelian region between the Adrar and Air is dominated by the Iwillimeden Tuaregs divided into those of the West (Kel Aṭaram) and those of the East (Kel Dennek). Numbers are difficult to assess. Some have estimated them as more than a quarter of a million. Probably there are, or were, some thirty thousand *Imashaghen* in Mali and forty-five thousand in Niger. To their number may be added a collection of *Ineslemen* groups, vassals and subordinate clients among the Arabs of the Sahel. More important than these are the negro Bella who are said to form more than half of all the Iwillimeden. (1)

Doubt exists as to the exact circumstances which led to the formation of the Iwillimeden. The true facts are not known to either those few Europeans who have delved into their past, nor to the Tuaregs themselves.

Some have seen the expansion of the Iwillimeden as a key event in the Sahel. (2) One explanation for their expansion seems to have had the Kunta as its formulators. (3) Tadamakkat (as-Sūq) was, they maintain, re-peopled by the Tuaregs after the Moroccan conquest of Gao under Judar Pasha in 1591, but after a time the power of the Moroccan Pashas grew weak, and As-Sūq was abandoned anew. The Adrar was occupied by the Imededghen, Kel Tadamakkat and the Ikatawen. An uneasy agreement governed the relationship of these tribes. The Ikatawen were chased from the Adrar by the Kel Tadamakkat who dominated the mountains with the Imededghen. Their supreme chief was called Alad.

A Moor arrived in the Adrar. He was an adventurer of the Brākna, the Barābīsh or the Awlād Mubārak. He seems to have come from Walāta. He was called Muḥammad. Nick-named Wa-n-Ara ('of the generation') or War-ilemmed ('the one whose name is unknown'), Muḥammad was the bravest of the brave. As a reward for his services Alad gave his sister Elad to the Moor and by her he begat three sons.

When Alad died, Elad according to Tuareg custom claimed her rights to the *eṭṭebel,* and the eldest son of Muḥammad War-ilemmed was chosen to be chief.

But when he died the Tuaregs disputed whether his other two sons had any right to succeed. They wanted the throne to pass to the son of Elad's sister. The sons of War-ilemmed said, 'No we wish that, according to the Arab custom, it should be the son who should succeed the father.' Their view was not accepted, and the two sons of War-ilemmed were banished to the region of Tessalit. It was in the latter locality that the youngest son of War-ilemmed, called Karidenna, united the Kel Tenere, the Ahaggaren and the Ifoghas who had arrived in Air under their chief Rayak. The assembled company were warriors, and their presence troubled the Kel Tadamakkat. They made the excuse that they wished to recover a riding camel and sent a messenger to Tessalit. The messenger was slain. In revenge the Kel Tadamakkat raided Tessalit. Karidenna and his men fled to the north-west beyond Taoudeni as far as the Sāqiya al-Ḥamrā'. Karidenna prepared for war. With the onset of the rainy season his army moved south-east into the Mali Adrar as far as Kidal. They killed four hundred of their enemies. The following year they returned and slaughtered two hundred and forty Kel Tadamakkat. The *Imghad* vassals of the Kel Tadamakkat joined Karidenna and recognised him as their chief.

Karidenna raided for a third time. He camped in the Adrar at Tessalit, and the Kel Tadamakkat fled west from As-Sūq and payed tribute to Karidenna in order to be left in peace in the region of Timbuctoo. Karidenna's descendants were called the Iwillimeden (the sons of Ilemmed). They remained in the Adrar together with the Ifoghas who were the descendants of Rayak.

The Kunta were hostile to the Iwillimeden. They never viewed with much favour these Tuaregs who were to dominate the lands between Timbuctoo and Gao, adjacent to the Moroccans, and within the sphere of influence of the Sultanate of Air. The Kunta would have liked to extend their spiritual jurisdiction over the Iwillimeden. As the years passed they were to gain some success. But Shaykh Sīdī al-Mukhtār al-Kuntī (d. 1811) did not conceal his contempt. 'The dynasty of the Arma (Moroccans) was better than that of the (Iwillimeden) Tuaregs because the former adhered to the policy of a kingdom. As for the Tuaregs they conquered without knowledge of how to run the policy of a kingdom and the establishment of offices according to the *Sharī'a.* They ruin and do not build and construct. This is their habit and their custom . . . They have described themselves Iwillimeden aptly for their dynasty is the last to rule in this country.' What sense of War-ilemmed had he in mind? Possibly 'the nameless' or 'the learners' or a pun on an Arabic word found in early lexicons, *lamṭ* meaning turmoil, confusion and upheaval.

The Kel Es-Suq say little about the facts surrounding the origins of the Iwillimeden. They are inclined to quote the Kunta. It is not made clear whether the Iwillimeden had arisen from the bosom of the 'drum-group' of the Kel Tadamakkat, or whether they were a related clan or tribe which was already distinct.

The Kel Es-Suq records are recent. By the nineteenth century their subordinate status under Iwillimeden patronage had become a burden to them. Mawlay Muḥammad al-Hādī was uncomplimentary about his masters. Yet he felt it his duty to counsel the Kel Es-Suq to be patient. 'Their dynasty is now in utter ruins . . . They have been the dominant power for more than two hundred years. As for those who are among their subjects, such as the Kel Es-Suq, it is they who are the custodians of learning and religion.' Despite these criticisms by the Kel Es-Suq, evidence suggests that they enjoyed many privileges under Iwillimeden protection between the sixteenth and the eighteenth centuries.

Some Kel-Es-Suq maintain that Karidenna swore allegiance to the Sultan of Agades. 'Our forebears and successors have concurred that the Tuareg *Amīr* Karidenna journeyed from his country to Agades. In it he was the *Qā'id* (4) to the supreme *Imām* called al-Ghudalā. He went carrying the power of appointing the post of *Qāḍī.* It was soundly bestowed by his hand at that time. When he reached his home country he was received with a welcome. He gave the post of the *Qaḍā'* to our paternal uncle Taballa after the latter had promised that he would bring him seven riding camels which were almost too beautiful to describe, for they were those of the Banū Azgar . . . . When Taballa gave up the turban in this serious profession, he relinquished it to his brother saint, Muḥammad al-Bashīr. He did so with affection and deepest love.' Mawlay Muḥammad al-Hādī confirms this same tradition independently, 'Karidenna . . . . was the first to whom allegiance *(bay'a)* was sworn and attached to in this country, after he had obtained it from the Sultan of Agades in Air, who took the *bay'a.* His name was al-'Addal/'Udal, and he had taken it from the Sultan of Istanbul.' No specific date is given for this event.

It is important to distinguish Karidenna's oath of allegiance to the Air Sultan from that which he gave later in his life to the Moroccans. The Agades episode, if it is historical, must have taken place prior to 1655, the date when many Kel Tadamakkat under the pressure of the then well-established power of Karidenna and the Iwillimeden were constrained to leave the Adrar in May of that year together with their families and herds, (5) and to seek the hospitality of the Pasha in Timbuctoo. Karidenna would have been in the process of buttressing his chieftainship and could have enlisted the services of the *Ineslemen* of the Kel Es-Suq to organise his confederation.

Some thirty years later his own power had been gravely undermined. Due to drought and other causes he had been compelled to move westwards, first of all to Gao in 1680, where grazing was abundant. Driven out of Gao by the Moroccans in 1688, and with herds seriously depleted, the Iwillimeden came to terms with the Moroccan rulers. In 1690 Karidenna sought investiture at the hands of the Pasha.

The event was a festive occasion, and the *Amenukal,* newly installed, was escorted to his tent outside the city of Timbuctoo. (6) By a reversal of fortune it was resurgent force of Kel Tadamakkat, which at the beginning of the eighteenth century engineered the downfall of the Moroccan Armas on the banks of the Niger. The Iwillimeden had to content themselves with the occupation of Gao. The *Amenukal* of the Western Iwillimeden continued to seek formal investiture at the hands of the Pashas until the latter vanished from history.

Karidenna, if the above facts are historical, seems to have ended up as a heroic yet ultimately unsuccessful Tuareg chief. Before his death at the end of the seventeenth century, possibly just before it, he had seen his personal triumph in the Adrar-n-Ifoghas, recognition by the Sultan of Agades, the spiritual dominance of the Kel Es-Suq in his *Ineslemen* class, and towards the end of his days an almost total dependence on the Moroccan Pasha for support. However, there are so many gaps in the records that it is difficult to trace the course of his decline.

II

The Tuaregs have legends which are concerned with the exploits of Karidenna. They do not tally with those described. Some Tuaregs, familiar with Arab historians, are inclined to reject the fanciful etymological theories about the name of the Iwillimeden and to favour the view that this name has some connection with either the Lamṭa or Lamtūna. (7) The Lemta people are referred to by Leo Africanus and appear on European maps earlier than the reign of Karidenna. Among the Ahaggaren the ancient nobles are sometimes called Loummet; Ilamatay (Alamtan) appears in Agades Chronicles, and a kindred name is also known among the Ifoghas.(8)

Other Tuaregs (9) do not offer an explanation which conforms to Islamic history. Their oral traditions omit to name Karidenna. They depict a hero akin to the Hilālī, Abū Zayd. The Iwillimeden appear to mean the Tuaregs in general. They chased the Ihatan - the Songhai and Zerma sedentary population - from the areas which were to be the power centre of the Iwillimeden in the Adrar-n-Ifoghas and adjacent regions.

The ruling family of the Iwillimeden, they allege, came from the district of Arawān and the Hodh, from the Barābīsh, a Ma'qil group who came from Egypt. This is possibly an allusion to the story of the journey of the Banū Hilāl from the banks of the Nile. In the beginning this aristocracy was to be found in the area of Timbuctoo. They wandered east to a region called Taylalt. There they joined with local Tuaregs and with the Ihatan. The Tuaregs there were mixed with Bella. They boasted of being *Imashaghen* because their eponym was a giant named Majegh (Māzīgh). He had conquered Gao. The city had been forced to pay a stipulated tax of seven Bella girls. These *Imashaghen* departed with their captives until they reached a valley. The sun set, and their Kel Es-Suq marabout (*elfeqqi)* said to them, 'Continue on your way. I have a matter to attend to, but do not halt in the valley.' However, when he arrived there he found them camped there. He asked them why they had halted. They answered that their camels were tired. They spent the night there.

That same night the genie or giant (al-Jayn) Majegh had relations with all seven Bella girls, and they conceived. Upon arrival at their destination the mara - bout placed them in a house until their time of delivery. Their offspring grew up surrounded by Zerma and Songhai. The latter complained to the marabout about the behaviour of these halfbreeds. He answered, 'Leave them alone, they are in the process of learning.' For that reason they were called Iwillimeden ('those who learn'). The children grew up. They fought the Ihatan and banished them.

Among the Asbenawa of Air there is a legend that Solomon left his palace for forty days. An evil spirit called Saharu (al-Jayn?) entered his palace and assumed his shape. He took Solomon's royal seal to his concubine Aminatu. Then Solomon returned to his palace and found that forty of his wives and concubines had been made pregnant by Saharu. He expelled them from his palace but he gave them slaves, cattle, camels and herds of sheep and goats. They were banished to the wilderness, and Solomon made huts of palm leaves for them to dwell in. They gave birth to many children, both male and female, and these children intermarried. They dwelt in the desert and bred cattle and sheep and goats. The forty wives and concubines pair the forty virgins who became the wives of the forty companions of Dhiyāb b. Ghānim al-Hilālī, or his double, Abū Zayd.

Certain details of these tales appear in the writings of Muḥammad Bello in his *Infāq al-Maysūr.* (10) 'Those Tuaregs (*tawārik)* were remnants of the Berbers who dispersed in the days when Ifrīqiyā was conquered. The Berbers are a nation of the offspring of Abraham. It is also said that they are descended from Japhet and from Gog and Magog who were shut up by Dhū 'l-Qarnayn (Alexander). A party of them came forth to wreck havoc and destruction on others. They remained and intermarried with the Turks and the Tartars.'

'It is also said that they are from the land of the *jinn* (al-Jayn). A party went to Jerusalem and spent the night in a valley. In the morning they found that their womenfolk had been made pregnant by the men of that spot. They gave birth to them. They are a people who are by nature blood-thirsty, who loot and pillage goods and possessions and wage war.'

The Iwillimeden - the mixed company of Tuaregs under the welfare of their holy-man - were to be ruled by a prince called Innezbig. He seems to correspond to Muḥammad Wa-n-Ara or Karidenna. He asked the *elfeqqi* to recite the *elfetekken* to establish him as ruler. He went to war followed by all the Tuaregs, and he became their *Amenukal.* Innezbig was a lavish bestower of horses. The smiths and artisans rode them. Some went to Gao to collect the taxes, some to Timbuctoo, others to smaller localities. They were his police and tax gatherers, and they collected the rice, cloths or whatever was demanded of the chiefs of the sedentaries as payment of *tusay.* (11) The Tuaregs attacked Air to seize cattle. The Iwillimeden were nearly always victorious.

Innezbig fought his younger brother Khatatu. He is confused in this account with Tafrīja or Karoza, rival of Karidenna and his successors in other tales. His younger brother left their land and went to settle in the region of Tahoua. There was to be perpetual warfare between the Iwillimeden of the West (Kel Aṭaram) and the East (Kel Dennek).

This fable indicates the inconsistency of Tuareg traditions. It offers Innezbig as an alternative to Muḥammad wa-n-Ara or to Karidenna. It implies that the Iwillimeden were in the Adrar-n-Ifoghas prior to the eastward expeditions of an 'Arab' chief. Iwillimeden was a name given to all Tuareg established in ancient times in the region of the Adrar.

No Tuareg 'history' offers more than a hypothetical explanation of Iwillimeden origins. The tale of the arrival of an outsider who was a prince among the Kel Tadamakkat and a switch in the choice of succession could be a foundation myth or might have arisen in a number of tribes at differing periods.

The march of the ancestors of Karidenna from Igidi near the Spanish Sahara or from the area of Walāta or Timbuctoo is introduced in some accounts, in a format wholly supplied by romancers of the Kel Es-Suq and the Kunta. It is based on the exploits of 'Oqba al-Mustajāb. A jumble of Islamic heros accompany or herald the dynastic founder into the heart of the Adrar-n-Ifoghas. The arrival of the Iwillimeden hero is thus described by an *Ineslemen* counsellor of Fihrun, a chiefly descendant of Karidenna. (12)

'Karidenna arrived at the beginning of the seventeenth century. He was advised by the scholar and counsellor Ya'qūb al-Anṣari, a Companion of the Prophet, the ancestor of the Kel Intasar, the Idaw al-Ḥājj and the Kel Es-Suq. This scholar was a furtherer of the *jihād.* Karidenna built up a mighty army of Arab warriors under the command of 'Oqba al-Mustajāb Tadamakkat was under Songhai power though shared between Tuareg groups. Idolatory was the religion of its inhabitants. A fierce battle raged in As-Sūq. Its citizens were offered Islam or the sword. While ‘Oqba continued his march to the banks of the Niger, Karidenna settled in the permanent grazing areas of the Iwillimeden. The holy man Ya‘qūb al-Anṣārī despaired of the restoration of As-Suq. He devoted his life to religious instruction, and he attached his family to Karidenna.’

Some anthropologists believe that the era of the Iwillimeden determined a switch to succession from father to son, superseding that of the son of the eldest sister or devolution in a semi-matrilineal manner within Tuareg political organisation (13) It then became a norm over a large part of the Tuareg Sahel and Sahara. The year 1650 or thereabouts was a landmark in Tuareg social history. (14)

We have no authentic historical information at all to either affirm or qualify this assertion though there seems to be some valid ground for believing that from the sixteenth century onwards Sultanates where son succeeded father were increasingly favoured.

In the preceding century leading Muslim reformers and men of influence had either condemned or had been noncommittal on this issue. ‘Abd al-Karīm al-Maghīlī in his ‘Replies to Muḥammad Askia’ was opposed to any form of succession other than the patrilineal *Sharī‘a.* The social ideals of the Songhai rulers were so powerful that they could not be ignored by adjacent Tuaregs. Those who followed al-Maghīlī pressed imposition of patrilineal inheritance. The subject was also raised by Muḥammad al-Lamtūnī in section six of his questions addressed to al-Suyūṭī, ‘Among them are some who do not follow the rules of inheritance. What a man leaves when he dies goes to his sister’s sons or to men of power and influence.’ The point is raised in general terms, and al-Suyūṭī leaves the question unanswered.

There were two camps among the *Ineslemen.* One was more radically minded and militant, swayed by al-Maghīlī; the other concessionary to local custom, unless directly condemned by al-Suyūṭī, and less interested in reform by force than by persuasion or evolutionary change. The Kel Es-Suq typified the latter.

Karidenna has been credited with the introduction of a ‘Mauritanian type’ class structure among the Iwillimeden, but how or why is obscure. The formation of his Sultanate was not the partial imposition of an alien aristocracy, as characterized by the *Amīrates* of the Banū Ḥassān in the Western Sahara, but principally an internal change within the Tuareg communities themselves.

If all the legends which explain the epic of Muḥammad ‘the nameless one’, Innezbig the progenitor, or the triumphal march of Karidenna to a Tuareg throne are compared, they are united by common features. They have been shaped by

Ineslemen ideas, borrowed from Islamic literary or oral prototypes and imposed on a dynasty of chiefs about whom almost nothing is known outside *Ineslemen* tales. Karidenna is among the faceless ones. Bedecked in borrowed trappings he is the combined production of the Mauritanian Moors, the Kel Intasar, the Barābīsh, the Kel Es-Suq and their kinsfolk. (16)

IV

All accounts note a historic split in the Iwillimeden. This split survives today. But while the Kel Es-Suq maintain that the split began in the lifetime of Karidenna, well before the end of the seventeenth century, the Kel Dennek are tempted to date it much later in his life and to ascribe it to his nephew al-Tafrīja. The Kel Es-Suq call this nephew - or his brother - Karoza, and they attribute the split to issues which involved the Sultan of Agades.

The Kel Aṭaram maintain that the split took place at the end of the eighteenth century, long after the death of Karidenna (either 1698 or 1715). There is no hope of bridging the chronologies. Western authorities are inclined to accept the thesis of the Kel Dennek, although they do not satisfactorily explain the motives for the split.

It was beyond the powers of the Kel Es-Suq *Ineslemen* to help shape a Sultanate for Karidenna like that of Agades in its prime, let alone that of the Songhai Empire. Scholastic in their tastes, compelled to dwell in camps, there is a certain unreality in their flights of mysticism and hair-splitting jurisprudence amidst mounting social chaos.

The droughts of the seventeenth century attained a peak in the early eighteenth century between 1711 and 1716. The hungry and scattered Iwillimeden cast themselves on the mercy of the Pasha of Timbuctoo. The investiture of Karidenna in 1690 was a sad end to their precocious hero. In the eighteenth century the Kel Tadamakkat and the Iwillimeden were to be a thorn in the flesh of the Moroccans on the river. But as Mawlay Muḥammad al-Hādī represented the situation it had grown steadily worse for those *Ineslemen* who had genuinely attempted to spread the observation of the *Sharī'a* and simple Islamic teaching. Only among the Kel Dennek in the east, in Azawād or in the camps in the Ifoghas did some Islamic culture revive in the late eighteenth century. The *Ineslemen* like the *Imashaghen* depended on slaves. Recurrent droughts and the drift of the *Ighawalen* to the southlands disrupted scholarly activities.

Tuareg society, unlike that of the Moors, the Arab world, or the Sudanic kingdoms, rarely illustrates efforts to organise a larger, more complex society in which power is sustained by commerce and religious authority. Where such efforts have been made the initial inspiration has usually come from foreign quarters. Hence the truth or the fable of the exploits of Muḥammad War-Ilemmed, Karidenna and his descendants, the legendary Moorish prince who tried to weld a patrilineal Sultanate from a tribe.

NOTES

1) *Nomades et Nomadisme au Sahara,* U.N.E.S.C.O., 1963, p. 172

2) See extended discussions and articles in *Revue de l'Occident Musulman et de la Méditerranée,* Aix-en-Provence, No. II, ler semestre, 1972.

3) See Richer, *Oulliminden,* pp. 50-56.

4) On the administrative and military (?) investiture of Karidenna as *Qā'id,* see Cortier, *D'une rive à l'autre du Sahara,* pp. 395-396.

5) *T.S.,* p. 484, Fr. translation.

6) See E.W. Bovill, *The Golden Trade of the Moors, (Caravans of the Old Sahara),* p. 198.

7) Iwillimeden and Ilemtien (Lamtūna etc.) differ in that in *Tifinagh* script the former is almost invariably spelt with a *d,* the latter with a *t.*

8) See the lineages of the Kel Intasar and the Kel Es-Suq, pages 141-143, where Lamtūn often appears.

9) For example, those of the Iwillimeden recorded in *Iwillimedan* presented by Altinine ag Arias, Niamey, 1970, pp. 43-67.

10) *I.M.,* Whitting, pp. 13-14.

11) An annual tribute payed by vassal clans to the *Amenukal.* The size of the tribute varies. It is normally collected by the clan chiefs who send it to the *Amenukal.* The payment may be made in millet, butter, goats, cotton and other ways. See J. Nicolaisen, *Folk,* Vol. I, 1959, pp. 112-113, and M. Benhazera, *Six mois chez les Touareg du Ahaggar,* pp. 53-54.

12) See note 9.

13) See the works of F. Nicolas and J. Nicolaisen and pages

14) See note 2.

15) See H. Lhote, *Contribution à l'Etude des Touaregs Soudanais,* p. 354.

16) See V. Monteil, 'Sur quelques textes arabes provenant du Soudan', *Bulletin du Comité d'Etudes Historiques et Scientifiques de l'A.O.F.,* 1938, pp. 499-517, and P. Marty, *Les Kounta de l'Est, les Berabich.*

A note on Iwillimeden, Lamtūna and Lamṭa

The presence of Lamtūn in genealogies links these alleged forebears with those among the Moors of the Western Sahara and with the ancestress (Lamtūna) or ancestor (Lemta) of the Ilemtien of the areas of Ghadames and Ghat. (see J. Nicolaisen, E.C.P.T., p. 405-411). The variant spellings of this name are given by Père de Foucauld in his *Dictionnaire Touareg-Français* Tome III, 1951, pp. 1086-1087 and in his *Dictionnaire Abrégé Touareg-Français de Noms Propres,* Paris, 1940, pp. 153-154. By extension it would seem to indicate the noble Tuareg of the Sahara in general. (Foucauld and Nicolaisen.)

Iwillimeden appears to have no connection with Lamtūn (a). See De Foucauld's *Dictionnaire,* 1.501, and *Dictionnaire Abrégé,* p. 196. On linguistic grounds Tuareg theories of some connection between Lamtūna and Iwillimeden would not seem likely, particularly as the Ilemtien of the Adrar-n-Ifoghas, who may well have a historical link with the Lamtūna or Lemta, were subordinate to, and quite distinct from, the Iwillimeden.

There remains the possibility that the Lamṭa and Iwillimeden are in some way connected. Here again the hypothesis has major weaknesses:-

1) The Lamṭa did not have the aura of grandeur of the Lamtūna among the lettered *Ineslemen* who, if they had any say in the dubbing of Karidenna's/Innezbig's lineage by a medieval name would have been likely to have preferred the latter. In Tifināgh the names Ilemtien and Iwillimeden are distinct.

2) A *ṭā'* in medieval Arabic names tends to become an emphatic *ḍ* - the letter *ḍād.* Thus Mas(h)ṭūfa (var. of Massūfa) have, it would seem, become Mashḍūf in recent times. One would expect Lamṭa to have become Lamḍa - with an emphatic *ḍ,* not a *d* as in the Tifinagh spelling of Iwillimeden. The Lamṭa had some link with the Lamṭ (oryx), from whose skins they made their shields (see T. Lewicki, *West African Food in the Middle Ages,* pp. 92-93 and 199). The word *labṭi* is also found. This word may just possibly be connected with the Tāmashegh word *ilemḍân.* (Foucauld, *Dictionnaire,* T. III, p. 1080).

3) How is the total absence of Iwi-/War (Banū) in Lamṭa in early texts to be explained?

It would seem nonetheless that some etymological relationship between

Iwillimeden and Lamṭa cannot be wholly ruled out, that a connection between Iwillimeden and Lamtūna is very unlikely, and that in all probability none of the various Tuareg or Kunta theories of the origin of the name can be accepted on evidence available. It is possible that manuscripts in the De Gironcourt papers may help, especially Ms. 2405, pièce no. 1, *Tārīkh Ulliminden* by Ibris Lotokoro (1830-1910) and Ms. 2411, piece no. 182, which supplies the lineage of Karidenna and Krṭa (Karoza?), but I have had no opportunity to examine these manuscripts, which are in any case recent. Inaccuracies which occur in them regarding Songhai rulers do not encourage optimism in regard to their accuracy in reporting the Tuaregs and their histories.

Note on the Iwillimeden and the Kel Es-Suq in the *Tadhkirat al-Nisyān.*

This anonymous work, an alphabetical inventory of Pashas and religious dignitaries of Timbuctoo and Jenne between 1590 and 1750, translated by O. Houdas (Paris, 1901), makes passing reference to the Iwillimeden, confirming several dates in the Kel Aṭaram succession from Karidenna (var. Kalidden/Kaladden).

During the Pashalik of Sanībar (Sinībar) in 1695, an expedition was sent to Tondibi near Gao to punish the "Tuaregs" and the "Kel Es-Suq". Despite the doubts of Houdas (see French translation pp. 99-100) I am certain that the Kel Es-Suq *Ineslemen* are intended here, while "Tuaregs" denotes Iwillimeden *Imashaghen.* No further details are provided, but it would seem that the influence of the Kel Es-Suq must have been considerable during the period of Karidenna's rule after his 'investitures'. Some conflict of interest between Timbuctoo and the Agades Sultanate may explain the expedition, and it is tempting to see the Kel Es-Suq as allies of Agades in a conflict with the Pashas of Timbuctoo to exert pressure on the Iwillimeden.

For a detailed clarification of this period see Henri Lhote 'Contribution à l'étude du Touareg soudanais II, *Bulletin de l'IFAN,* 1956, pp. 396-403.

CHAPTER VIII

LATER SCHOLARS OF THE KEL ES-SUQ

> 'As for those who are among their subjects, such as the Kel Es-Suq it is they who are the custodians of learning and religion, but they have no military power even for those who are in a subject status, their dependants for example, for they have gone to the utmost limit in their search for peace and the suppression of military might, fearing reproof in order to make firm the establishment of a quietest retreat and on account of a belief of hope for God's creation.'
>
> Mawlay Muḥammad al-Hādī al-Sūqī

In previous chapters I have assessed the impact of the early Tuareg scholars of Tadamakkat on the religious beliefs of the Mali Adrar and Air. It has been seen that certain of these scholars claimed descent from the Prophet's household. In origin they came from families long established in Sijilmāsa in Morocco or in the Arabian peninsula. Other scholar families seem to have been of Tuareg blood, descended from lettered families among settled groups of Azgar, Targa, Lamtūna and other tribes in Tadamakkat.

The scholars who lived after 1600, who call themselves Kel Es-Suq to distinguish themselves from the Kel Tadamakkat who were warrior nobles, have familial ties with their medieval ancestors or predecessors. But they are different from them in several respects. The status of these later scholars was one of inferiority. They were to all intents and purposes vassals of the Iwillimeden. Elsewhere, for example in Agades, they had to compete with newcomers who challenged their spiritual status and monopoly. Among the most important were the Kunta who entered the Tuareg lands from Mauritania or from Tuwāt.

The later scholars of the Kel Es-Suq were very dispersed. Many forsook the Adrar-n-Ifoghas and emigrated to every part of the Sahara and the Sahel. Tadamakkat was somehow forgotten in their travels and their wanderings, but they managed to preserve something of its medieval culture by creating new centres of learning. They did so in new townships and villages in the area of Azawād north of Timbuctoo, in the oasis of Ghadames in Libya, and in a few scattered localities in the Mali Adrar. Some of the Kel Es-Suq scholars lived and taught in camps throughout the territory claimed by the Iwillimeden. I hope to show by three examples - the Kel Es-Suq of Arawān in Azawād; the most noted scholars who lived among the Iwillimeden; and one or two scholars of the Ifoghas - that the Islamic heritage of Tadamakkat was never totally lost despite wars and famines. The later scholars of the Kel Es-Suq made an important contribution to Tuareg life. In their knowledge of Arabic language, jurisprudence and mystical texts they were at least the equals of the Kunta. Some would rate their achievements higher than theirs. Nonetheless, only by the discovery and publication of their texts will it be possible to equitably assess the true value of their scholastic contribution.

II

Azawād and Tadamakkat

There is Arabic textual evidence to indicate that elements of the Kel Tadamakkat and Kel Es-Suq were well known in Azawād before Karidenna. The 'Walāta Chronicle', for example, explicitly states that during the reign of Askia Dā'ūd (d. 1582) a raid against Ḥassānis in Walāta district included squadrons of Massig (Lemzazga Imashaghen), Kel Tadamakkat and Tad 'Amart, Banū 'Āmir mixed with Tuaregs.

Local chronicles and oral traditions in Azawād report that the definitive founder of Arawān was the Quṭb Aḥmad b. Addah al-Sūqī, who left As-Sūq about 1575. He travelled via Tuwat to Arawān about 1592, performed the pilgrimage to Mecca in 1593, then married into the Kel Intasar and died in Arawān about 1627. He was affiliated to the Qādirīya, and he was a contemporary of the Muslim reformer of the Kel Intasar, Muḥammad Quṭb al-Anṣārī whose legacy will be discussed in Chapter X. The Kunta were nowhere in the vicinity, since their own accounts tell of the foundation of their centre at al-Mabrūk far later in 1133/1720-21. The area of Azawād was a centre for mystics of Tadamakkat or As-Sūq some time prior to Karidenna. These contacts may be explained by the renewal of west to east commercial routes of long standing and the wandering of scholars.

It is unwise to accept too much historical significance in reports of 'mass' expulsion of Kel Tadamakkat to the Timbuctoo area at the hands of the Iwillimeden. It is also unwise to date the entire decay of the commercial life of As-Sūq to a vague period in the middle of the seventeenth century. I have shown how Tuareg scholars vary in their explanation for the 'fall of As-Sūq'. Some hold Sunni Ali to be instrumental in its ruin, others maintain that Karidenna and the anarchy of his dynasty were to blame. Mawlay Muḥammad al-Hādī gives some blame to both, also to a feud between the Kel Imeglalen (either 'people of the swords' or 'the gardeners') as an important factor in the ruin of this city.

Other evidence shows the survival of As-Sūq well into the eighteenth century, long after the Iwillimeden had emerged. It is provided in the text of the Walata biographical corpus of scholars *Fatḥ al-Shakūr* written in 1214/1799-1800 by Muḥammad b. Abū Bakr al-Ṣiddīq al-Bartīlī. The following is the biography of al-Ṭālib Sīdī Aḥmad b. al-Bashīr b. Muḥammad b. Muḥammad Mu'min al-Kel Sūqī:-

'He grew up in the town of the people of al-Sūq (Tadamakkat) his town. Then he came to Arawān when he was twenty-five years old. The reason for his departure from his town was that he left to seek for a pious man whose name was Sīdī Aḥmad al-Hoggārī (of the Hoggār) who was known among the people of Ra's al-Mā'. He had sons there known by the people of Ra's al-Mā'. When he came to him, he commanded him to go in the direction of Arawān, and he stayed with the Kāhīya (the Moroccan Arma) chief of the town. He studied the 'litany' (*wird*), and he learnt it from Sīdī Aḥmad b. 'Abd al-Qādir b. Aḥmad b. Aḥmad al-Raggādī and one of the 'seven readings' from Shaykh Sīdī al-Amīn b. Ḥabīb al-Jakanī and Sīdī Ibrāhīm b. al-Imām al-'Alawī, may God Almighty have mercy upon them both. They gave him their *ijāza.* He studied the (*ḥadīth*) readings of al-Bukhārī and Muslim, the *Shifā'* and the *Khaṣā'iṣ* (al-Kubrā) and else besides on the authority of the Qāḍī Sīdī 'l-Wāfī b. Ṭalibna al-Arawānī. He also studied exegesis in Arawān. Most of the books he used were works of exegesis, tradition of the Prophet and readings of the Qur'ān.

He was a person who spoke little about that which was not his concern. He hardly left off pious devotions, during the night and in the day-time. One would only see him reading and reciting aloud and voicing his devotions. Often he would chant the Qur'ān in the reading of Qālūn. He would hardly ever ignore one who spoke opposite him but he would command him to think of God in his devotions. Frequently he would recite sermons to the common people. He preached to every one of them. To them he would quote the (Kitāb) *al-Targhīb wal-tarhīb* and the *Kitāb* of al-Samarqandī and *al-'Ulūm al-fākhira fī umūr al-ākhira* and *Sharḥ al-Ṣudūr fī aḥwāl al-mawtā wal-qubūr* and *Tanbīh al-mughtarrīn.* He mentioned that one of the saintly and pious told him before he had attained the age of fifty years that the pious saints had met and had appointed him to be among the 'people of *taṣrīf*' (wilful disposal). He also mentioned that he was ill in the year *Tikar,* and that the famous authors of works known to us used to come to him to visit him regularly during that sickness of his. The last of those who stood by him was the Imām al-Ḥaṭṭāb. They asked him about that, and he said, "I was asking God's blessing on them." He also mentioned that he saw (the Caliph) Abū Bakr al-Ṣiddīq. He said, "Between me and you is blood relationship."

He used to honour the people of God and the Prophet's household and the progeny of his Shaykhs. The daughter of his Shaykh was the responsibility (?) of one of the Ragāgida, so he used to give the husband many male camels and the raiment of the daughter and the maintenance expended on her. He was generous, and he gave so much away that he gave thirty she-camels between two camps in the desert. He had at hand some two flocks or herds pasturing freely. One of them he gave away, and he sat as the herder of those camels. Often he used to say that one of his Shaykhs ordered him to spend (his wealth), and said to him "Give it (away) for indeed you are sitting on a treasure (of the spirit)." He was in confidence and trust with and among the common people and among robbers and ruffians. How did he stand among the men of God? His son Muḥamma[d] al-Amīn said, and one whom I trust mentioned to me that he heard from Sīdī Muḥammad al-Ṭāhir b. Sīdī 'Alī that he said to him, "I have seen none equal to my Shaykh Sīdī Aḥmad al-Kel-Sūqī." He said to me, "When I differ regarding a word with the novices and scholars, and we betake ourselves to research in books, I do not desire to be a victor or to master them. My sole desire is to know the truth and tc learn what is correct whether I be right or proved wrong in it." His death - may God Almighty have mercy upon him - was in the forenoon of Sunday in 1184/1770/1. He was buried opposite the mosque of (the town) of Bū Jbayha. Among those things noted after his burial was that his cries of "Glory to God" were to be heard in his tomb, with regularity by the people. Very often during his life-time he used to sit in the place wherein he was buried. He lived to be eighty-four, and he was born at the very beginning of the twelfth century (of the Hijra).'

There are other points of interest in this passage besides chronology and biographical details. The ability of *Ineslemen* to interchange between a pastoral and semi-urban life is to be noted. Sīdī Aḥmad left As-Sūq for learning and religious reasons. No mention is made of economic disaster nor of Iwillimeden expulsions. It is also noteworthy that the goal of his journey was a Tuareg scholar of the Hoggar. Despite the Moroccan orientation of the Pashas, at this period there was contact between declining Tadamakkat (As-Sūq) and the Tuareg Kel Es-Suq centres of Bū Jbayha and Arawān (the Kel Arawān), east and west through the territory of the Iwillimeden. This relationship was not new, nor was it to be totally interrupted.

III

Scholars of the Kel Es-Suq among the Iwillimeden

Among the Iwillimeden whom they served the Kel Es-Suq scholars were both Mālikī jurists and mystics of the Qādiriya. This balance of academic disciplines was also characteristic of the Kunta, but there is no evidence to suggest that the Kel Es-Suq had simply acquired it from the Kunta. To quote Mawlay Muḥammad al-Hādī, 'It is essential to know what to be thankful for. It is labour in jurisprudence *(fiqh)*. It is discourse about the basis of Islam. That basis is not sound without its knowledge, nor is there Sufism without *fiqh* since God's rules which are literal and external are only known by it. There is no *fiqh* save with Sufism and mystical insight. Both exist due to faith. They do not exist without the co-presence of the latter. On account of this it is said, "He who follows *fiqh* and possesses not mystic knowledge is a free-thinker, while he who is a mystic and does not follow *fiqh* is in error and commits a sin. He who combines them arrives at the truth and is in true faith."

The Kel Es-Suq Daghūghīyīn who originate as *Shurafā'* from Mawlay Idrīs have already been introduced in Chapter IV. This claim stood them in good stead during the days of the Askia. To quote Ḥammād b. Muḥammad b. Muḥammad al-Sūqī, 'When the tyrannical prince harmed people they were not safe from his oppression save for the *Shurafā'*, so claim to Prophetic descent multiplied.' In their ancestry the line of 'Alī b. Yaḥyā b. Ibrāhīm al-Daghūghī ensured their status. Yet as Tuaregs they could not, did not desire to wholly repudiate their matrilineal heritage. A key figure in their lineage was Fāṭima 'the virgin' (*al-batūl)* the Prophet's daughter to whom great honour was shown. Their title of *Sharaf* was not only in flesh and blood (*ṭīn*), but also in scholastic achievement (*'ilm*). Both blood and learning were inherited like the *eṭṭebel* and proved the truth of the ancestry which they claimed. Fāṭima is singled out for praise in an ode by Hāmma al-Daghūghī:-

> Oh, my succour (Muḥammad), I am from the few of your descendants,
> Pleasing to you and pleasing to her (Fāṭima) - the virgin.
> Oh, my succour, the fire of Hell will be turned away from those
> who stem from you.

This same Suqi scholar, Ḥammād b. Muḥammad, elsewhere reports a tradition about Sīdī al-Mukhtār al-Kuntī that 'when he came to a Tuareg camp, and he saw women assembling to visit him and to acquire his *baraka,* he asked, "Is there one from among you with a *Sharīf* in her womb?" He ordered that she should not come to him save walking upon rugs. This was due to the honour towards the being in her womb. She was the mother of Fāṭima al-Zahrā', the daughter of our uncle Tabbala. The latter married her. Then he divorced her when she was pregnant with Fāṭima al-Zahrā'. She returned to her family, the people of that camp. He stayed there before she gave birth.'

Side by side with Prophetic lineage is that of the ancestress Akallu. Some held that she had no spouse, but most claim that she was married to 'Uthmān, a *faqīh* who bore the title of Iddan-tamazgidda (of the mosque). Scholars's mothers were as important in their lineage as their fathers and were often better known. Despite this Prophetic connection, in earlier times the title of *Amīr* was held not by a man but a woman. According to Ḥammād b. Muḥammad, 'This (fifteenth-seventeenth centuries) was the time when the *Imāra* was in the hands of womenfolk. Sometimes it is recorded that only males were worthy of mention. We are told of the *Amīrates* of Tadhandit, the mother of Kāwa. Mention is made of the sons of Taghidat and the sons of Takhatta.' Mawlay Muḥammad al-Hādī appears to allude to this situation where he remarks, 'Our ancestor Muḥammad al-Mukhtār - nicknamed Ahalis - neither denied nor confirmed the status of *Sharīf* to anyone because he himself, it was said, had forebears who were offspring of Muḥammad b. Aghdanfas (Aghfatnas) the brother of the ancestress Taghidat.'

Unfortunately the dates of most of the later Suqi scholars are unknown. The names given by Ḥammād b. Muḥammad seem to span the centuries, from 1600 to 1850, nor is it clear where most of them lived, although some were certainly in the Adrar-n-Ifoghas or in camps of the Iwillimeden.

Among the elect was al-Bakrī b. Agg Ayyay, who may have lived in the late seventeenth century. Many of his texts were later quoted. Another was Inalbush, from whose writings a fragment refers to the Kel Es-Suq, 'As for the fathers of the Sūqīyīn, among them are those who inherit an uninterrupted and unbroken tradition as to their Prophetic descent, like the offspring of our grandfather Ibrāhīm al-Daghūghī and the progeny of Ayitta to whom we owe the birth of descendants and others besides.' A leading Qur'ānic commentator was Mahdī b. al-Ṣāliḥ al-Mufassir. Aḥmad known as 'Āmm, the saintly and pious, the son of Muḥammad Aḥmad called Hamma-hamma who both in poetry and prose claimed his descent from 'Alī, the Prophet's son-in-law. Muḥammad b. Dāniyāl (Daniel) was an authority on *Sharī'a* jurisprudence. Aḥmad b. Muḥammad b. Wa-n-Ṣaṭṭafan made rulings and openly alleged the assumption of direct descent from the Prophet' household. A famous *Qāḍī* of uncertain date was Shaykh Shalhu who performed numerous miracles.

Another famous *Qāḍī* was Ḥanna b. Immattal, jurist and mystic, who may have been Muḥammad Ḥanna, Shaykh of Mawlay Muḥammad al-Hādī. He was born sometime in the eighteenth century. According to Mawlay Muḥammad al-Hadi this Shaykh allegedly ruled that the dissolution of a marriage was anathema in law and maintained that its 'adornment was the very essence of mercy.' He wrote a book setting forth his views but it was badly received, and he was obliged to hide it. Among the greatest scholars and saints were Muḥammad b. Intaklusut, Muḥammad b. Hulāy, Ibrāhīm b. Wadāy, a poet, Sīdī Muḥammad b. Issāy and his grandfather Inbadhdha. Other saintly men were Aḥmad b. Makhā and his grandfather Malū, and Muḥammad known as Ḥāmma (al-Daghūghī) who was a poet. His son al-Na-'ām was also famous. Other scholars of repute were Muḥammad b. al-Sālī, Muḥammad Aḥmad b. al-Thānī, and Muḥammad known as Ugannat.

Only the names of these scholars are at present known. Unlike the Kunta, wh became famous for actively spreading the Qādirīya, the Kel Es-Suq specialised in Arabic rhetoric. They perfected their calligraphy. They were inclined to mysticism, but at the same time turned to many legal problems which faced Tuareg society, problems which could not always be solved by reference to the law manuals or to the opinions of al-Maghīlī and al-Suyūṭī.

IV

Scholars of the Kel Es-Suq among the Ifoghas

With the rise of the Songhai Empire, in the fifteenth and sixteenth centuries a party of Ifoghas Tuaregs from the Adrar allegedly emigrated to the Libyan region of Ghadames. Then later in the middle of the seventeenth century, following the conflict between the Kel Tadamakkat and the Iwillimeden, a number of them moved west to Timbuctoo, while others moved to the Tassili-n-Ajjer and Ghadames. Local traditions of Ghadames maintain that Sīdī Aḥmad al-Faqqī al-Sūqī and his Kel Es-Suq came there from Timbuctoo about 1600, prior to the triumph of Karidenna.

Upon his arrival at Ghadames his party of Kel Es-Suq joined the Ifoghas already established in the vicinity. These Kel Es-Suq became famous for their piety and fixed their *Zāwiya* at Timasinin near Fort Flatters. So great was their prestige that one of their number, Sīdī al-Bakrī married a noble Tuareg woman of the Kel Ahaggar, and his son became the *Amenukal.* Their power and influence began to decline at the end of the nineteenth century.

While there is no reason to dismiss some of these Ifoghas traditions there is also evidence to suggest that those Ifoghas in the Adrar-n-Ifoghas were in part absorbed matrilineally into the Kel Es-Suq and played a part as *Ineslemen* during the time of Karidenna or after him, until their position was undermined by the Kunta. Among their religious leaders was the *Sharīf* Agag al-Ghazālī, who came to be venerated by the Iwillimeden and the Kel Es-Suq as well as the Ifoghas. He is said by some Kel Es-Suq to have been a contemporary of Karidenna, although there is no documentary evidence to substantiate this claim. It does seem, however, that he lived when the Iwillimeden Sultanate first came into being.

Some account of the life of the *Sharīf* al-Ghazālī is reported in the so-called 'Traditions of Tarrazart'. (1)

'Of those reports which have reached us, and we have heard on the authority of our elders, is that a man called al-Ghazālī who was the father of the tribe called the Ifōghās, journeyed from the land of Air. He was with a tribe called the Ihalashshaten and another called the Iderfen.

They journeyed from that land, leaving it behind. Upon their heels was a tribe called the Ikadammaten. Eventually they made their camels kneel at the well where they drew their water. The father of the Ifōghās, al-Ghazālī, said to them, "I shall set a trap for them. In it we shall slay their prince. I shall put antimony in my eyes, I shall go out to him and sit before him. When he looks at my eyes coated with antimony he will die on the spot."

So he dyed his eyes with antimony and went out to meet him. When he sat down before him and looked at him he died on the spot. By reason of the death of the prince of the Ikadammaten they did not raid those tribes, and they refrained from further harming them.

After that the father of the Ifōghās, al-Ghazālī, set forth again. He was followed by the tribe of the Ihalashshaten and the tribe called Iderfen until they reached a country called Itighazart. Then a group of people rode out from among them, and they followed after those others who had fled from their own pursuers from Air, that is to say the Ikadammaten. That group numbered one hundred men. They arrived at a well called Fattarmen and Iftumaggen. Fifty of them left them, and fifty of them remained.

Now those who left followed a route above a mountain which was called Fatfati until there met them on that route a small herd of she-camels of a tribe named Tigasast. They asked them where they were making for. They said to them, "We are making for the country of the Iwillimeden, since our country has brought us injury and loss. We therefore loathe it, and we have departed making for this country."

They said to them, "If you are making for the country of the Iwillimeden, we, likewise, have left in order to go to them. We journeyed until we reached a people of the tribe of the Ikadammaten. They raided us, and they took away our wives and offspring, and they took our slave girls captive. So help us recover what they have taken away from us, namely our wives, our slave girls and our offspring so that we and you will be as one 'hand', (2) and we shall co-operate against our enemies, and we shall journey with you to the country of the Iwillimeden."

So they did that for them. They aided them to the extent of their need until they arrived at that country. A party of them rode to the prince of the Iwillimeden, and he gave the father of the Ifōghās, al-Ghāzalī, three tribes - named Iderfen (3) and Ihalashshaten and Ikadammaten. The prince said to him, "This is the reward for your coming to me. My portion for these who have gone forth are these camels known as the Tigasast.'"

This tale of unknown date introduces the saint Egag al-Ghazālī as a father figure of an *Ineslemen* tribe within the Iwillimeden. In the account the latter appear as a protective power drawing others into their orbit, not as a force which expelled tribes long established in the Adrar-n-Ifoghas.

While the Ifoghas *Ineslemen* of the Tassili-n-Ajjer have no vassal *Imghad,* and seem detached from their neighbours, the Ifoghas of the Iwillimeden country, to whom the Taghazart tradition refers, appear to have evolved quite separately from their former kinsmen in the north, and to reveal marked differences explained by historical, social and environmental reasons. The Ifoghas of the Adrar were once subordinate to the Iwillimeden, and this text seems to confirm it. They paid tribute to them until the Iwillimeden became so weak that the Ifoghas were able to assert their independence and have their own *Imghad.* Unlike the northern Ifoghas, who are divided into three or four fractions, those of the south are divided into seven. Their names differ from those in the vicinity of Ghadames. The Kel Es-Suq formed an essential *Ineslemen* element in their social organisation, and their Sufi affiliation was to the Qādirīya *ṭarīqa* not the Tijānīya like those in the north.

NOTES

1) *D.G.*, manuscript No. 135, Traditions du Terrazart.

2) 'hand' here has almost the sense of 'tribe', since *tawsit* (var. *tawshit)* not only has the sense of 'la Grande Taoussit' where all people descend from a common eponym, but also the palm of the hand from which branch the fingers.

3) *Ederef,* fem. *Tedereft,* pl. *Iderfen,* 'those who have been manumitted'.

CHAPTER IX

THE JIHĀD OF ḤADĀḤADĀ AND THE ḤĀJJ OF TADELIZA

ما بين تنبكتو إلى بينبو × وطدق وجاكت إلى يقرب

'The land twixt Tinbuktū as far as Baynabū, Ṭaduq and Jākat and up to Yaqrabu.' (1)

Verses attributed to Ḥadāḥadā c. 1650, who claimed this land as his domain.

I have argued that by about the year 1650 there had evolved in the Tuareg communities a pacific and subordinate sacerdotal class devoted to study and religion. These *Ineslemen,* especially the Kel Es-Suq, had ruled out warlike acts as an option open to them in order to obtain just treatment from their masters who were *Imashaghen.* Despite this there were already signs that among other groups who were *Ineslemen* of the Iwillimeden, there were leaders who held a different opinion. Their thesis was that holy war (*jihād*) was a legitimate occupation of the *Ineslemen,* either as allies of the *Imashaghen* or the Sultan of Agades, or as their opponents. Armed revolt was lawful and worthy of adoption by men of religion. This school of thought was to find increasing favour among the *Ineslemen.* Some of them had grander dreams, the creation of an Islamic Tuareg empire from Mauritania to Tibesti.

A sparsely documented series of religious wars began just before the split among the Iwillimeden. Specific local sources in the Sahel assign some importance to these wars. They regard them as an integral part of the feud which led to the formation of the Kel Aṭaram and the Kel Dennek. Other sources ignore them, if only for the reason that they date this split nearly a century and a half after the wars allegedly took place. However, for the Kel Dennek Ait Awari, more especially the Kel Aghlāl, the participants are key figures in their lineage. Records perpetuate a religious and legal dispute between them, their *Imāms,* the Kel Es-Suq and the Sultanate of Agades and the *Ineslemen* who argued the legitimacy of its throne and spiritual authority. One rare document - an impressive poem by a Ḥājj from Tadeliza - shows that Tuaregs of that time were masters of the Arabic language and were skilled in its rhetoric and satire in extended verse. More important it is a genuine contemporary historical document among the very few.

II

The Imazwaghan

A number of Tuareg tribes call themselves the Imazwaghan - those with a 'clear' or 'ruddy complexion'. They are the Kel Agala 'People of the South', the Kel Temerkest, the Ait Awari and the Kel Aghlāl. By extension *emezwagh* (pl. *imazwaghen*) can have the sense of 'white race'. It is akin to the Ḥassānīya term *bīḍān,* used in the Saharan west to distinguish the Moors from the negroes. This group, or one akin to it, is mentioned in medieval sources. Ibn Ḥawqal among his list of Tadamakkat Tuareg tribes includes the *Īmazwāghan* among the Ṣanhāja. For the Tuaregs of today, the Ait Awari *Imashaghen* and the Kel Aghlāl *Ineslemen* are perhaps the most significant *Imazwaghan* in post-medieval Tuareg history.

The origin of the Ait Awari is far from clear. An Oriental region is indicated in the tale of a certain emigrant from their home in Medina. He was called Ja'far. Upon his arrival at Agades he was given a sword by his brother. It was a symbol of his heroism. Another version tells of the sword being presented to him by the first Sultan of Air. Later Ja'far left for Tuwāt.

The name Awari or Awaray is known in the Western Sahara. Īwaray occurs as a name in lineages of the Kunta and the Tajakant. The Kel Aghlāl claim that their ancestor came from the Mauritanian Adrar. Muḥammad Ghilli - 'Muḥammad the White' - their eponym, is the same as Muḥammad Ghullu, the founder of Shinjīṭī. But they are by no means in total agreement. Some Kel Aghlāl who speak with authority call their western ancestor Muḥammad wa-n-Akalal, Muhammad 'the great weeper', a name which brings to mind the nickname of the ancestor of the Kunta, Sīdī Aḥmad al-'Bakkāy'. Aglālī or Aghlālī, it is claimed, is the same as the Morrish Ghallāwī.

The Kel Aghlāl do not differ from other *Ineslemen.* They speak Tamashegh, write Tifinagh, and they accept patrilineal descent. A familial link with the Aghlāl, the Awlād Muḥammad al-Aghlālī in Timbuctoo-Walāta, might be suggested as their possible origin.

As we have seen, Sunni Ali's slaughter of the Ṣanhāja of Timbuctoo increased the coming and going of lettered groups. The Aghlāl (Laghlāl) were among their number. Their installation as a family in the qṣar of Walāta has been dated about the beginning of the sixteenth century, but there are indications that the Aghlāl were influential in that region at an earlier date. The mosque of Sankoray in Timbuctoo was probably constructed in the fourteenth or fifteenth centuries.
Its first known *Imām,* who was a member of the Massūfa Aqīt family was appointed in 1480. Yet the mosque building was paid for and aided in its construction by

a woman of the Aghlāl (Aghlālīya). She was a person of note during that time. Timbuctoo was governed by Ṣanhāja - at least one from Shinjīṭī - under the overall authority of the Imagsharen Tuaregs. At a slightly later date, following Sunni Ali's expulsion of Berbers from Sankoray, it is recorded (2) that in 913/1507/8, a certain Alfagha (*faqīh)* 'Abdullāh b. Muḥammad al-Aghlālī assisted in the writing of a document in the biography of the Songhai ruler Askia Muḥammad. These lettered persons were links in a tradition of learning which united the Saharan west with the Saharan centre.

III

Karidenna versus Karoza

According to the Kel Aghāl of Abalagh district the split in the Iwillimeden took place in the middle years of the seventeenth century. Framed in the myth that it was the intervention of a serpent which confounded the disputers, the new alignment left the Kel Aghlāl on the side of Karoza, a brother or nephew of Karidenna. In some ways the account of the Kel Aghlāl is the same as that of the Kel Es-Suq. But while the latter came to oppose the claims of Karoza and in their later accounts call him a miser while they praise and extol Karidenna, the Ait Awari swore allegiance to Karoza, and the Kel Aghlāl became his champions. This choice placed them politically in the opposite camp to the Kel Es-Suq and those Air *Ineslemen* who were supporters of the Agades Sultanate.

About 1650 the Kel Aghlāl participated in a military operation launched by the Ait Awari against Ṭaduq. In Tuareg legends Ṭaduq was founded by Abū Yaḥyā, grandson of Ja'far of the Ait Awari. However, it is more likely that it was an early colony of the Kel Es-Suq which later came under the influence of the Ait Awari. The chief of the Kel Aghlāl was Muḥammad Māsīl who had been invested by a *Qāḍī* named Ḥamidtu (Khamittu). The chief of the Ait Awari *Imashaghen* was named Muḥammad Waysimuden (Usāmata?). In some genealogies he is the son or descendant of Abū Yaḥyā b. Ja'far. Ḥamidtu, Muḥammad Māsīl and their company were to follow the dictates of an ambitious fanatic called Ḥadāḥadā (Khadăkhadă).

There is some mystery surrounding his origins. All agree that he came from the west (Maghrib). A majority of the Tuaregs affirm that he was one of the Barkuray (Iberkorăyăn), an ancient tribe which included elements of the Ikettwan, Immedadghen (Muddūkan?) and the Zwāden who were to be found in the Hodh, Azawād and the Fezzan. Iberkorăyăn, however, may not mean more than the pejorative term for unlettered *Ineslemen,* and some believe that the word is derived from the Zarma *boro kwaray* - 'white man'. Hence the confusion and disagreement as to the district where Ḥadāḥadā was born. Other Tuaregs think that Ḥadāḥadā was one of the 'Israelite' Īdaw Isḥāq, or Iswaghen, a group near Menaka assimilated to the Tuaregs, but who speak their own dialect or language. Ḥadāḥadā was lettered although his opponents deemed his learning superficial. He was very ambitious, and he advocated the diffusion of Arabic in an Islamic empire which he dreamt of establishing from Timbuctoo to the heart of Air, most of the area loosely controlled by the Iwillimeden.

The extent of his success is unknown. There is a consensus of agreement that he ruined the town of Ṭaduq. It resisted him so he decided to destroy it. Twelve tribes left the town at his behest or due to his sword, among them the Iderfen, the Kel Es-Suq, the Ikuhalayen and many freed slaves. The town was then razed to the ground. Other destructive acts in Air at Jīkat and elsewhere are laid to his charge.

In Chapter V I have described how some Tuaregs maintained that Ḥadāḥadā caused the death of Sīdī Maḥmūd al-Baghdādī who had encouraged the Kel Away to fight the Barkuray because they had not accepted his doctrines. Some circles close to the Agades Sultanate supported this claim because the death of the greatest saint of Air could be laid to the charge of Ḥadāḥadā, Ḥamidtu and the Imazwaghan of Azawagh. However, the few references to Ḥadāḥadā by Suqi writers who would be predisposed to favour the Sultanate do not excuse the Sultan Aḥmad b. Taluẓa for the death of Sīdī Mahmūd, nor do they blame Ḥadāḥadā for the deed. Mawlay Muḥammad al-Hādī remarks that 'the bands of the Balkurayin, shed the blood of Muslims on three occasions - as a trial and an affliction from God - like the party of Ḥamidtu (Khamittu) who was the first, at the commencement of the dynasty of the Iwillimeden. During the time he was impelled to spread his evil abroad, the party of Karẓ (Karoza) was severed from the lord of the Iwillimeden, Karidenna. . . . This was due to the killing of the son of one by the son of the other so a feud broke out between them . . . . Then came the party of the one who inherited his evil, namely Ḥadāḥadā.'

From this brief statement a short gap between the revolts of Ḥamidtu and Ḥadāḥadā is implied, and nothing is said of the martyrdom of Sīdī Maḥmūd al-Baghdādī.

Relations between the *Qāḍī* Ḥamidtu and Ḥadāḥadā seem to have been close. Relations between the chief *(Imām?)* of the Kel Aghlāl and Ḥadāḥāda were also close. According to the Kel Aghlāl, the successor to Muḥammad Māsīl in their patrilineal succession to the *Imāmate* was also called Ḥadāḥadā. He was given this name in order to ensure God's favour and blessing. His successors were al-Ḥasan,

Aḥmad al-Ṭāhir and Muḥammad Isūfu (Isūkhu?) The Kel Aghlāl *Imāmate* was patrilineal while the choice of *eṭṭebel* among the Kel Dennek, *Imashaghen* successor of Karoza was only partly so. Often force of character alone dictated who was to be chief of the Kel Dennek.

IV

The Ḥājj of Tadeliza

Despite the confused details about Ḥadāḥadā and his movement, an ode survives addressed to Hamidtu and Ḥadāḥadā. (3) It was composed by al-Ḥājj Muḥammad b. Tighna of Tadeliza. The original was recopied and embellished with glosses and commentaries, some in Tamashegh, to facilitate comprehension. The text is unique, its authenticity indisputable.

At a little distance from the 'Sultan's palace' in the valley of Tadeliza there is a small cemetery adjacent to a mosque outlined by stones in the sandy valley bottom. Some of the tombs are old but have no inscriptions. Two tombs are much larger than the rest, and they bear inscriptions. The larger is enclosed by roughly laid and oval shaped retaining walls. The tomb has the epitaph incised in large letters, 'The *Faqīh* al-Ḥājj Muḥammad'. The second tomb which is a little smaller, but close to the first and similar to it in appearance has one name - 'Tighna'. The villagers of Tadeliza agree that the first tomb is that of their great *marabout*. But they know nothing about who he was or when he lived.

This Tadeliza Ḥājj composed the ode. On the final page of the surviving copy (4) the copyist, Ilyās b. al-Sharīf Ibrāhīm b. Shaykh Uwayis al-Jakṭī of Jīkat, states that the poet was the 'restrainer of the people who swerve from the truth'. He was a grammarian, 'the Sībawayhi of his age' - alluding to the Persian Sībawayh (d. c. 793 AD) whose 'book' settled the principles of Arabic grammar among the philologists of Iraq. 'The poet was Muḥammad b. Aḥmad b. Ḥāmid known by his mother, Tighna. He came from the town of Taddīzə (Tadeliza).' It is stated that he was buried there. The copy of the poem dates from the late seventeenth or eighteenth century.

The ode has some ninety-seven, partly illegible, verses, and it may once have been longer. It displays a mastery of Arabic rhetoric and diction. (5) The poem is a lampoon. Ḥamidtu and Ḥadāḥadā are castigated on a number of issues, some religious, some academic including the ability to versify correctly. Muḥammad b. Tighna reveals himself to be the defender of the Sultan of Agades, the upholder of his status as *Imām* conferred upon him by the Caliph. He brands Ḥamidtu and Ḥadāḥadā as heretics.

Both had offended against the *jamā'a* of Islam and had acted rashly against the *Imām* - Sultan. In a gloss the Sultan is specifically named as al-Tafrīja b. Yūsuf. Ḥadāḥadā and his company had declared the Sultan's *bay'a* invalid and had asserted their own entitlement to *bay'a.* They had written an epistle to the Sultan which was 'crudely scrawled'. Much of the poem is a rebuke. The two rebels had joined company with evil doers who had raided the Sultan's domains. The Sultan was entitled to punish them. What seems clear from the poem is that he did not always have the power to do so and that his writ beyond the city of Agades was nominal. In certain verses the tone is almost conciliatory. It is the proper procedure to complain of injustices to the Sultan irrespective of the means he has, or lacks, to combat it. Obedience to him as *Imām* is a duty laid down in the Qur'ān. It is his prerogative to declare and fight a holy war. Hence claims by others like Hamidtu and Ḥadāḥadā to be *Mujāhidīn* cannot be sustained. If the Sultan in the role of *Imām* needed help to fight a holy war then he should be assisted not hindered nor disputed. This view had been held by greater scholars who outshone Ḥamidtu and Ḥadāḥadā yet were known to them both. Among these scholars was Muḥammad Ingilla who was possibly one of the Kel Es-Suq Daghūghīyīn. (6) The facts being so the two rebels were at worst heretical innovators, at best conceited individuals. Furthermore, the behaviour of their *Mujāhidīn* nullified their claims. They had shed innocent Muslim blood, committed atrocities and destroyed books. They had treated all other Muslims as infidels.

Muḥammad b. Tighna draws attention to the crudeness of the poetry of his adversaries, arguing that the command of Arabic language - the pride of Ḥadāḥadā and his fanatics - was of an elementary kind. He and his colleague Ḥamidtu could string words in a loose phrase. It might appear to be poetry but it could only deceive the unsophisticated.

The Tadeliza Ḥājj next affirms the basis of the Sultan's authority. More royalist than the king, he points out the sinfulness of rejecting the Sultan's right to obedience. Only one school of thought adopted the view that it was lawful to do so, the Mu'tazilite school. It is not clear however, whether Muḥammad b. Tighna means the philosophical rationalists of the 'Abbasid era or the Kharijites who were often called the *Madhhab al-I'tizāl* in North Africa. Even though the Sultan and his officials might fail or behave below ideal standards, it was the duty of subjects to be patient since infallibility was the virtue of prophets. Lesser men might fail. It was a duty to follow the dictates of higher authorities when it came to ritual observances and the rules of the *Sharī'a.* This point of view had been challen ged by the *Qāḍī* Ḥamidtu who, it appears, had rejected the need for an establishment, from the Caliph down, in order to supervise feasts and religious observances or to declare a *jihād* in the name of Islam. Scholars had repeated that such was the obligation on believers laid down in the *Sharī'a,* and they had

3. The Tomb of Tighna at Tadeliza

4. The Tomb of Muhammad B. Tighna at Tadeliza

written books and pamphlets setting forth their opinions on all these matters.

Certain details in the poem of Muḥammad b. Tighna enable it to be approximately dated, and to fix the revolts of Ḥamidtu and Ḥadāḥadā into some kind of historical context. Their campaign postdated the death of the scholar al-Najīb b. Muḥammad Shams al-Dīn al-(Ta)gaddawī, al-Unṣammanī (Wa-n-Anū Ṣamman) who has been mentioned in Chapter III (7) Al-Najīb died some time after 1597. Muḥammad b. Tighna states in his poem that Najīb composed a treatise which dealt with the duties of princes. Perhaps there is some confusion here with his predecessor al-'Āqib, also of Anū Ṣamman, whose writings concerned the duty of the Friday prayer. At the time of Ḥadāḥadā Anū Ṣamman was a ruin. Its destruction may have occurred during the struggle for power between the Sultans Yūsuf and Ibn al-Mubārak between 1597 and 1625. Yet is scholarly associations were sufficiently alive in people's memories to suggest that the lampoon of Muḥammad b. Tighna could not have been composed long after 1600-1625.

If the gloss is correct the Sultan defended was Muḥammad al-Tafrīja whose dates in the 'Agades Chronicles' span some thirty-one years between 1033/1624/5 and 1064/1654. Karidenna died at the very end of the seventeenth century so the conflict between him and Karoza, in which the *Qāḍī* Ḥamidtu seems to have been involved, could have occurred between 1640 and 1650. Ḥadāḥadā's campaigns attained their peak during these years. It was then that Ṭaduq was destroyed, also holy places on the edge of Air and possibly in the heart of the Massif. It is by no means impossible that the reference in the *Tārīkh al-Sūdān* (8) to the surprise attack of the Iwillimeden on Timbuctoo in 1647 could have some connection with Ḥadāḥadā's movement. His *jihād* could have been very grave. The flight of the Kel Tadamakkat to Timbuctoo in 1655 could have been aggravated if not heralded by his fanatical activities. Among the expelled Tadamakkat were the chief of the Iderfen and two of the Ishuyukhen of the Kel Es-Suq. Both groups suffered when the town of Ṭaduq was razed by Ḥadāḥadā.

V

The aftermath of the jihād of Ḥadāḥadā

Nothing is known about the fate of Ḥadāḥadā, nor what became of his companion Ḥamidtu. Their story is lost amid the confusion surrounding the early history of the Iwillimeden and how Karidenna emerged as their major figure. It is not known when Muḥammad b. Tighna died. There is no date on his tomb. He seems to have written other books. One is introduced in a tiny fragment. (9) It sheds a little more light on the leaders of the Tegaregarey Imazwaghan at this time. The fragment has no name and no date:-

'To noble and upright brethren, to al-Ḥasan and to Aḥmad and to Muḥamma. Tizwāghīn. Perfect peace and increasing regard. To proceed. May I inform you tha we have discovered documents containing answers of the Ṣanāhija to that documen of the *Amīr* (10) - may God aid him. We have understood its contents. Reflect if God so wills and store up what we mention to you. Learn that we have pondered the matter of the Ṣanāhija, and we have closely and thoroughly examined it. We have discovered that they have a predecessor in the matter they allege regarding the office of *Imām*. This office they inherit, one ancestor or predecessor from another. They are from the seventy-second party, who are mentioned in the *ḥadīth* "The Banū Isrā'īl separated into seventy-one parties, and my *umma* will split into seventy-two". This was reported by the Shaykh and saint Muḥammad b. Taghin (Tighna) in the book *talfīq al-fawā'id.*

The Ṣanāhija are a host of tribes which have dispersed in all directions from the land of Air. Among them are those who dwelt to the east, and they were the allies of the princes of Air. Among them are those who dwelt to the west, and they were the allies of the chiefs and Sultans (*ṭubūl*) of the Iwillimeden. Despite that, they chose one from those who was most learned and superior among them, and on their own initiative, they assigned to him the power to impose penalties in their affairs. Him they call the *Imām.* This they have inherited from father to son since they arose and ever after it. Such is proof enough for anyone who has the least ability to perceive what befell some of the princes of Air and Ḥadāḥadā and Ḥamidtu, and what took place between them and the jurists and Shaykhs in correspondence. It is well known and famous . . . . . .'

The exploits of Ḥadāḥadā and Ḥamidtu seem to be part of a general pattern which prevailed in the Sahel in the seventeenth century. From Mauritania to Chad there were a number of reformist movements led by *Imāms* who were puritanical, who branded other Muslims as evil doers, even as infidels who merited death. They stressed egalitarianism and a rejection of all establishments which had been invested or blessed by non-Sahelian authorities. Their forces widely ranged. Cities such as Timbuctoo and Agades were exposed to raids or pressure from these movements which crossed the Senegal and Niger rivers, penetrated the Air Massif or traversed the whole Sahara in a series of long distance attacks. They were symptomatic of a new militancy abroad among the hitherto submissive *Ineslemen.*

NOTES

1) Most of these localities are in Air. Jākat is variant of Jīkat, Baynabu is a grazing ground for the Kel Ferwan Tuaregs, and Yaqrabu is perhaps an abbreviation of Kurubobo.

2) *T.F.*, Arabic text p. 74, Fr. Translation p. 141.

3) See pages 128-134. The original text is in library *A*, although a photo-copy is to be found in *A.N.*, Niamey.

4) See page 134.

5) The metre of the poem is *Rajaz*. The poet has made his task more difficult by introducing a choice of rhyming patterns, both 'fettered' (*muqayyada)*, when the verse ends with a consonant, and 'loose' (*muṭlaqa)* when it ends with a vowel. The latter is sometimes an *'Alif,* an appendix to the rhyming letter (*rawī*), and it is not infrequent for the letter of prolongation *(ā)* to act as a pillion (*ridf)* immediately preceding the rhyming letter. The use of rhetoric is deliberate. The poem is a satire aimed at those who do not command Arabic rhetoric, who abuse its basic rules, and more particularly the errors of measure, incorrect inflection and *ikfā',* the substitution of some cognate letter - the most common being the interchanging of an 'm' and 'n' (*mīm* with *nūn*) - for the rhyming letter. This is a very grave fault but not surprising among Tuaregs where in their own poetry much use is made of assonance. The poet employs a rhyme of up to three or four letters in the final word in each hemistiche, a technique named *luzūmu mā lā yalzam* where a poet unnecessarily imposes on himself difficulties and limitations in respect of the rhyme, and enforcing word harmony. This technique was carried to an extreme by Abū 'l-'Alā' al-Ma'arrī (d. 1057) in his *Luzūmīyāt* which embody his philosophic scepticism.

6) See page 144.

7) See page 38.

8) See H. Lhote in his 'Contribution à l'étude des Touaregs soudanais', *Bull. de l'I.F.A.N.*, T.XVII, sér B, no 3-4. 1955, pp. 340-355.

9) A manuscript preserved in Collection *A.* and copied for the author by Muḥammad al-Mukhtār of Tchin Tabaraden.

10) Possibly this poem by Muḥammad b. Tighna.

The reply of the Ḥājj of Tadeliza to Ḥadāḥadā and Ḥamidtu (*See pages 213-220 for Arabic text*)

In the name of God, the Compassionate, the Merciful, the blessing and peace of God be upon our Lord Muḥammad and upon his family and his companions.

1. Praise be to God who has commanded obedience and subordination to princes.
2. Then the blessing and peace of God for ever be upon the Prophet who devised a steadfast law.
3. He is the Messenger and Chosen one, the glorified, the lord of all creation, Muḥammad.
4. And blessing be upon his family and his Companions, of all men the best, and their followers, just and pious.
5. To proceed. - Here is the reply I have directed against Ḥadāḥadā (1) and Ḥamidtu. (2)
6. Both have acted as unbelievers, have offended the *jamā'a* of Islam, and rashly acted against the *Imām.* (3)
7. They have declared his allegiance unlawful and compelled allegiance to themselves.
8. They have forsaken homage in word and deed, with thoughtless rashness, they have countenanced error and have spoken ill.
9. To the Sultan they have sent an epistle, crudely scrawled. How many are their follies and their blunders thus disclosed!
10. The writer knoweth not the art of poetic style, and we behold his clumsy art.
11. His verse is merely words which have been scattered here and there. Yet he believed it to be poetry. By it he tumbled backwards.
12. Time after time, you were the Sultan's worry. He threatened you with his troops like copious rain.
13. Leave your evil doers in your habitation, stay aloof from the company of the wicked, act as one who flees.
14. Yet you rely upon them, you mix with them and you live among them.

Gloss: in Arabic or in Tamashegh, written in Arabic script:-

(1) Name of a jurist from the Maghrib. (2) Name of a jurist from the Maghrib. (3) *Imām,* the Sultan al-Tafrīja.

15. You know that the fire of wrong-doing touches with maddening dreams him who has not wronged.

16. As our Lord God spoke in His revealed book in words of disapproval.

17. You wronged the Amīr who was no doer of wrong, of the reality of his power you had no knowledge.

18. By God, my brother, you are indeed aware that his army you beheld not.

19. Save, a little after you raided, once, twice and a third time. He demanded help.

20. Oh, how worthy! Behold the doers of iniquity and unjust among you - nay, it is furthermore reported that they help and follow you.

21. Then, with that aid they raid the *Imām.* You will deem his vengeance bitter.

22. His fierce army is numerous and impetuous. Sometimes his will, through incapacity, is unachieved.

23. To succour manifold men, assembling those who care not for mischief, is his will.

24. If you envisage the contrary of the vile, a numerous army prepared and equipped for holy-war,

25. Encompassing you in ways and tracks. By God, shame confronts you in your circumstance!

26. Do you not see that which the Queen of Sheba, Bilqīs, saw. Have you no measure to judge her tale of submission to Solomon to compare it with your own?

27. Nonetheless; would that oh, Ḥadāḥadā and Ḥamidtu you were ones to complain to army chiefs; and then to the Amīr himself, to make known your complaints.

28. The world, past and present, is not free from enmity, oppression and wrong doing, corrupt living and unjust, unlawful deeds.

29. It is only princes who uncover such. To them complaint is lodged. It is they who bring the evil to an end.

30. Disregard of a complaint to him openly, and by clear statement means an increase in evil ways and disobedience.

31. You said, oh, Ḥadāḥadā, you claimed you raid in a jihād, morning, noon and night. You are, oh, Ḥādaḥadā, as one who doeth mischief, becoming in the morning a sinner, no fighter in a jihād.

32. In your raidings you avenged not, nor did you raid in a jihād. Against Islam alone did you both launch your attacks.

33. You said the jihād was a duty on your part - for my part all I can say is, "If only you had acted jointly with the Amīr, the Sultan!"

34. Such a jihād we may perceive in texts written by the greatest scholars in their books.

35. Was not the office of *Imām* a Muslim obligation? Indeed it was, similarly the jihād is a conspicuous obligation.

36. There is no region where a man of military might has power which may fully suffice, nor can he accomplish every task.

37. He must turn aside to combat and suppress internal feuds, because among scattered bands and companies he is not at peace.

38. The scholars have written words about those who hold in trust and guard security. They have quoted them from men who were dependable and to whom they are attributed.

39. Obedience to the *Imām* is an incumbent duty. It is firmly stated in God's holy writ.

40. How many learned scholars have we welcomed in this town of Agades, of this there is no question!

41. Some of them you have known among you both. Their renown and reputation have surpassed you both and them you honoured.

42. Like our Shaykh Muḥammad Ingilla; his knowledge like the sea, and other scholars likewise from among his people.

43. Everything which you have said was in no way indicated. They did not point it out. Your way of life with wrong doers was not the path they followed.

44. Is your view worthier, reputable and more correct than such as is recorded in a forebear's book?

45. Not at all! Not among the scholars of this age, not to speak of those who lived in far, far earlier times.

46. By God, is it the path of the jihād which you have trod? Rather, it is the company of injustice which you multiplied.

47. Your army did not spare its mischief when it committed evil. It ruined books. It raped and fornicated, then it butchered.

48. Nay, not only this - the sick and the young, those who were unlawful to be slain, all were scattered, - the readers of Qur'ānic science, the council of the learned and the law.

49. You complained of one who acted wickedly in his way, abhorred his act, yet it was you, too, who acted just the same.

50. Granted as you have said we are people of injustice - what then is the meaning of your raid shortly after the peace and cessation of hostility?

51. You released and brought down evils with vile actions. This you did against all Muslims in their mosques.

52. Every one amongst us and among you. Their blood and their honour is to your charge on judgement day.

53. The base and evil ones in their injustice, wherever it may fall, have not refrained from raiding, from ravaging a Muslim.

54. The 'warf' of verse in every couplet is abominable, both in word and meaning. It is corrupt and it does not stir the spirit.

55. Thus he the poet 'wove' it, by chance and guesswork, hypothetical, and in mere rhyme alone he introduced its content.

56. Licensing *al-ikfā'*, beating to sound of anvil and to rhythmic tread.

57. Other things besides those mentioned, he introduced of prosodic vice, the needs of poetry, too he has not comprehended.

58. All these he introduced in measure, and in incorrect inflection. Rather he brought us the language of a beduin rude.

59. By God, my brother, you have not versified, so know it. The art of poetry is not within your grasp!

60. You launched forth in a sea whose bottom you were not fit to sound; you sensed not the scope and span of human speech.

61. Do you think that he who letters and words compares and fits, held simply in suspense, has versified or has an art achieved.

62. A gaping hole made in a line or so written on a leaf only deceived, or caused to stumble, the most vulgar and most ignorant of men!

63. There is a measure for poetry by which it may be tried and tested. Afterwards, how much true learning it possesses is pondered, comprehended and assessed.

64. Its masters shine. They are masters of skill and splendour. They have ground like flour the fancies of the cowardly.

65. How presumptuous are those who are 'half-breeds' in their speech, who are addicted to the art of verse,

66. then send it to his excellence the Amīr as if he were the one able to perfect its shape!

67. Your attack and intrusion on the Sultan is barefaced conceit, self-deception and a devilish urge.

68. We behold in every book that the holy law commands conduct and manners seemly and becoming.

69. According to just measure and full due. How should one honour then him who is of highest rank?

70. Who is of princely status. How much is due to him in honour and esteem in truth and in sincerety?

71. Our Sultan, may God preserve him and increase his justice, for He appointed him to be Sultan, may He

72. Gird him with support and high esteem, strengthen him in triumph over his enemies.

73. Fulfill his desire in this world and the next, in matters sacred and profane, by His supreme Messenger.

74. Much has the Sultan dispelled of hardship, affliction and injustice. Much of men's grievances has he alleviated by the law.

75. He has imposed on men the observance of the *Sharī'a* and blocked the path to evil deeds and ways.

76. He has aided the Truth and those who hold it. Injustice and evil he neither tolerates nor condones.

77. Nay, if he sees that Islam demands it, he rouses his armies like the lofty mountains.

78. He sends them towards the band of war-makers. You, oh, Ḥadāḥadā and Ḥamidtu were their close associates.

79. The Truth is found in pure and godly speech, in the ruling of the tradition of the Prophet.

80. Therein injustice is made apparent, likewise sins. To them the princes the loan of good is owed. (?)

81. The scholars are unanimous regarding its obligation, quoting it verbatim in their texts.

82. In Islamic learning there is no justification shown, for your withdrawal from obedience to the Sultan.

83. Save rules according to the school of the Mu'tazila. If the injustice of the king who sits in his battle-hut be established.

84. That is the path to error and perdition. The word of the Prophet, the true guide declared it false.

85. He who disobeys the prince, has disobeyed God Almighty likewise, such shines forth in the meaning of tradition.

86. Gratitude is a duty of a subject if the Sultan acts justly, and patience is a duty if he acts unjustly.

87. Infallibility is peculiar to prophets not a virtue of Sultans nor of saints.

88. Nor is it the prerogative of the Caliphs, nor, after them, the governors. In the *Sharīʿa* scholars do not see such law prescribed.

89. Nay, Sultans by the permission of their superiors perform the Friday prayers, and hold the feast and wage jihād. The followers of princes should likewise act.

90. They have no duty save pious prayer at other than the statutory hours. Among the men of tradition is found learning and preferable opinion.

91. With it they are contented. The *Sharīʿa* is its foundation, in its entirety, similarly the books of jurisprudence in its branches.

92. And the view of the scholar of Anū-Ṣamman, the Faqīh Najīb. He was a man of noble standing. The ruins of his town ought not to cause surprise.

93. Since how many are the towns and villages which have been ruined, and their people have taken away their learning with them!

94. The land shrinks within its bounds, be it composed of provinces, or be it a region or the towns of honoured scholars.

95. (Missing . . . .)

96. The blessing of God, our Lord, and His peace be on the chosen Prophet, he who is exalted.

97. And upon his family and his noble Companions in the beginning of affairs and in their ending.

Conclusion of the poem

Here ends the ode, God be praised and by His good help. It was versified by the *faqīh* and scholar Muḥammad b. Aḥmad b. Ḥāmid, known by his mother Tighna. May God illumine his tomb and bestow mercy and bless the forebear in the progeny. (It is written) by the hand of the needy of God, Ilyās b. al-Sharīf Ibrāhīm, the son of Shaykh Uwayis, al-Jakṭī, of Jīkaṭ his home town. May God have mercy on our fathers, our Shaykhs and our brothers and all Muslims. Amen. Oh, beholder. A pious prayer is your obligation for a happy ending and for protection in the two abodes while I live or die. The written word remains for a time when its writer is buried beneath the ground. The blessing of God be upon Muḥammad whenever the needy recall it and the forgetful neglect to mention it.

Gloss.

The poet is the restrainer of the people who swerve (from the truth) and who err, 'master' of his age and its Sībawayhi - Muḥammad b. Aḥmad b. Ḥāmid known by his mother Tighna. He came from the town of Taddīza. (Tadeliza) where he is buried. May God have mercy upon him. Amen.

CHAPTER X

A SHORT HISTORY OF THE KEL INTASAR

> 'To the *jamā'a* of the Kel Intasar. He calls them to arbitration and submission to God's judgement. He accuses them of impiety because of their evil conduct, road-cutting, blood-shed against Muslims unlawfully. Tell me any cause committed by the Kunta so that you might have grounds to lash them and to assault them by your hands and tongues.'
>
> Shaykh Sīdī al-Mukhtār al-Kuntī.
> (d. 1811)

The Kel Intasar are the most westerly of the Tuaregs. They live near Lake Faguibine along the Niger to the west of Timbuctoo and in scattered centres as far east as Gao. In certain respects they resemble the Moors of Mauritania. They share a common border with the Hodh. Many of them speak Ḥassānīya Arabic as well as Tamashegh. Not wholly Tuareg, not truly Moor, they are essentially Western Saharan in their history. Yet, to exclude them from a study of Tuareg Islam would be unjustified. Their contribution to its Arabic literature has been considerable, and many of their dynamic ideas made a notable impact on the Tuaregs of Azawagh and Air.

In order briefly to assess their contribution I will need to cover rapidly, something of their early history, but I wish to concentrate particularly on their leaders of the seventeenth, eighteenth and nineteenth centuries. My last chapter introduced the concept of the militant *Ineslemen* as a factor of importance in later Sahelian Tuareg society. The Kel Intasar are a very good example of the interchange of pacifism and militancy as options open to devout Tuareg Muslims. In all likelihood the Kel Intasar inherited much from the Almoravids whose memory seems to be embodied in the person of Lamtūna who often appears in Kel Intasar genealogies.

The Kel Intasar were among the earliest Tuaregs to assert 'Arab' connections. They were adjacent to the Lamtūna and Western Massūfa who had formed the bulk of the Almoravid armies. There is no evidence from Arabic geographers and historians to indicate an *Ineslemen* class among them, scholars who were pacific, who renounced warfare, or depended solely on a militant aristocracy of Tuaregs or Arabs to defend them. The mystic orders of Islam had not yet made their influence felt among them.

There is a plausible case for a purposeful transcription in their name from the Banū Yntsr of al-Bakrī to the Banū Yntṣr of al-'Umarī (circa 1342-9) The change in the letter 's' in these two texts may be a signal of Arabisation. In the eleventh century the Banū Yntsr were in the Nīsar (YSR) desert along the present Mauritanian and Mali frontier. In the fourteenth century they were in the north of Mali and formed part of the Imagsharen Tuaregs, an aristocracy of *Imashaghen.* The Significance of the change of 's' to 'ṣ' may mark a social change of importance. The Banū Yntsr had probably become associated with the Anṣār - the 'helpers' of the Prophet. They were 'sons of the Anṣār', their patrilineal descendants. The warrior Kel Intasar increasingly became *Ineslemen.* By the seventeenth century, the process was virtually complete, but signs suggest that the evolution had begun far earlier.

A number of Tuareg clans or tribes who were vaguely centred in the area of Ghana, Walāta and Timbuctoo, took up new habitations to the east and to the north of the Niger Buckle. In the fourteenth century, the writings of geographers and travellers like al-'Umarī, or Ibn Baṭṭūṭa, reveal not only the presence of the Kel Intasar towards Gao but also the Ṣanhāja Massūfa, who dominated life in Walāta. Commercial activity flourished, jurists formulated the law, and many made the pilgrimage to Mecca. About 1400 Timbuctoo began to supersede Walāta and other towns of the west, perhaps a side effect of the Hafsid renaissance in Tunisia under Abū 'l-'Abbās (1370-1394). Walāta was a refuge for scholars who fled from persecution in Timbuctoo. It was to be spiritually revived by the arrival of the ancestors of the Eastern Kunta towards 1500. But, in the main, by that date the centres of Islam for the Tuaregs lay to the east of Timbuctoo and no longer to the west of it.

Some vague memory of the early history of the Kel Intasar survives in the semi-legendary documents which they cherish. The Kel Intasar consult these texts, not only to discover their pedigree but also to trace what links they have with the senior *Ineslemen* in Tuareg society, the Kel Es-Suq. For the Kel Intasar scholars and the Kel Es-Suq share many common lineal traditions, but at the same time display marked ideological differences. Both were latterly confronted by the Kunta (Kanāta) who from the seventeenth century were to trespass on the domain which these *Ineslemen* had built up in the Sahel. Some Kel Intasar maintain that their ancestors were among the earliest Muslim conquerors:-

Among that which is authoritively quoted from Muḥammad b. al-Hāshim on the authority of Muḥammad, known as the *Quṭb,* quoting the lordly Shaykh 'Alī b. al-Najīb who quoted Shaykh al-Amīn Aḥmad b. Muḥammad b. Aḥmad al-Mujtahid.

As for the history of Ibn al-Najīb, - written in 1122/1133(?) (eighteenth century) he mentioned the treck, quoted from forebear to successor. As for the commencement of the departure of our ancestors from Medina, their flight from it, leaving behind their houses and their date palms. It was after the conquest of Egypt and the flight of al-Muqawqi s (Cyrus, the patriarch of Alexandria) to Alexandria, and after the return of their army commander 'Abdullāh b. Sa'd b. Abī Sarḥ. (It was) after the peaceful submission of the Nubians and after the peace made between 'Abdullāh b. al-Ḥijāb and the Yahma (?) who were a party of the Nile negroes.

When the army returned after the conquest of those regions in Africa, and the Berbers fled from them to the Sūs, a mountain land where they dwelt, and still do, they - the Anṣār - returned to Medina, and feuding broke out amongst them. It lessened in the days of al-Ḥasan b. 'Alī b. Abū Ṭālib. With the death of Mu'āwiya b. Abī Sufyān feuds resumed and troubles rent this Muslim *umma* in the reign of al-Walīd and his minister . . . .;

The next passage of the text is missing but elsewhere it is claimed that the tradition of the Anṣār (Kel Intasar) of Timbuctoo affirms a journey from the city of Medina to a new settlement in the region of Walāta and Timbuctoo.

A gap in Arabic records separates the genuinely historical Banū Yntsr of al-Bakrī and al-'Umarī, and the far later semi-historical chiefs of the Kel Intasar. The western Massūfa, the Idaw al-Ḥājj and the Idaygub (Īd Ya'qūb), and some Tuaregs to the east of Timbuctoo maintain a certain Ya 'qūb to be their common eponym. The mythical ancestral claims of the Kel Intasar and certain of the Kel Es-Suq meet in this person or in his equivalents Abū Bakr al-Anṣārī or 'Amr b. Ḥazm al-Anṣārī. The essential claim is that at some time a predecessor came from Medina and settled a colony of Anṣār to the north of the Niger in Azawād and later in the Adrar-n-Ifoghas.

Kel Intasar lineages differ, (1) but the name Lamtūna or Lamtūn is common to them all. The appearance of this name indicates a point of intersection in Mauritanian and Tuareg genealogies. Another key eponym is al-Muẓaffar, 'the victorious', a title similar to Muntaṣir and Yantaṣir, embedded in the very name of the tribe. He is said to have left Fez for the Hoggar where he joined the Idnen who were then masters of those mountains. He moved south to Bourem where he joined the *Shurafā'* who lived under Songhai rule, and he died there and was buried at Afeitao near Rergo.

His most famous descendant was al-Muzammil, whose son or grandson was called Infa who became chief of the Kel Intasar and of many negroes in that region near Bourem. Infa lived during the sixteenth century. He arrived in the region to the north of Timbuctoo, about 1560. There he settled. He dug wells, purchased cattle and married a Tuareg wife from the Idnen who dominated that region. Intermarriage with the Imagsharen also occurred. Legends likewise exist of an Anṣārī captive girl who married a Tuareg noble and gave birth to a son. The latter imposed Arab customs and succession on his father's people. This story is the obverse of the exploits of Muḥammad wa-n-Ara and Alad, yet it tells of a comparable result, the acceptance or imposition of a patrilineal succession of the Kel Intasar Tuaregs. Infa was buried at In Gouzma or Arawān.

Muḥammad (al-Mukhtār), his son, was buried at In Telliq. His most famous son was Muḥammad Quṭb, who is sometimes referred to as Quṭb. He lived at the beginning of the seventeenth century, and he was a contemporary of Aḥmad b. Addah al- Suqī who made Arawān into an important religious centre. Quṭb al-Anṣārī was a semi-nomad. He dug many wells, organised caravans, and his district knew great wealth attracting other *Ineslemen* and Ishsherifen to its vicinity. Quṭb drew up a constitution for the Kel Intasar. They were forbidden to carry arms and devoted their lives to breeding cattle, to cultivation where possible, to commerce, study and prayer. The Kel Intasar followed the constitution to the letter. Their Tuareg protectors were from the Kel Tadamakkat. These *Imashaghen* refrained from molesting the Kel Intasar who served them. Reciprocity was established. Quṭb vigorously preached Islamic virtues to lax Tuaregs in Azawād. He died towards 1650 and was buried north-east of Bamba.

What determined this renaissance of the area of Arawān under the two Quṭbs, Muḥammad Quṭb al-Anṣārī and Aḥmad b. Addah al-Sūqī? The expulsion of the Kel Tadamakkat *Imashaghen* from Iwillimeden territory could hardly have inspired it, since by 1655 both men had died. One factor was the opening of the salt mine at Taoudeni and the increase of commerce through Arawān-to the north, and through Bū Jbayha, to the east, particularly in the sixteenth century when the routes to Morocco were increasingly dangerous and subject to pillage. The former Songhai salt mine at Taghāza had been made unworkable since 1556/1557 by the Moroccans. In 1582 it was abandoned. Taoudeni took its place, and it had advantages which Taghāza lacked. The distance to Timbuctoo was much shorter, and as Taghāza by this time had been exhausted, Taoudeni held out prospects of increased production. Work seems to have begun there in 1556. This activity must have given a boost to life in Arāwan and its vicinity. Walāta was in decline. It would have tempted scholars to move to Arāwan. The commercial decline of Tadamakkat at this period also tempted scholars to journey westwards. The concentration of activity in the heartland of the Kel Intasar and their neighbours inspired Quṭb and his tribe to devote more and more time to the life of the *Ineslemen.* It involved them in commercial and legal work as well as in Qur'anic studies and in teaching.

It is not clear whether the holy men Abbāna Zuhra, al-Ḥājj Bulla, and Muḥammad al-Amīn were children or grandchildren of Quṭb. The first two were probably his sons, the third possibly his grandson. Abbāna Zuhra mastered the Tuaregs by his sanctity and prestige, while Bulla was reported to have died near Kufra in Libya on his return from the pilgrimage. Perhaps the most important of the trio was Muḥammad al-Amīn. He was nicknamed 'Abbāna' or 'Ibbīna' (our father), and he lived towards the end of the seventeenth century. He was buried at Tadrart, a hill north-east of Timbuctoo. The most noted of his descendants was Aḥmad (Ḥammāda) agg Muḥammad al-Amīn.

Ḥammāda was born about 1690 and died about 1760. Although he lived near desert wells he also camped by the Niger and close to Ra' s al-Mā'. He was a noted *Qāḍī.* He became famous in the annals of the Kunta because of a debate between him and Shaykh Sīdī al-Mukhtār al-Kabīr in which the latter is reported to have achieved a resounding success. Be this as it may, the Kel Intasar continued their pressure on the river and had conflicts with the Kunta who were establishing agricultural settlements on the Niger or in its islands. The sons of Ḥammāda had the task of checking Kunta encroachment.

One of them, Dawa Dawa (Muḥammad al-Amīn) totally reversed the policy of his ancestor Muḥammad Quṭb. He shared authority with his brother Huwalan (Ihallūn) upon the death of their father. The arrangement was a curious one; Dawa Dawa became a military leader, while Huwalan continued pious study or tribal administration. There was a certain similarity to the movement of Ḥadāḥadā. It was the Kel Intasar response to Kunta harassment, which was also troublesome to the Moorish tribes centred near Lake Faguibine. The Kel Intasar were threatened by Moors and Kunta, and their future demanded the combination of two roles in one - the *Ineslemen* and the *Imashaghen.*

Dawa Dawa trained his novices in military tactics. In a battle at Timessukaten near Lake Faguibine the Kunta were decimated. A similar fate awaited the Barābīsh, the Mashḍūf, the Awlād 'Allūsh and the Peuls. All were driven away from the lake and the Kel Intasar settlements. Dawa Dawa died about 1812. He was buried at In Kundar, north-west of Bamba. This Anṣārī warrior-saint was enterred in a locality of memories of 'Oqba al-Mustajāb. A new 'Oqba, it was only fitting that he should rest there. About the year 1815, Huwalan (Ihallūn) his faithful colleague and brother died and was buried at Farash.

This dual leadership was to continue under Muḥammad Aḥmad, the eldest son of Huwalan, (Ihallūn) (2) and Muḥammad 'Alī, the eldest son of Dawa Dawa. They fought the Peuls of Māsina, in retaliation for a raid on the Kel Intasar and the imposition of an annual tribute of two horses. The warrior *Ineslemen* pressed their attack to Hamdullahi, the capital of Shaykh Ḥamad of Māsina, beyond the Niger lakes and Mopti. The young brother of Muḥammad Aḥmad, In Ghallala was the leading warrior chief. Muḥammad Aḥmad died in mysterious circumstances during a camel race about 1835.

In Ghallala succeeded him. He ruled jointly with Muḥammad 'Alī. They repulsed the Awlād 'Allūsh. Both died about 1848 and were buried at Dawra. They were succeeded by Muḥammad Ṣāliḥ and In-Gūna. One of the five sons of In Ghallala was 'Uthmān, a wandering mystic scholar in the region of Timbuctoo and Walāta. Muḥammad Ṣāliḥ and In-Gūna together warred against the Kunta.

Many fine Arabic odes in which the Kel Intasar lampooned their opponents survive from this period. One lampoon by Shaykh Muḥammad al-Mukhtār al-Ḥawwid al-Anṣārī aimed at the Kunta - more particularly the Banū Mullūk - is both savage and vivid, rich in equestrian imagery.

In truth, our joy and boast is the Banū 'l-Anṣār.
Among whom are the descendants of Zayn al-'Ābidīn.
They ride forth in a troop on horses.
Standing on three feet, they wait,
And with the fourth they softly tread the ground.
They are controlled. Fear not a restive stubborn steed.
Of perfect beauty they are large and tall and lean.
Among them can be seen steeds, young and old.
Some are black, others deep red or white and grey.
In their pickets, at the ready, tethered they stand.
We led them forth against the chestnut
And the strong-limbed horses. We armed raiders struck them.
Their horses were tied together (so it seemed),
As up they rose; arching a body we had smote.
We attacked at a time they felt secure,
Just before dawn. Then we dispersed within
The land of Taghā, straying on our way . . .

At Kurzediay they inflicted a disastrous defeat on the Kunta of Aribinda. Muḥammad Ṣāliḥ died, childless, about 1874. In Gūna remained sole chief of the Kel Intasar until he died in 1898. Heredity was the principle of succession of the Kel Intasar, but it was that of the family unit and not of the individual and took into account not only the wish of the preceding chief but also the election by the *jamā'a.* A drum (*ṭabl*) was the symbol of the chief who had the sole right to beat it.

These Kel Intasar - called Gallād by the Kunta - together with a number of Eastern Anṣārī groups along the Niger at Tagarōst and Gao represent a positive political, social and scholastic achievement in Tuareg Islam. Their piety and learning has been as vigorous and dynamic as their power to fight or to adapt to sedentarisation. Many of their ideas and policies were to be adopted by the Kel Dennek in the eastern Sahel.

NOTES

1) See pages 141-143.

2) It is possible that Muḥammad Aḥmad b. Huwalan (Ihallūn) is the excentric academic in *Fatḥ al-Shakūr* who worked all night and defied sleep as a habit 'to excess, until I learnt that he tied his hands with a rope and attached them to the ceiling of his house so that sleep would not overcome him.' Several scholars of the Kel Intasar (Gallād) receive mention in this work.

Lineages of the Kel Intasar and Kel Es-Suq

The lineage of the *Kel Tejanit:*

Sīd Aḥmad b. 'Abd al-Raḥmān b. Muḥammad 'Umar b. al-Ṭayyib b. Ḥillāy (?) b. 'Uthmān b. al-Ḥājj Bulla b. Quṭb b. Ag Infa b. Bulla b. al-Muz(z)ammil b. al-Muẓaffar b. al-Wildān b. Abī Bakr b. Yūsuf b. 'Abd al-Ḥasan b. Abī Bakr b. Yaḥyā b. 'Alayya b. Ma'bad b. Alḥad b. Taḥakkat b. Maktūd b. Qanwān b. Nazzār b. *Lamtūn* b. Nasab b. Yaḥyā b. Manṣūr b. Abī Bakrin al-'Arabī al-Anṣārī b. Kinānah b. Khuzaymah b. Mudrika b. Naṣr b. Ma 'add b. 'Adnān b. Udad b. al-Haysha' b. Sābat b. Salām b. Khamal b. Qaydār b. Ya 'qūb b. Ismā'īl b. Ibrāhīm - the Friend of God.

Written by Sīd Aḥmad b. 'Abd al-Raḥmān b. Muḥammad 'Umar al-Anṣārī of Timbuctoo at Lazaret Camp, Niamey, 1974.

The lineage of al-Bukhārī b. Muḥammad b. al-Ṣāliḥ b. Muḥammad Aḥmad b. Muḥammad al-Mushtaba b. Ḥammād b. Abbāna b. Sīd Quṭb b. Muḥammad al-Mukhtār b. Infa b. al-Muzammil b. Muḥammad Aḥmad b. Āyāra b. al-Muẓaffar b. al-Wildān b. Abī Bakr b. Yūsafa b. 'Abd al-Ḥasan b. Abī Bakr b. Yaḥyā b. 'Alayya b. Ma'bad b. Alḥad b. Taḥakat b. Maktūd b. Qanwān b. Nazār b. *Lamtūn* b. Sanba b. Yaḥyā b. Manṣūr b. Abī Bakr al-'Arabī al-Anṣārī b. Kinānah b. Khuzaymah b. Mudrikah b. Naṣr b. Ma'add b. 'Adnān b. Udad b. al-Haysha' b. Sābat b. Salām b. Khamal b. Qaydār b. Ya'qūb b. Ismā'īl b. Ibrāhīm - the Friend of God.

Written by al-Bukhārī b. Muḥammad al-Anṣārī of Timbuctoo, at Lazaret Camp, Niamey, 1974.

Lineage of the *Igellād:*

Muḥammad al-Muṣṭafā b. Ag Ayy b. Aḥmad b. Ḥammād b. Abī Bakr b. Mūsā b. Muḥammad al-Mukhtār, known as Ayatta b. Ibrāhīm b. Dāwūd b. Sa'īd b. 'Abd al-Raḥmān b. 'Abd al-Jabbār b. Tamīm b. Ḥātim b. Ḥayy b. Yūsuf b. Yūsha' b. Ward b. Baṭṭāl b. Aḥmad b. Muḥammad b. 'Īsā b. Muḥammad b. al-Ḥasan b. 'Alī b. Abī Ṭālib b. 'Abd al-Muṭṭalib.
Unsigned, 1974 at Lazaret Camp, Niamey.

Lineage of the *Kel Tākarannāt,* more particularly that of 'Īsā b. Aḥmad al-Sūqī al-Daghūghī:

'Īsā b. Muḥammad Aḥmad b. 'Abd al-Salām b. Muḥammad Aḥmad b. Muḥammad al-Ṣāliḥ b. Falka b. Aḥmad Baba b. Ajkan b. Aḥmad Āta (?) b. Muḥammad b. Ayd-In-Tākarannāt b. Muḥammad b. Ibrāhīm b. 'Īsā b. Ishulum b. Nūḥ b. *Ya 'qūb* al-Ṣāḥibī, *al-Anṣārī.* He is from the tribe of the Kel Es-Sūq known as the Kel Tākarannāt. Unsigned, 1974, at Lazaret Camp, Niamey.

Second lineage of the *Kel Tākarannāt:*

Muḥammad Aḥmad b. 'Abd al-Salām b. Muḥammad Aḥmad b. Muḥammad al-Ṣāliḥ b. Falka b. Aḥmad Baba b. Abbakkin b. Aḥmad In-Āta b. Muḥammad b. Idda-Tākarannāt . . . . . b. Ibrāhīm b. 'Īsā b. Ishulum b. *Ya 'qūb al-Anṣārī.*

Written by Muhammad 'Abbās b. al-Kabīr. 1974, at Lazaret Camp, Niamey. See Barth, 1858, Vol V, pp. 559-560.

Lineage of tribes of the *Kel Es-Sūq* of Kidal:

'Īsā b. Aḥmad b. al-Ḥasan b. al-Mabrūk b. Aḥmad b. Muḥammad al-Ṭāhir b. Wan-Gilla b. A'ālli b. Aḥmad b. al-Ḥusayn b. al-Ṣāliḥ b. Bāy b. Āl b. Mūsā b. Abī Bakr known as Dhī 'l-Fīla (he of the female elephant) b. 'Uthmān b. Tadkān b. Ẓidart b. *Agār**(?) b. Ibrāhīm al-Daghūghī b. Sa'īd b. al-Mahdī b. 'Abdullāh b. 'Abd al-Raḥmān b. 'Alī b. Mawlay Isḥāq b. 'Abd al-'Alī b. Aḥmad b. Muḥammad b. Mawlay Idrīs b. 'Abdullāh al-Kāmil b. al-Ḥasan al-Muthannā b. al-Ḥasan al-Sibṭ b. 'Alī b. Abī Ṭālib b. 'Abd al-Muṭṭalib b. Hāshim.

This lineage is sound, authentic in the eyes of the *'ulamā,'* and there is no divergence of view regarding it. As for Ibrāhīm al-Daghūghī many tribes of the Kel Es-Sūq are related to him among them Ahl al-Kātib named Kel Iḍā'(?), the Kel Ihyūn. All of them are tribes. One tribe from among them, the Kel Tibrāq, another the Kel Tagilalt, another called the *Kel Iskan* and another called Agdash, and another called Kel Zamgī. There are other tribes I do not recall. With us in Niamey are Ifōghas *Shurafā'.* Some are the off-spring of the Ait al-Sharīf, some are Tāghet Mellat, one of the tribes of the Ifōghas who are not *Shurafā'.*Another tribe of the Ifōghas is called Kel Telābet who are related to the Anṣār and a tribe of the Kel Ghill (?) who are related to the Anṣār, and a tribe from the Idenān who are also related to the Anṣār, and a tribe of artisans who are carpenters and smiths, called In Haḍḍ who claim to be *Shurafā*.'

Unsigned, 1974, at Lazaret Camp. Niamey.

Lineage of the *Kel Intasar* as preserved in the copy of a manuscript at Lazaret Camp, Niamey, 1974, and in the private possession of Muḥammad b. Nūḥ al-Anṣārī:

al-Hājj Int-Ḥammād b. al-Mundhir b. Ibrāhīm b. Muḥammad b. 'Uthmān b. Muḥammad al-Āmin (nicknamed Ibbīn) b. al-Ḥājj Bulla b. Quṭb b. Muḥammad b. 'Uthmān b. Infa b. Muḥammad al-Muṣṭafā b. al-Muzammal b. Muḥammad Aḥmad ag Āyr b. al-Muẓaffar b. al-Wildān b. Abī Bakr b. Yūsuf b. 'Abd b. al-Ḥasan b. Abī Bakr b. Yaḥyā b. 'Alī b. Ma'bad b. Laḥḥad b. Taḥakkat b. Maktūd b. Qunwān b. Nazzār b. *Lamtūn* b. Sanbah b. Yaḥyā b. Manṣūr b. 'Abdullāh b. Abī Bakr b. Muḥammad b. 'Amr b. Ḥazm al-Anṣārī b. Lūdhān b. 'Abdūd b. Zayd b. Tha 'labah b. al-Khazraj b. Sā'idah b. Ka'b b. al-Khazraj b. Ḥārithah b. Tha'labah b. 'Amr Mazīqā (?) b. 'Āmir Mā' al-Samā' b. Ḥāritha al-Ghiṭrīfah b. Imri' l-Qays b. Tha'labah b. Māzin b. al-Azd b. al-Ghawth b. Nabat b. Mālik b. Zayd b. Kahlān b. Saba' b. Yashjub b. Ya'rub b. Qaḥṭān b. 'Ābir b. Shalikh b. Arfakhshadh b. Sām b. Nūḥ b. Lamk b. Mattūshalakh b. Akhnūkh b. Yard b. Mahlil b. Qaynan b. Yānish b. Shīth b. Ādam.

The Kel Es-Suq

A tentative lineage of Ibrāhīm al-Daghūghī and his descendants

(Based upon the text of Ḥammād b. Muḥammad al-Kelsūqī)

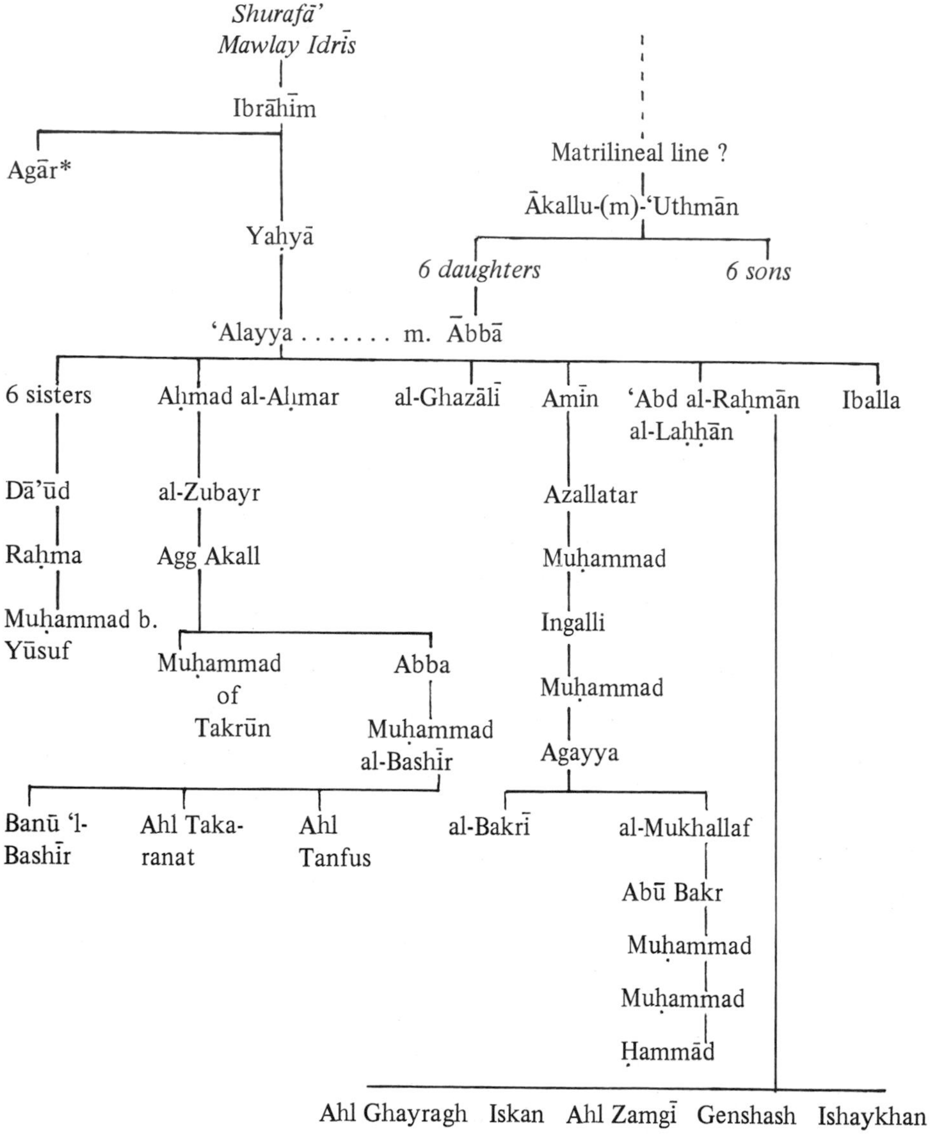

CHAPTER XI

THE JIHĀD OF MUḤAMMAD AL-JAYLĀNĪ

> 'Come up ye horses; and rage ye chariots; and let the mighty men come forth; the Ethiopians and the Libyans that handle the shield.'
>
> Jeremiah, 46 v.9.

At the end of the eighteenth century there were wide Tuareg expectations of the appearance of the *Mahdī*. Any leader of importance whose aims embraced war against unbelievers or social reform could expect his supporters to see in him marks which proclaimed him to be this usherer of the end of the age. Unsophisticated Tuareg zealots did not hide their ambitions to this role. They were attacked by Kunta scholars and by the leader of the Fulani Sokoto *jihād* Shehu 'Uthmān Dan Fodio who had emphatically disclaimed such pretensions. The Shehu dismissed the claims of a Maganga Tuareg called Hamma. (1) This false *Mahdī* was put to death. As the activities of these excentric agitators were disturbing to the devout their claims needed to be refuted.

Some Tuaregs of the Kel Dennek and those of Air were profoundly influenced by the Fulani Caliphate in Sokoto. They saw in its concept of the *jihād* a class struggle whereby the *Ineslemen* could assert their total independence from the *Imashaghen* and establish a new order based on the creation of a settled society in the Tuareg Sahel. It should be well-organised but wholly independant of the Sultanate in Agades and of the disorganised Iwillimeden aristocracy claiming descent from Karidenna, Karoza and their successors.

The Tuareg *Ineslemen* who took this activist view rejected the pacifism of the Kel Es-Suq and favoured an alliance with Sokoto as the surest path to success. The alliance was dictated by their own interests. It could be dissolved if it suited them, and they regarded the Sokoto rulers almost as equals. When the latter sent them panegyrics or words of counsel they were accepted as of right. If they disagreed with Sokoto they expressed their disagreement. These Tuareg *Ineslemen* bore the title of *Ṣanāhija*. It had a proud medieval Islamic ring. It distinguished them from the Tuareg *Imashaghen* and from those heretical Tuaregs who followed a *Mahdī* whose credentials did not square with orthodox Islamic prophecy. A letter (2) written about this time sets out the point of view of the orthodox Tuareg Ṣanhāja *mujāhidīn*:-

'From the *Qāḍī* Aḥār, son of the late Maḥmūd, to his brother and the beloved in God, the Shaykh and jurist, the knowledgable and understanding Washar b. al-Ṣāliḥ 'Abdullāh, known as 'Abd. Peace be upon you, perfect peace in plenty.

I have heard your news involving the combats of the Tuareg (*Imashaghen*) with the *Ṣanāhija,* and I offer my condolences to you, in tender condolence . . . and in brotherliness regarding him who has died from the poor believers and the brethren and those who are weak . . . God grant them their reward. O God, I ask You, do not tempt us, after they departed in the way of Truth, that through disloyalty, we should incline to the love of sin. By the high title of our lord and loved one Muḥammad - the blessing and peace of God be upon him.

To proceed. It seems to us that your affliction is that which we feared. It is due to mixing with the doers of iniquity and those who depart from the Truth and God's reality. However, the Prophet - the blessing and peace of God be upon him - said, "Acts are judged by their intentions," . . . "Every man has his intentions . . . to the end of the *ḥadīth.*"

If you ask about our news, we are in the best of circumstances and health, but what you have suffered we too have suffered because that which brings you joy from acts of goodness brings us joy likewise, and any evil which besets you due to evil deeds, afflicts us also. You and we are one body. If you ask about that agreed upon by the scholars of the Sudanic region and ourselves - the *Ṣanāhija* - regarding the claim that their master is the *Mahdī,* - is this claim established, or is this matter correct? - then know that it is false, because it conflicts with *ḥadīths* regarding the *Mahdī.* He will go forth from Medina fleeing to Mecca . . he will swear fealty between *al-Rukn* and *al-Maqām* . . . and there are other *ḥadīths* regarding his name and the name of his mother and his father.

The scholars concur also that if the fighting (by the *Ṣanāhija*)of the Tuaregs is on account of their non-recognition of their *Mahdī* - whose status as *Mahdī* is unconfirmed, and all the scholars have rejected his claim - and if it be to defend themselves and their property due to great amount of warring by the Tuaregs, and their oppression and notorious hostility, then it is not hidden from the man who has the least insight that this is a lawful act for them (the *Ṣanāhija*) and permissable, since to wage *jihād* on those who wage war unjustly is among the most important reasons for holy war. It is every man's bounden duty . . .

If such be the case, then it is unlawful that any of the Muslims should fight the *Ṣanāhija,* on account of the battles which took place against the Tuaregs, since their circumstances are not a secret. All who die by helping the Tuaregs act with hostility against Muslims who defend their persons and property. They die for helping the oppressor against the oppressed. God is sufficient for them because the oppressors disobey God's will.

We ask God for peace in both abodes with all Muslims. This is that which is agreed upon by the scholars of this Sudanic district and ourselves. However, if you have anything of use to give from your knowledge in regard to these depths whose bottom is so deep - God, God, O, God, then send us a note which will be a wise counsel for us and furnish further knowledge.

This said, I wish you heartiest greetings and peace and a happy outcome in these battles. By God, I enjoin on you to advise the 'free men' (Tuaregs ?) to repent to God and to none other, and to forsake followers of heretical customs, and to restrain their hands from vanities. They should eschew iniquities and restrain their feet from following him who claims for himself that he is a *Mahdī*, like the lord of Maganga, because his deceits are many in our experience . . .

II

Muḥammad al-Jaylānī

The *Mahdī* of Maganga and his mysterious fate did not upset the complex relations between the Shehu and his pious and orthodox Tuareg neighbours. Many Air Tuaregs were in sympathy with the aims of the Shehu, especially the Kel Ferwan and the Sultan of Agades, Muhammad al-Bāqirī. There were also some devout leaders who took a different view. Foremost among them was Ibra of the Tamezgidda, whose connections with the mosque at Agallal made him a powerful religious leader to be reckoned with. He was to be an ally of the Sultans of Gobir and Katsina and his final defeat was only achieved by the Shehu's successor, Muḥammad Bello. But one Tuareg leader, who was an ally of Muḥammad Bello, became a legend in Niger owing to his forceful personality and his revolutionary ideas for the Tuaregs of the Sahel.

Muḥammad al-Jaylānī (Jīlānī) agg Muḥammad Ibrāhīm agg Muḥammad Iskakkaghan was born into the Ait Awari about 1777. Virtually nothing is known about his early life. Folklore tells of his religious vocation, the dreams and visions he had and the traditional Islamic background to his studies. He became the first *Amenukal* of the Kel Dennek to assume at the same time the office of *Imām*.

It has already been explained that the eastern branch of the Iwillimeden (the Kel Dennek) had probably separated from the main body of the Iwillimeden of Menaka sometime prior to 1715. The Kel Dennek settled in the region of Azawagh to the north of Tahoua. The Iwillimeden split produced deep social changes. According to the Kel Dennek the rebellious nephew of Karidenna, at-

Tafrīja (3) succeeded in gathering support for his cause by granting major concessions to the *Ineslemen.* If they aided him he promised them certain privileges which hitherto had been the monopoly of the *Imashaghen.* These included the levying of taxes arbitrarily fixed by the ruling *Amenukal,* the right to carry arms, and to participate jointly in raids.

The well-armed Kel Dennek Ineslemen were increasingly tempted to reject the suzerainty of the *Imashaghen.* A new militancy among the Ṣanhāja *Ineslemen* was manifest. All they needed was a powerful leader, and Muḥammad al-Jaylānī was to be that leader.

The Tamezgidda were the first to feel his might. While *Imashaghen* of the Kel Dennek were absent fighting in the west Muḥammad al-Jaylānī repelled the Tamezgidda *Imashaghen* near Tillia. One success led to another. He raided the Kel Aṭaram Iwillimeden twice, and he reached the river Niger after the defeat and death of Kāwa who was the Kel Aṭaram *Amenukal.* The Kel Dennek *Ineslemen* held sway at this time over huge tracts of southern Niger.

The struggle for liberation from the *Imashaghen* appears to have welded the Ait Awari *Ineslemen* into a really united fighting force. The chief problem which Muḥammad al-Jaylānī, their leader, faced was how to maintain this unity and enthusiasm. One way to consolidate it was to turn his attention southwards towards the black and rocky terrain of Adar. He therefore declared a *jihād* against the pagan Aznas there.

Muḥammad al-Jaylānī was fired by the example of 'Uthman Dan Fodio. The Shehu had recently conquered pagan Gobir. Muḥammad al-Jaylānī conquered Adar, despite the initial opposition of Ya'qūb, the Muslim Amīr (Sārky) of Adar, who had the Tuareg Kel Geres as his allies. A tax of fifty cowries per capita was imposed on the population, and the forced conversion of the pagans to Islam was promoted. But the goals of Muḥammad al-Jaylānī were far more ambitious and more radical.

Certain of his excesses have undoubtedly been exaggerated by later writers, by his foes and the extravagance of folk-tales. It was said that he prohibited all singing save religious chanting. No drumming was permitted and even the braying of asses was to be suppressed. The Tuareg women were strictly secluded. There was a lucrative manufacture of 'magic' amulettes, cures were reported, and foemen were afflicted by calamities. To quote Sīdī 'Umar b. 'Alī b. al-Shaykh al-Kuntī of Timbuctoo, 'All the Tuaregs were in fear and awe of him, and they named him *al-Jayn,* while the Arabs named him Bū Guṭṭāya - 'master of customary law and tradition.'

Muḥammad al-Jaylānī's most original ideas were to be seen in his social ideal of the equality of all classes and ethnic groups in the *jihād* in God's 'way', his branding of the irreligious *Imashaghen* as infidels or at best 'serfs' (Buzus) of God, and his plans to settle and urbanise the Tuaregs and the other inhabitants of Adar in a classless society.

Between 1809 and 1815 Muḥammad al-Jaylānī fortified himself at Kureya, just east of Tahoua. Towns, villages and walled enclosures were built. An indelible mark was left on the landscape of Adar. During the whole of this phase of his career, and long after it, the advice of Muḥammad Bello, who was to succeed ʿUthmān Dan Fodio in 1817, was vital in shaping the policy of Muḥammad al-Jaylānī. Despite his plans to settle he had to remain mobile for military reasons and because of large cattle herds.

Correspondence between Sokoto and Tuareg chiefs and religious leaders in Air and Azawagh was common but few surviving Arabic documents supply detailed discussion on social questions. An exception is a long epistle (4) sent by Muḥammad Bello in reply to a letter of Muḥammad al-Jaylānī who had raised a number of pressing problems in his community. It is clear from this correspondence that the Tuareg *Imām* intended to promote the permanent settlement of his supporters and to reduce his dependence upon cattle herding. In this way it would be possible for Muslim observance to be maintained and an Islamic community established.

The questions posed by Muḥammad al-Jaylānī accompanied the gift of oryx shields to Muḥammad Bello. The Tuareg *Imām* had been moving with his herds and was much fatigued. He had fashioned a fortress of bushes but was unhappy that mutual assembly was so inhibited by the seasonal search for pasturage. Opinions were divided about settlement among the *Ineslemen,* and an outside opinion was of value. 'In this matter Ahyā and his companions have confused me. He said that the state of affairs in settled localities is otherwise. The desert is the ruin of religion, the feebleness of Islam and its negation.'

Muḥammad Bello was quick to reply that living in settled villages and desert life were markedly different in law and circumstances. 'In general, he who is a beduin does not undertake interests and matters of life and livelihood save as a nomad. Urban life is not part of his need, nor is it his concern. He who is a village or urban dweller does not undertake nor concern himself with matters of his livelihood save in an urban society and environment. The life of the desert nomad is none of his business.'

According to Muḥammad Bello, the Prophet and his followers who fled to Medina were citizens, nonetheless, to his knowledge no general command had been issued to the nomads to forsake their desert habits and settle in towns or villages. . However, there was a *ḥadīth* of the Prophet, quoted by Abū Dā'ūd and Anas, which predicted urbanisation. This came about after the early conquests when garrison towns were established in Basra, Kufa, Fustat and Damascus. These *Amṣār* attracted both villagers and beduins. Dwelling in villages and towns was to be preferred to residing in the desert except during feuds or in time of dissension.

The argument, to some extent, was one of degree of preferability. What was certain was that the Prophet, or traditions attributed to him condemned excessive breeding of cattle since to do so would be detrimental to the furtherance of the faith.

'Abū Ya'lā al-Mu'ammal made it known, on the authority of Ḥasan, and the 'Companion of Paradise', and his son Abū Manṣūr, quoting 'Uqba b. 'Āmir. He said, "The Messenger of God said, 'The destruction of my community lies in the book of God and in milk.' They said, 'What is the book and the milk?' He said, 'They will learn the Qur'ān, and they will comment and interpret it in a way contrary to its correct interpretation, and they will love milk, and they will leave communities and live in the desert.'"

After further *ḥadīths,* which favoured community life since it facilitated statutory prayers, Muḥammad Bello argued that it was better to dwell in towns than in villages and to dwell in the latter was better than to dwell in the desert. 'The concern of the *Sharī'a* to promote community life is well known. Due to this the jurists have ruled that it is lawful to transfer a foundling from the desert to the village and from the latter to the town but not the opposite. There is no doubt man is urban by nature. Human perfection is not reached save through urbanisation and civilisation.'

Were there certain circumstances which favoured withdrawal into the desert? There were, but they were limited or specific. The Prophet permitted the city dweller and the villager to dwell in the desert two months. After that they would become beduin. Then there were periods of feuding, and *ḥadīths* existed which specifically referred to these tragic occurences, recommending the desert as a suitable place to escape from them. 'The virtue of (a place) of retirement is to be found during days of feud and dissension, albeit man should be among those to whom is given the ability to put an end to a feud.' There are certain circumstances when it may be obligatory for urban dwellers to go into the desert, and there are others which oblige desert dwellers to resort to urban life as a collective obligation.

A crucial factor in determining the establishment of a settled community was the prevailing situation in the *Dār al-Islām,* namely whether war was imminent or whether peace or relative peace prevailed. The *jihād* against an enemy, or the defence of Islam's frontiers, necessitated combining as a group in some localities and settling there, or the *Amīr* might need to build a fortress over his military camp where he could take refuge, or he might be obliged to establish fortresses where the frontiers were drawn.

The *Amṣār,* the military towns of the Companions of the Prophet were of this type. Thus Basra blocked the border facing India, Sind and China; Kufa was a military centre which blocked the frontier facing the Persians, the Kurds, the Daylamites and the Turks. Fustat (Old Cairo) blocked the frontier of the Byzantine Greeks in Alexandria, the Copts and the Nubians. Damascus faced northwards towards Byzantium itself. Such 'fortresses' had their prototype in the 'trench' dug by the Prophet to guard Medina against the attacks of the Meccan infidels.

A majority of *Imāms* had need to fortify their centres. As Muḥammad al-Jaylānī was both *Imām* and *Amenukal,* this situation was applicable in his case. Muhammad Bello supported his argument by quoting al-Maghīlī whose teachings were held in high esteem by Muḥammad al-Jaylānī. Al-Maghīlī had taught that it was the obligation of an *Imām* to build a strong fortress and to fill it with instruments of war, food, supplies and other necessities. It should be a place of refuge and 'a protective enclosure.' The latter description was coined by a Mauritanian scholar, Muḥammad b. al-Mukhtār b. al-A'mash, quoting the jurist Abū 'Abdullāh Muḥammad, the son of the famous *Qāḍī* 'Iyāḍ of Ceuta. There was little doubt that such a fortress and its construction was a duty which Muḥammad al-Jaylānī as *Imām* of his community was obliged to fulfil.

A more difficult problem to solve was how to collect taxes which were legal and in accordance with the *Sharī'a.* These included *zakāt* (statutory alms tax), *fay'* (lawful booty) and the inheritance of the *bayt al-māl* (the exchequer). The latter had to be sufficient to support the maintenance of troops to safeguard Muslim interests. If it was empty then the burden of fulfilling Islam's needs would have to be fairly distributed among the community. Taxation was only lawful provided five conditions were fulfilled; the *bayt al-māl* was empty; that charity was to be given to the deserving; it should be expended only as necessity demanded; the imposition of a tax should be upon those who were capable and not in dire want, and that the destitute should not be obliged to pay it; and fifthly and lastly, that it should be subject to review. 'A time might come when there was no need for taxation owing to an increase of what is to be found in the *bayt al-māl.*'

If the *bayt al-māl* was empty then assistance by the *Imām* himself and those of his subjects, who were capable, was incumbent. The building of a fort or maintenance of a headquarters in Islam's interests might involve unavoidable impositions. Muḥammad Bello advised Muḥammad al-Jaylānī to act in accordance with the experience which he himself had gained during his Sokoto *jihād*. 'God Almighty be praised when He granted me victory in the land and removed the people of infidelity and corruption, I strove with endeavour to build cities and mosques and to manifest the emblems, symbols and rites of Islam, and to found centres and capitals. I made clear to the people of the towns what affairs and duties were their religious obligations and worldly interests. I entrusted to each and every occupation those capable of fulfilling it, such as the office of *Imām,* the preacher and the judge, the *muḥtasib* (overseer of markets), the teacher and the instructor, in the school and in the *jihād* and in defending Islam's frontiers and other circumstances, such as the burning of pest from cultivation, and in commerce and in other activities besides these among those which are essential to the interests of the community.'

Muḥammad Bello then drew Muḥammad al-Jaylānī's attention to the problem of safeguarding a people whose habits were adjusted to a desert or Sahelian pastoral environment and social system. The appointment of a Shaykh or *Amghar* over each tribe was essential, a respected elder who could command and be commanded. A tutor or teacher was needed to educate the children, and a learned man chosen to act as an *Imām* for their statutory prayers and to teach their novices and to instruct them in all they needed to know in their religious practises. The people of the desert needed to be taught the use of implements and utensils. They should be discouraged from breeding large herds of cattle, and they should be commanded to increase the number of their camels, to prize and make full use of their horses and their sheep since these were the main source of supply for waging the *jihād.*

The arguments in favour of horse-breeding were stressed with particular emphasis. In fact it may be said that the prohibition for overbreeding cattle was among the most radical parts of the programme for the pastoral nomadic communities. Cattle should be sacrificed for the furtherance of the *jihād*. 'This tribe of ours has become infatuated by the love of cows and cattle, despite the fact that the Prophet did not own them. Nay, it has been reported that he slaughtered a cow for his women-folk. Abū Manṣūr al-Daylamī quoted Anas b. 'Abbās b. Mālik as saying that the Prophet said, "My *Umma* will not suffer humiliation as long as they keep horses picketed (in a *Ribāṭ*) ready to fight their foe. If they forsake this duty and cling to the tails of cattle, God will bring humiliation upon them. He will not remove it from them until they return to horses." There are many *ḥadīths* in praise of horses. Let the famous *ḥadīth* suffice you that the Messenger of God said, "Horses have good knotted in their forelocks until the day of judgement. Their owners should treat them with care." There have come down many *ḥadīths* in reproof of cows and cattle. Here is one to suffice you. "Their keepers will never be free of weakness.

It will not depart from them." Mention has been made of this. "They will undertake the *jihād,* and they will perish." Such is to be found in another *ḥadīth* and more besides.'

Muḥammad Bello concluded his letter by informing Muḥammad al-Jaylānī that he was leading the desert dwellers northwards advising them in spiritual and worldly matters, ensuring their support in his own *jihād* and enlisting their help for Muḥammad al-Jaylānī against his opponents. Since the desert dwellers, the nomadic herders, tended pasture lands which could support the settled population, he had decided to devote two months to putting their affairs in good order. As for the settled urban or rural population their duties were well known to them. If God so willed they would fulfil their obligations.

There seems little doubt that this advice had its effect and set the course of action which Muḥammad al-Jaylānī was to choose. His *jihād* and that of Muḥammad Bello were more or less the same. It would appear that Sokoto and its ruler were committed to aiding the Tuareg warrior *Imām* wherever his ambitions might lead. He was encouraged by such support. Schooled in a tradition which, because of his lineal links with the *Ṣanhāja* Barkuray, must have preserved memories of perennial Saharan religious movements and the teachings of al-Maghīlī and others, Muḥammad al-Jaylānī was convinced that his aims and ultimate goals should be Islamic. What he did not seem to realize was his limitations - and those of his allies, the Shehu ʿUthmān Dan Fodio until his death in 1817 and after him his successor Muḥammad Bello.

III

Muḥammad al-Jaylānī and Ibra

In 1813 the Tuareg *Imām* had turned his attention towards Air. He had attacked the Kel Geres and intervened in the feuds between the Itisen and the Kel Away. Inevitably his activities became the serious concern of the Air Sultanate. Entries in the Agades Chronicle (5) mention a sequence of events:-

'Then followed the combat of al-Jaylānī (Jīlānī). He caused many of the Kel Geres and Itisen to perish. In it died al-Ṣādiq b. al-Shaykh 'Umar in the year 1228/1813. The year 1229/1814 was when the Sultan Muḥammad Gumā killed Abū Bakr, the lord of Akaduday (?) A dissension occurred. Its cause arose among the Kel Away when some of their tribes went to the side of the Itisen. Al-Jaylānī was with them with many troops making for Air at the end of that year.'

It should be pointed out that these battles only concerned those Tuareg groups in the region of Air. Later, certain southerly groups of Kel Geres and

Itisen and their leaders were to join forces with Muḥammad Bello and Muḥammad al-Jaylānī.

The defeated Kel Geres of Air were to be instrumental in the eventual defeat of Muḥammad al-Jaylānī. Their chief escaped from the battle and sought refuge with the Tamezgidda and Kel Fadey who were powerful in the region of In Gall and Tagedda. An alliance was formed between the Kel Geres and Tamezgidda. It was to be so powerful that Muḥammad Bello was compelled to intervene to save his Tuareg allies from disaster.

The Tamezgidda are probably of Ahaggar or Azgar origin. They claim to stem from the Ihadenharan who formerly lived in the oasis of Janet and before that in Awjila, the half-mythical home of the Tuaregs. The ancestress of the Kel Fadey was the twin sister of the ancestress of the Tamezgidda. The latter once nomadised in the north of Air. Then in the days of the chief Muḥammad wa-n-Tagedda they established themselves in Azawagh. It was in the beginning of the eighteenth century. With the Kel Ferwan they were the 'lance and the whip' of the Sultan of Agades. The Tamezgidda - as their name 'people of the mosque' denotes - were devoted to religious practices. They were clients of two of the greatest centres of Air Agallal and Takriza, and the tribes associated with those centres were related to the Tamezgidda.

Air apart, there were also close ties between the southern Tamezgidda and the chiefly families of the Iwillimeden. Hotly though the two might contest the north of Adar, gifts were exchanged, and the Iwillimeden on occasions sought Tamezgidda mediation with the Sultan of Agades. When Muḥammad al-Jaylānī fought for the freedom of the *Ineslemen* among the Ait Awari there were signs of a similar social split among the Tamezgidda. It never reached grave proportions, yet one of their *Ineslemen,* Ibra (Ibrāhīm) due to the circumstances of the times, achieved a status not wholly dissimilar to his rival, Muḥammad al-Jaylānī.

The pious chief of the southern Tamezgidda was called Aḥmad al-Walī. He was not unsympathetic to the Islamic goals of Muḥammad al-Jaylānī. However, it was towards his son Ibra - who was born about 1785 - that the Kel Geres, the beaten Kel Aṭaram Iwillimeden and the Lisawen turned for spiritual and military aid to gain revenge. Supernatural powers which Muḥammad al-Jaylānī was deemed to possess could only be neutralised by those of another as great, if not greater than the ally of Muḥammad Bello.

The first engagement of the Tamezgidda against Muḥammad al-Jaylānī was unsuccessful. It took place at Tin-Makha. What precisely took place is far from clear. Some accounts speak of an attempt at an agreement between Aḥmad al-Walī and Muḥammad al-Jaylānī. Ibra seems to have been present at the engagement and not in Air. He was the commander of the forces of the Tamezgidda and their allies. Aḥmad, his father, had attempted to prevent their joint attack against Muḥammad al-Jaylānī but Ibra had refused. Aḥmad had finally given his son permission to launch the campaign on condition that he accompanied him and conducted secret discussions with Muḥammad al-Jaylānī to discover the reason for his wars. The latter came out to meet the Tamezgidda chief. While they were whispering together Ibra and his army suddenly attacked. The forces of Muḥammad al-Jaylānī quickly reacted. A skirmish took place, while the two leaders were engaged in secret confidences. Ibra's forces only held out for a few hours. He was decisively defeated. His father Ahmad died by the hand of an unknown killer. Ibra and the Kel Geres escaped. Little happened for some time while Ibra made new plans. News of the events reached Sokoto and the victory of Muhammad al-Jaylani was warmly applauded. Muḥammad Bello encouraged him and congratulated him. An ode composed by Muḥammad Bukhārī (d. 1840), vizir of Sokoto, was lavish in its praise.(6)

> The guardian of honour and the smiter of the courageous.
> Yet sweet in his fine qualities and tender to his friend.
> Bitter is his taste for those who are filled with hatred.
> Oh, hero, oh brother of reliance and trust, who excells
> himself in the day of passion and the clash of points.
> There is not to be found in all the tribes, one, who
> in excellence and bounty and courage is like Muḥammad
> al-Jaylānī.
> If you camp with him as a peaceful stranger you will
> possess large goblets or a steed.
> Oh, rider, tell Ibra and all those who are with him,
> men of deviation (from the truth) and doers of iniquity.
> I am in fear lest there should alight on their
> Camp some of the hatred of that lordly scholar.
> A host, a swarm, a multitude - Ṣanhāja - will be
> Set ablaze, ignited like new fires.
> Such are a people who (oh Ibra) forsook your father,
> felled and butchered, on the day they met, food for
> the vulture and for the hyenas.
> Ask about the battle of Abrik, the day he (Jaylānī)
> Marched to the Kel Geres, when he gave them a draught
> of the cup of perdition and of humiliation.

The continuous successes of Muḥammad al-Jaylānī, however, were not to last. His unwilling ally Ya'qūb b. al-Muṣṭafā, the *Amīr* of Adar, was defeated at Daré by dissidents rallied by Ibra in Damergu. In 1816 the battle of Jibale or Tinghasa was fought. It was a disaster for Muḥammad al-Jaylānī. The Ait Awari *Ineslemen* warriors were slaughtered, but their *Imām* with survivors of the disaster fled to the territory of Sokoto where they were welcomed by Muḥammad Bello. Ibra seized Kureya, and the *Imashaghen* reoccupied Azawagh.

The *jihād* seemed a lost cause but this was far from true. It was integrated into the politics of Sokoto. Furthermore Ibra found himself facing new enemies among the Iwillimeden. Their leader Bōdel, who was an ally of Muḥammad Bello and also helped by the Ilaswen of Adar, twice defeated him. The Kel Geres switched sides, and those of Godi became active supporters of Sokoto. For some time Ibra had suspected that ʿUthmān Dan Fodio and Muḥammad Bello had enlisted the help of the Sultan of Agades to restrain his Tamezgidda. This policy seemed logical since the economics of the salt trade and other commercial ties prevented the Sultan of Agades from antagonizing Sokoto, while the Kel Geres and Itisen were held in check by their need for grazing during the dry season on the fringes of Sokoto's borders. The defeat of Muḥammad al-Jaylānī did not appear to have impaired his spiritual status. It is reported that Khanza, the father of Azemzem (Ajimjim), the *Imām* of the Aṭaram Kel Es-Suq, said in Sokoto that the Ait Awari hero had the power to change himself into a bird, and that at night he went to Mecca to return to Niger the following morning.

The flight of the Tuareg *Imām* to Sokoto and his weakened position among the Ait Awari who were reduced to refugee status, poses the question whether he became nothing more than a puppet of ʿUthmān Dan Fodio and Muḥammad Bello, a young idealist caught up in the religious fervour of the age and dominated by Muslim personalities of far greater importance. Perhaps it was his rival that Ibra was thinking about when he wrote in a letter to Muḥammad Bello:-

> My guinea fowl has flown and returned to your pocket.
> I want you to send it back to me.
> If you cannot, I myself will come and put my hand
> in your pocket to take it.

Muḥammad al-Jaylānī was capable of independent judgement and was prepared to argue with Muḥammad Bello however much he respected his opinions. The following Arabic letter sent to Muḥammad Bello gives the impression of a leader conscious of his power. (7) He was able to quote from the accepted religious manuals if it suited his interests.

'In the name of God, the Compassionate, the Merciful. From Muḥammad al-Jaylānī to the Commander of the Faithful, Muḥammad Bello. - Peace be upon you and the mercy and blessing of God. To proceed. The reason for this communication is your questioning my motives to act over the disposal of the possessions of the Tuaregs who fled to the *bilād al-ḥarb* - the territory of the infidels - and who aided its inhabitants against Muslims and who challenged the rules and limits laid down by the *Sharīʿa,* and who left them in our country. So I used such property for the Muslims.

If I am unjust in acting so, I do not feel I am. My sole motive was due to what I saw in your writings and epistles sent to me and in the works of Shaykh 'Uthmān b. Fūdī and those of 'Abdullāh b. Fūdī - namely, that the property of the doers of iniquity, falsehood and corruption, who have done more harm than good, are not inviolate nor sacrosanct - not even mothers of children. You wrote to me one letter after another saying that property of the Tuaregs (*Imashaghen)* are forms of legal booty. I have watched you seizing and appropriating their property every day, and you care not a whit. You have even seized the property of those who travel on commerce to the country of the Burma before they waged war against Muslims and before their apostasy.

Al-Maghīlī indicated that the property of apostates should not be restored to them because what has remained charged against them is so much the greater. We have not observed any disparity or difference between what they have left in our country and what they have taken away with them. Those men who know, inform me that you dispose of the properties of those of the Tuaregs who went to Katsina in the year Jāna (?). We heard no disapproval from you until today, when 'Garrīd' came and told me that one of your scholars called Sūqi spoke harshly on account of it, and deemed me to be among the unjust doers whose land is ruined by their wrong-doing. He had said to them, "You will come to Sokoto fleeing from the unbelievers - due to your wrong-doing, like the injustice of the people of Al-Qaḍāwa [Alkalawa?]." Then your 'Garrīd' came, and he told me it. I said to him, "Yes, but you have no pretext nor reason in the *Sharī'a* for seizing the horses of the Tuaregs or other such possessions which they have left with you. If such is really the situation, then it is a very grave matter."

Glory to God, how is it that you left me to remain in my iniquity and false ways and yet you did not reprove nor forbid me in that respect, even for a day! Have you not seen the words of al-Maghīlī, "Your motive for action is linked inseparably to your act. If such be good, then the reward and recompense is due to you on account of both. But if it be evil, then the punishment is likewise on account of both."

Do you not know that I have put numerous questions to you for fear lest I commit a wrong? You did not answer most of them. Any error I have committed regarding those possessions, then you are the cause of it, so find a cure for sin! God be with you, go in peace.'

The circumstances of this letter are admittedly obscure. Muḥammad al-Jaylānī paid great heed to Muḥammad Bello, yet he knew the rulings of al-Maghīlī and acted upon them and resented accusations that any acts of his were contrary to the *Sharī'a*.

The Tuareg *Imām* was an active but troublesome ally. He was to show his mettle once again some thirteen years later on the battle field. In 1836, the final battle with Ibra was fought. Ibra's opponents were a formidable alliance - Muhammad Bello, Muḥammad al-Jaylānī, and the Kel Geres of Zodi and Wa-n-Agoda. Ibra had as his allies, 'Alī, the Sultan of Gobir and Rawḍa, the Sultan of Katsina. The battle took place at Dakoro (or Gawakuke) south-east of Madoua. It was a disaster for Ibra, even more so for his allies. Ibra was spared on account of his *Ineslemen* status. Muḥammad Bello reputedly said, 'I do not desire the blood of Ibra for he is a *murābiṭ* like myself.' Ibra died at Birni-n-Adar sometime after 1850. The Tamezgidda *Imashaghen* had lost many of their finest warriors, but their *Ineslemen,* who were less actively engaged, were by comparison little affected. (8) The exact date of the death of Muḥammad al-Jaylānī is unknown. He died near Sokoto in Dundaye district.

IV

The Mahdī of the Kel Dennek

The Kel Es-Suq and Kunta portrayed Muḥammad al-Jaylānī in the blackest hues. Mawlay Muḥammad al-Hādī called his movement the 'mischief of the party of the magician Aḥmad al-Jannān' - a distorted name for al-Jayn or Muḥammad al-Jaylānī. The Fulani *jihād* was condemned in like manner, and as the 'magician' in question had joined it as an ally, the aims of the Ait Awari *Imām* could arouse no sympathy among the Kel Es-Suq who were pacifists or influenced by the ideas of the Kunta. As for the latter, they had little reason to wish for his success. They wanted to retain the Ahaggar as a field for missionary activities. The Ahaggar Tuaregs had few scholars, but, in the eyes of the Kunta, many virtues. A Tuareg Islamic rival could upset this relationship and injure the Kunta cause, particularly the influence they had among the Kel Aṭaram Iwillimeden.

There was a widespread report that Muḥammad al-Jaylānī had claimed to be the *Mahdī,* or that his followers had given him this title. There were many leaders who were regarded as a *mahdī* in the sense of a 'guide' in the true path of knowledge, a title of respect given to a teacher or a shaykh of outstanding spiritual or intellectual merit but without any association with specific technical concept of the eschatological *Mahdī.* The religious fervour of ʿUthmān Dan Fodio had helped to foment ideas that at the dawn of the nineteenth century the end of time was at hand. Muḥammad Bello sent delegates and seekers to the East to meet the unknown *Mahdī* and to pay him homage.

Nowhere in the writings of Muḥammad al-Jaylānī is there the slightest indication that he regarded himself as the *Mahdī.* Yet in Kunta texts - preserved in Timbuctoo - he is bitterly attacked on these grounds. His movement is deprecated, his life regarded as detrimental to the Sokoto Caliphate, and atrocities were laid to his charge. The Tuaregs had been bewitched and misguided by a fanatic who though one of themselves proclaimed himself to be none other than the *Mahdī*, a *Sharīf* and an Arab of the noblest lineage.

This claim is extremely unlikely. Muḥammad al-Jaylānī would never have received the support he asked from Muḥammad Bello had he made such a claim. He was from a scholastic family. He was as well aware as the Kunta Shaykhs, Muḥammad Bello and other *'ulamā'* that neither in birth nor in circumstances did his person qualify to be the *Mahdī* who was awaited. What seems probable is that he has been confused with certain other contemporary Tuareg zealots - the erroneous name Aḥmad al-Jannān is indicative - who did make this claim and were attacked by 'Uthmān Dan Fodio in his book *Taḥdhīr al-Ikhwān* (1814). As we have seen a noted example was Hamma, the *Mahdī* of Maganga. The Shehu dismissed his claim by the same arguments which the Kunta were to use to denigrate Muḥammad al-Jaylānī. Tuareg scholars were as knowledgable of the invalidity of Hamma's claims as were their colleagues among the Kunta or in Sokoto.

Muḥammad al-Jaylānī and Ibra, his rival, were sophisticated religious leaders of a wholly different type. Despite the paucity of the records they emerge as classic examples of a certain type of Tuareg Muslim hero, a militant *Anislem* who was versed in Islamic history and less rare than is commonly supposed. Among all the Tuareg *Imāms* of Niger Muḥammad al-Jaylānī is the one who left the deepest mark in popular tales. His twentieth century successors were to be divided. Some were equally militant against the 'infidel' French, but lacked his dream of social revolution and equality with the *Imashaghen.* Others were to see in the less militant example of the Kel Es-Suq and the Kunta a better way to confront the most powerful opponents the Sahelian Tuaregs ever faced.

NOTES

1) 'Uthmān Dan Fodio, *Taḥdhīr al-Ikhwān* (1229/1814) and 'The Thirteenth Century in Muslim Eschatology, Mahdist Expectations in the Sokoto Caliphate' by M.A. al-Hajj, *Research Bulletin,* Centre of Arabic Documentation, Institute of African Studies, University of Ibadan, Vol. 3, No. 2, July 1967, pp. 100-115.

2) Preserved in collection *A*.

3) Without repeating arguments in Chapters VIII & IX regarding the date, cause or historicity of the evolution of the Iwillemeden, the following summary of the three principal and irreconcilable accounts of what took

place is restated for ease of reference:-

a) The death of Karidenna was either 1698/9 (Sic. Barābīsh Chronicle) or 1715. His investiture as *Amenukal* by the Timbuctoo Pasha was in 1690. *(Tadhkirat al-Nisyān).*

b) The *Ineslemen* theory for the split, the tradition found, amongst others, in the histories of the Kel Es-Suq and Kel Aghlāl. Karidenna sought investiture *(bay'a)* and the swearing of homage to the Sultan of Agades. He was opposed by his brother (?) or nephew (?) Karoza. The Sultan gave authority to Karidenna, a feud followed, and Karoza was expelled to Air - later to Azawagh. According to the Kel Aghlāl, Karoza's successors were:- Mūda, In Niyāl, Khatūtu, Alegharam, Bōdel, Musa, Muḥammad, Ismāghīl, al-Khurayr, Bāzū.

c) The Kel Dennek theory of the split. At the end of the seventeenth century Karidenna was *Amenukal* of all the Iwillimeden. His nephew At-Tafrīja sought to form a nucleus of partisans, the Kel Nan, Tigguermat and others including *Ineslemen.* He broke with the other Iwillimeden at Menaka and fought his uncle Karidenna. He left for Azawagh. The succession to At-Tafrīja is claimed to be Karoza, his son, then Mūda, brother of Karoza, Agush, Attutu (Khatūtu?) son of Mūda, al-Gharīb (Alegharam?), ... Bōdel, etc. The sequence and spelling of names approximates to those of the *Ineslemen* sources. Tafrīja versus Karoza is the main difference.

d) The Kel Aṭaram theory of the split. Kāwa at the end of the eighteenth century was challenged by Kātim, father of Bōdel, of the Kel Nan together with five or six noble tribes and *Ineslemen* and *Imghad.* A bloody battle took place near Ansongo. The dissidents left Menaka for Azawagh. This event led to the major Iwillimeden split.

It is now generally accepted that the Kel Aṭaram theory refers to an episode long after the initial scission. The theories of the *Ineslemen* and the Kel Dennek are basically plausible. They principally differ over whether the Dennek leader was At-Tafrīja or Karoza. This effects the chronology of the split, even if they cohere in a vaguely 'historical' explanation which can be accepted tentatively as some approximation to events between 1650 and 1715.

4) See in particular Muḥammad Bello, *Jawāb shāfī* and *Jumal min al-mabānī fī nasā'iḥ li Muḥammad al-Jaylānī,* copy in the Nizamiya School Sokoto, and texts in the private collection of *A.*, more particularly with Shaykh Muḥammad al-Mu'min.

5) See *C.A.* by Urvoy, Manuscript *F.*, p. 163.

6) Poem in Collection *A.* Other copies of it exist in the *Préfecture* of Tchin Tebaraden, Niger Republic.

7) Text in Collection *A*.

8) See *T.D.N.C.A.*, p. 237. One of the finest descriptions of Ibra is by Barth:-

'While I was indulging in pleasing reveries of new discoveries and successful return, I was suddenly startled by three hosemen riding up to me and saluting me with a "Lá ílah ilá Allah". It was Dan Ibra (or Ibram, the 'Son of Ibrahím') the famous and dreaded chief of the Tamizgída, whom the ruler of Tin-téllust himself in former times had not been able to subdue, but had been obliged to pay him a sort of small tribute or transit money, in order to secure the unmolested passage of his caravans on their way to the Sudán. The warlike chief had put on all his finery, wearing a handsome blue burnús, with gold embroidery, over a rich Sudán tobe, and was tolerably well mounted. I answered his salute, swearing by Allah that I knew Allah better than he himself, when he became more friendly, and exchanged with me a few phrases, asking me what we wanted to see in this country. He then went to take his turn with Mr. Richardson. I plainly saw that if we had not been accompanied by Ánnur himself and almost all our luggage sent on in advance, we should have had here much serious colloquies.'

CHAPTER XII

THE TUAREG JIHĀD AGAINST THE FRENCH

'At this very moment we are at the end of the world. Islam prohibits all that is forbidden. I am not a *feqqi* who is knowledgable in scripture. I am a practiser of religion, and I obey God's commands. The religion of Islam is God's way. Do that which God has told you to do, observe the fast if you can, give the alms tax, perform the obligatory prayers. By this the quality of being a true Muslim is defined.'

Digga agg Khammad Ekhya.

The early years of the twentieth century were exceptionally disastrous for the Tuaregs of Azawagh and Air. Loss of their independence, their wealth in herds and slaves and their ability to raid made life a burden for the *Imashaghen* and impelled the *Ineslemen* to seek a warrior leader or a solace in reclusive religion. (1) Between 1911 and 1914 one of the worst droughts in Sahelian history forced many Tuaregs to press south to the Niger river and its banks. Then, when the world was at war, the Sanūsīya of the Fezzan, eager to avenge the wrongs inflicted upon them by Italian Colonialism, enlisted the Tuaregs as allies. Religious sympathies, specifically Sanūsī or vaguely Islamic, were aroused in all classes of Tuareg society. It produced an almost spontaneous outburst of sentiment.

It is usually accepted that the 'marabouts' played an active part in increased Tuareg resistance to the French. It has been argued by Finn Fuglestad that it was the Colonial Power which had first encouraged them to assert their influence and to take the initiative away from the *Imashaghen.* (2) In his view, their ascent commenced with the arrival of the French who were its sponsors and deemed it expedient to further their political ends. The 'marabouts' in the few years of French occupation attained virtual equality with the *Imashaghen.* The latter who had lost their prestige were compelled to respond to the calls of the 'marabouts' for a *jihād.* To refuse to have done so would have been cowardice. It would have undermined their status as chiefs, and it would have disgraced them in the eyes of the lower classes in Tuareg society.

This argument of Finn Fuglestad has the merit of simplicity but it is hard to accept in view of what is known about the lives of several of these 'marabouts' or the evidence offered by earlier Tuareg historical texts. The rise of the *Ineslemen* from a lower and semi-vassal status among the Iwillimeden dates back to at least the seventeenth century, and it has been shown in my last chapter that it was a major force in some districts of the Kel Dennek at the height of the Sokoto *jihād*. Sahelian societies do not operate a wholly static class structure whereby *Ineslemen* cannot assume the role of *Imashaghen*. Tuaregs like the Kel Intasar, the Kel Aghlal and the Ait Awari revealed a past capability of the Islamic lettered to transform themselves into a warrior élite. No special relationship developed between French and *Ineslemen*. Even where the latter did not take up arms they adopted a correct aloofness towards the unbelievers.

Unanimity of sentiment can be observed in the *jihād* of Fihrun against the French in Filingué. Fihrun was born about 1885, and he became *Amenukal* of the Kel Aṭaram *Imashaghen* in 1902. In 1905 fierce combats took place between the Iwillimeden and the Kunta who had been armed by the French. This anti-Kunta sentiment among the Tuaregs became so strong that they sought for arms in the Hoggar and in Agades. Battles with the Kunta led to strained relations between Fihrun and the French. At first he had been willing to cooperate with them in order to gain a free hand to raid the Kel Air, but early hopes were soon turned to hatred.

Fihrun was exiled to Timbuctoo in 1912. He flattered his captors who brought him to Gao. In February 1916 he escaped and rallied the Iwillimeden of Menaka. He declared a *jihād* despite the sympathetic dissuasion of his *Anislem* of the Kel Es-Sūq Ajemjim, who argued that only the arrival of the *Mahdī* could defeat the French. Fihrun politely ignored his counsel and marched in the direction of Filingue, and his aims were to conquer Dallol Bosso, the granary of Niger. Seizure of it would offset the effects of the drought. It would also be of strategic value and if captured would have diverted the French army from other Tuareg areas. It would incite the Kel Dennek of Tahoua and the Kel Geres to revolt. Fihrun's attack on Filingué in April 1916 was broken by the superior armament of the French garrison. (3)

His *jihād* was badly organised. He had no hope of rallying the Soudie Hausa to his side. Finn Fuglestad regards it as a coincidence that his attack on Filingué took place when more important operations were planned in Air. (4) Yet there is little doubt that Fihrun was known to the Sanūsī and the Tuareg revolutionaries in Agades. Other *Imashaghen* of the Iwillimeden were to fight the French in the territory of the Kel Dennek. Khurayr, their *Amenukal* fled to Ghat, where he died. Tuareg auxiliaries, Kel Geres and forces under the ruthless command of Sadoux destroyed camps, devastated entire regions, and leaders who had surrendered were summarily executed. The pacific but basically hostile *Ineslemen* around Tahoua watched the infidels take a terrible revenge on the Iwillimeden who had attempted to resist them. To the north of Air the *jihād* was fiercer and more skilfully planned. The sword of Islam in the hands of the Tuaregs there had been tempered in the Sanūsī Fezzan. It had a sharp blade and was of tougher steel.

The Tuareg military hero of the revolt was Muḥammad Kawsen agg Muḥammad Wa-n-Tagedda. In reality he was a lesser figure than some of his admirers in Niger make him out to be. There were other Sanūsī personalities and other characters in the Air *jihād* who were of importance. Nonetheless, so powerful an influence did his personality exert on Tuareg resistance in Air and the Libya border areas that it would be as pedantic to remove him from the heart of the story as it would be to omit 'Uqba b. Nāfi' from the semi-legendary exploits of the Arabs on the Libyan and Niger borders twelve centuries before.

There is disagreement regarding his birth. He was an Ikazkazen from Damergu, and he was born about 1880. Some allege that he was a Buzu. Whatever truth there may be in this report, it certainly does not seem to have impaired the status he occupied in the eyes of his allies, nor did it lower his esteem in the key role he was to play in the plans of Tegāma, the Sultan of Agades. The latter was in reality as much a hero of Tuareg resistance in Air as Muḥammad Kawsen.

A few remarks need to be made about the Ikazkazen, Kawsen's tribe. Their history is not clear. They are divided into two main divisions, the Kel Tamat (acacia) who are mostly in Air, and the Kel Ulli (goats) who are mostly centred in Damergu. (5) Some maintain that they are Ahaggaren, others that they are Libyan Tuaregs from the region of Ghat. They form part of the Kel Away confederation. The Kel Tamat may have arrived in Air in the eighteenth century, the Kel Ulli a century later. The Iguirnazan are among their *Imashaghen* in Damergu, and Kawsen was born into the latter. The Ikazkazen also have links with the Ishsherifen, for, it is said that the son of Sīdī Maḥmūd al-Baghdādī married a wife among the Ikazkazen. (6) At the same time another *Sharīf* called Agg Aḥmad came from Janet near Ghat. He married a wife of the Kel Takarat Tamezgidda. Their son was Muḥammad Wa-n-Tagedda. He came to Air and Azawagh. His descendants formed the tribe of the Ishsherifen Tamezgidda and the Ishsherifen were considered part of the Ikazkazen.

This mixed background to Kawsen's origin is matched by the reports of his marriage and offspring. He is said to have married a wife near Tanout and had one child by her. Another daughter called Nana was born in Tibesti. Kawsen is also reported to have married a daughter of one of the *Ineslemen* 'Abd al-Qādir. If this be true then it might explain an Agades oral tradition that he was a 'marabout' turned warrior. In 1901 Kawsen emigrated to Kanem to enroll at Guro, a strategic lodge of the Sanūsī. He was one among a general Tuareg exodus at that time. Several factors brought it about. One was the tribal dissension in Damergu, another was the French occupation of Zinder and the passage of the Foureau-Lamy mission through Agades. Hostility was heightened by the presence of Sanūsī emissaries in Damergu. Resisiting bitterly, the Tuaregs left *en masse* for

Guro where they joined the Arab Awlād Sulaymān who were blocking the French advance from Chad. Many of the Tuaregs were to return to Damergu after the fall of the Sanūsī citadel of Bīr Alali in 1902.

The concept of mobility, of withdrawal and return, was characteristic of the Sanūsī order. 'It is not revolt which the chiefs of the Sanūsī preach, it is emigration. For, in their eyes, emigration is the sole means whereby true believers under Christian yoke may return again to Islam. This applies also to the equally abhorrent rule of Muslim rulers who, like those in Constantinople, Cairo, Tunis or Fez, are at the mercy of the European powers and are subject to their pernicious influences.' (7) Kawsen did not return to Damergu. He joined the Sanūsī as a member in 1909 and became the leader of a private army which offered its services to the Turks or to the Sanūsīya. In the Fezzan he gained the confidence of Sīdī Muḥammad 'Abīd, the Sanūsī *khalīfa,* a relative of the Grand Master, Sīdī Aḥmad Sharīf, who employed Kawsen in Ennedi until he was forced to escape to Darfur in the Sudan.

The Sanūsīya are sometimes presented as an aggressive and militant movement. This is misleading. As founded in the early nineteenth century by the Algerian, Muḥammad b. 'Alī al-Sanūsī, it was orthodox and of a conventional and austere Sufism. To achieve its goals it worked through lodges (*zawāyā*) which were centres of culture as well as religious instruction. Where these lodges were well established, Sanūsī withdrawal concepts could be implemented, but where they were remote and newly established the warlike or hostile sentiments of the newly converted could reverse policy or modify tactics. This was particularly noticable after Kufra became the seat of the order, replacing al-Bayḍā' (1843) and Jaghbūb (1856).

Its southern Saharan expansion took place under Sīdī Muḥammad al-Mahdī, son of the founder. Kufra was selected for several reasons. It was an important junction of desert routes and rapidly became a caravan centre. The Sanusi leader responsible for operations in Kanem (Bīr 'Alali) and among the Awlād Sulaymān, the Teda and the Tuaregs, was Sīdī Muḥammad al-Barrānī. In 1906 the French took Kuwwār and Bilma. In 1907 'Ain Kalak was occupied, and Sīdī Muḥammad al-Barrānī, the Shaykh of its lodge, was killed. Lodges of the order were destroyed in the whole region. It is hardly surprising that the originally pacific policy of the Sanūsiya underwent considerable modification among its Saharan supporters.

The Tuaregs of the Central Sahara had never been deeply attached to the Sanūsīya and had remained loyal to the Qādirīya and the Khalwatīya. The significance of attachment to one order as opposed to another has been much exaggerated. There was always contact and dialogue between them. Members of different orders worshipped in the same mosques, and where colonial powers tried to play off one order against another the result was usually a failure.

Commercial and cultural relations between Agades and the Libyan oasis of Ghat had been established for centuries. Ghat merchants and scholars resided in Air, and events in the Tassili-n-Ajjer region were of concern to the Tuaregs of Air, the Ikazkazen among them. If Air and the lands of the Iwillimeden were ever to be liberated from the French, Ghat and its neighbourhood would be the obvious base from which to launch operations. Agades would be the first goal. At the same time disruption of enemy communications through Damergu to Zinder would ensure the necessary time to establish a grip on Air and a base in the Massif. Kawsen knew Damergu, he knew Air, he was a friend of the Sanūsī, and he had served the Turks. He frequented Ghat. His military experience was useful, and he had already fought the French. He was a key man in any project to eject the occupying power.

In March 1916 Sanūsī forces captured the oasis of Janet. They did so in the name of the Sultan Ḥamūd who had previously resided there but had crossed over to Ghat after the French occupied the Tassili-n-Ajjer in 1911. While in Ghat, Ḥamūd joined the Sanūsīya, and he fought both the French and the Italians. Several operations were mounted from this base.

Meanwhile, for at least three years, Tegāma agg Baqārī, Sultan of Agades, had made plans with this Sanūsī allies in the Fezzan and Kufra to coordinate action with Kawsen. (8) Tegāma was a calculating Sultan. He was in secret correspondence with Kawsen and also with Sultan Ḥamūd in Janet. Kawsen approached Agades via Jado and Iferouan. The people of Agades were told to prepare a feast and to celebrate because a 'marabout' had arrived in Air. He was to be entertained in the guest house built for him by the Sultan. The French were unaware of the pending arrival of the 'marabout'. It is not clear who planned the fine timing of the plan, whether Tegāma himself or the Ikazkazen guerilla fighter. Kawsen's assault on Agades began in December 1916.

Kawsen had many advantages. The French garrison was besieged, he commanded a good deal of popular support; he was a master of lightening raids, and he was by no means ill-equipped. Yet, in the event, he failed. After eighty days' siege, the beleaguered garrison was relieved. The operation cost the French some losses and was so grave that it demanded an emergency switch of men from other parts of Africa. The British in Nigeria aided in providing communications and military backing since it was felt that had Kawsen succeeded the way to Kano would be open, to the Sanūsī and their allies. (9) Towards the end, short of men, food and with a demoralised band of fanatics Kawsen and Tegāma retired to Tibesti and the Fezzan. Kawsen who was tempted to visit Murzuk fell into a trap and died in 1919. Tegāma was captured in Kuwwār. He was taken to Agades and officially he committed suicide in French custody on the night of the 29th April 1920. He 'disappeared' but there is little doubt that he was put to death during his imprisonment. Tegāma was one of the most energetic Sultans of Agades, far from being one of the ineffectual figures these potentates are often claimed to be.

The reasons for Kawsen's failure have been variously assessed. A combination of bad Sanūsī intelligence, tactical errors, cupidity and in the last resort a hopeless inequality of forces, were among the factors which doomed the attempts by the Tuaregs to 'liberate' Air. The talents of Kawsen, the ability and regality of Tegāma and the courage of many of their men were not enough to defeat the overwhelming superiority of their enemies. As for the goals of the Tuaregs leaders, these are not clear, and it is possible that they themselves had no precise notions of them. The improbable theory of a 'Tuareg State' seems to have no substance. The maximum hope in this direction might have been a temporary re-establishment of an independant Agades Sultanate under Tegāma, such as his colleague Sultan Ḥamūd had attained in Janet. A letter addressed by Kawsen to his two Ikazkazen uncles, al-Ḥājj Mūsā and Adembar, dated October 1916 and sent from Agades is full of pious exhortations. The Azgar Tuaregs had fought a *jihād* and had achieved success. 'All the Muslims have risen up for the holy war. The Sha'mbas who were with the enemies of God are divided, some among them have fled and have gone in the direction of the sandy country towards Ghadames, and you will see in the letter of our brother al-Mukhtār b. Muḥammad some columns are departing in the territories occupied by the French, the enemies of God and of His Prophet. Know that the Turkish Government and the Germans await us in Kano where they have gone before us. All the country conquered between the 'sea' and Egypt has been handed over to the Sanūsī Government.' (10)

If the date of the letter is correct, and if it is authentic it must have been written before the assault on Agades, but some six months after the capture of Janet by Sultan Ḥamūd. Hyperbole must be allowed for. Even so it reflects a fanciful and ill-informed attitude among the Tuaregs sympathetic to the Sanūsīya. Religious sentiments which were genuine enough, even if some of the scholars of Agades had misgivings, evoked hopes which were impossible to fulfil. There was wide tribal representation in Kawsen's base force in Agades and an equally wide variety of tribes in Janet under the authority of the Sultan Ḥamūd.

The Air revolt was disastrous for the Massif itself. It nearly led to the re-settlement by the French of its whole population in the region of Damergu. At least 30,000 Tuaregs fled from Niger and settled in the Emirates of Kano and Katsina. Air declined, and the desert encroached in the areas of garden cultivation. Mosques were ruined deliberately, or due to neglect, and their archives were in major part lost or destroyed. The decline of Islamic institutions in Air was accelerated by a revolt controlled by an external Islamic movement which contributed little to Islamic belief and practise in Tuareg society.

II

By historical irony it was one of the Kunta - the traditional enemies of the Tuaregs - who was to be largely responsible for a Tuareg Islamic revival in Azawagh in the post-war period. He was called Shaykh Bāy al-Kuntī, and he lived between 1865 and 1929 mainly in the Adrar-n-Ifoghas.

Shaykh Bāy was arguably the most important religious teacher of the twentieth century in the Sahel. Many were his pupils, of profound significance his ideas. More than any other of the Kunta he combined the traditions of the *Zwāya* of the Moors and the *Ineslemen* of the Tuaregs. So well balanced, so well integrated were these two traditions that even if he had achieved no other triumph in itself this would earn him special mention among major figures of Tuareg Islamic history.

Born about 1865 his true name was Sīdī Muḥammad b. Sīdī 'Umar ('Amar) b. Sīdī Muḥammad b. Sīdī 'l-Mukhtār al-Wāfī. In 1896 after the death of his brother he became the spiritual chief of the Kunta of Azawād. Half-Tuareg in his background, having had Tuareg teachers, Shaykh Bāy of Telīa in the Adrar-n-Ifoghas, by his sensitive yet powerful personality left a mark on the poets, mystics and religious leaders in Azawagh and in the region of Tahoua. He drew away many of the Azawagh *Ineslemen* from the Kel Es-Suq yet some of the latter were eager to deem him one of themselves. A text by Ḥammād b. Muḥammad b. Muḥammad in praise of the Kel Es-Suq includes him among their number. He is described as 'coolness of the eye' al-Shaykh Bāy b. al-Shaykh 'Umar b. al-Shaykh Sīdī Muḥammad, al-Khalīfa, a renowned scholar and man of piety, who was exemplary in the honour he showed to the Kel Es-Suq, who acknowledged openly their status of Prophetic lineage and their scholastic worth. His forebears were bitter Kunta critics of Muḥammad al-Jaylānī, yet many relations of the latter became attached to Shaykh Bāy and were most fervent advocates of his pacific policies.

Cortier, who visited the Ifoghas in 1908, gave a first-hand portrait of this Kunta 'marabout':- (11)

'The marabout who enjoys the most considerable influence among the Ifoghas is 'Bāy', whose brotherhood or Zāwiya is at Telīa.

'Bāy' is a Kunta, son of Sīdī 'Amar, a Kunta marabout. Sīdī 'Amar first came and settled in the country of the Ifoghas and there he bought from the tribe of the Tarat-Mellat, for the price of fifteen goats, the whole Wād Telīa with its own wells and several neighbouring wells. The principal ones are In Ṣaṭṭafen (12) to the north of the valley of Telīa where are sited the tombs of Sīdī 'Amar and his son Sīdī Muḥammad, Telabbit, Agharagh, Khammeden, Brika (filled in), Allal (filled in), Barka, and the two wells of Telīa, one at the gates of the *Qaṣba,* the other in the middle. Sīdī 'Amar established himself at Telīa founded his fraternity or Zāwiya there and let his tents nomadise in the more or less immediate neighbourhood of his *Qaṣba.* He died at Telīa and was buried at In Ṣaṭṭafan. He left four sons, the oldest Sīdī Muḥammad who succeeded him as head of the Zāwiya; 'Bāy', the present marabout who succeeded his eldest brother; Bāba Aḥmad and Bakkāy. He also left some daughters, all now deceased. Sīdī Muḥammad, son of Sīdī 'Amar, died towards 1893 leaving six sons, Sīdī 'l-Mukhtār, Sīdī Aḥmad al-Bakkāy, Shīkh Bāba Aḥmad, two others who were younger and two daughters Lalla and a second, younger still. The two eldest sons are the only men at the present time, the four others are still youths.

At the death of Sīdī Muḥammad, 'Bāy' became the chief of the Zāwiya and tutor of his nephews. He himself will be replaced by Sīdī 'l-Mukhtār, eldest son of Sīdī Muḥammad. All the sons of Sīdī Muḥammad live near 'Bāy' as well as the two younger brothers of 'Bāy' himself. One of them, Bāba Aḥmad is in the tents of 'Bāy' at the head of a small Zāwiya subsidiary to Telīa. 'Bay' could now be some forty years old. He is short, thin, light complexioned, with a beard not yet white. He has no moustache. His outward appearance inspires great respect. He is always very richly dressed in indigo cloths of the Sudan, *doukkali* of Tuwāt and a *burnus* of silk, cut in Kunta fashion, not in the Tuareg fashion. He only shows his face publicly during the prayer. The remainder of the time he covers his head - either with a *ḥā'ik* or by a loose part of his clothing. Likewise he covers his hands and his feet, and when he stretches his fingers to be kissed by the Ifoghas, he hides them under a veil, furthermore the natives themselves cover the hand with their dress in order to touch the hand of 'Bāy'.

Before the French came in 1904, 'Bāy' was living in his *Qaṣba* at Telīa. He rarely left it, sometimes to go to his tents established in the Wād Telīa but never for longer than a day, so that he could always be in the place which served as a mosque at Telīa and to preside over at least one daily prayer, if not all five. Since 1904 he has given up his house of stone and *pisé* and leads a nomad life under a tent without ever wandering from the Wād Talīa. Few persons are admitted into the presence of the 'marabout. His abode infuses and inspires devotion, and upon entering his presence the Ifoghas cannot restrain their tears. He speaks little, for long hours keeps silence, and now and then utters a word of deep significance. Unceasingly he counts his rosary of amber and coral. 'Bāy' has always refused to receive a stranger. He has not presented himself to the French and did not even wish to accept the visit of the Dawi Maniya who came on a raid in 1904, replying to them that their demands would be met but that he had no need to see them in person.

He lives the life of the perfect scholar, speaking both Arabic and Tamashegh, reading and understanding the Qur'ān and all the Arabic books. His camp consists of a tent where he dwells and a great tent used as a mosque. There is to be found his famous library. His books fill three great boxes as well as two woollen bags and two skin bags, enough to load three or four camels. Amidst his books he lives in great simplicity. He eats no meat, drinks no milk and contents himself with *agarouf* (13) and crushed dates.

'Bāy' exerts a considerable influence over the Ifoghas and his repute extends into all the Sahara. Incessantly the Tuaregs come to consult him, ask him to pray, have amulets written by him, greet him and bring him gifts. At his door there is always a goodly number of people waiting for him to come out in order to kiss his hands. His political action is wholly pacific, besides he has never participated in a raid, and he confines himself wholly to his religious calling, a man of prayer, books and pious works. He is so gentle and pacific that he even prohibits the hunting of lions which sometimes attack his cattle. Whenever his counsel is sought he always advises peace, seeking to avoid bloodshed, wars, arguments, unjust acts, and he discourages raiding and pillaging.

Having brought up and educated Mūsā ag Amastan, *Amenukal* of the Ahaggaren, of whom he is to some degree spiritual father, he urged him to submit to the French and to live in harmony and cooperation. It is due to his constant counsels that Mūsā shows himself to be merciful, conciliatory, pacific and an opponent of bloody combats. (14) Conversely, he has always reproved the pillaging of 'Ābidīn al-Kuntī, his cousin, and Ḥammūdī the chief of the Kunta.

'Bāy' is very rich due to gifts he has received. He has sheep, goats, cows, horses, she-camels and slaves, but he bestows alms in abundance, and day and night he bestows hospitality on all who come. In his Zāwiya he instructs all those who desire to receive his lessons, and, incessantly he has around him children or youths who seek to learn science and wisdom.

Since the occupation of Timbuctoo, the French have never entered into relationship with 'Bāy' whose allied influence could - for us - be of indisputable value. In 1904 he was treated as though he were an enemy. At the start at least, Europeans should avoid seeking to see him face to face, but he does not lack persons of worth and influence in Timbuctoo, by whose mediation it could be possible to reach an agreement with 'Bāy' and, to our advantage, canalize the indisputable and weighty influence which he exerts in the entire desert.'

Unfortunately little, if any, attention was paid to the wise advice of this French officer. Nonetheless, it was Shaykh Bāy more than any other who advised Mūsā ag Amastan, the Ahaggaren *Amenukal,* to avoid involvement in any of Kawsen's plans. His influence also swayed many of the *Ineslemen* of the Kel Dennek in favour of no direct involvement in the revolts against the French, either in the region of Filingué or around Agades. Some of the *Ineslemen* fought as individuals but in the main they preferred to express their hostility by passive resistance, withdrawal and aloofness. There is little doubt that many of the ideas of Shaykh Bāy had profoundly influenced their manner of thinking.

III

The end of the first World War left the *Ineslemen* of the Kel Dennek with a wholly new situation to face in Azawagh. They had been relatively unaffected by the war but their *Imashaghen,* against whom they had fought in the days of Muhammad al-Jaylānī, had been slaughtered. As Tuaregs and as pious Muslims they could not welcome the French. Yet, it was the latter who had brought about their final freedom from the *Imashaghen* who had once controlled them. The war had been traumatic, and it had followed immediately on grave drought and shortage of food. In the post-war years these *Ineslemen* found solace in a withdrawn religious community living with their herds in closely-knit family campments. Their Shaykhs were influenced by many Kunta and Mauritanian scholars but their eyes were also turned in the direction of Kano, Sokoto, Morocco and the Middle East.

Urvoy concludes his account of the events of the war in Azawagh and Tahoua with an illuminating report on the numerical and social balance of the Kel Dennek in the post-war years. (15) Counting their Bellas they numbered less than 50,000. The tribes of the *Imashaghen* totalled with their Bellas some 5,200. Only a few hundred were true *Imashaghen.* They had lost their political power and influence. By far the most numerous and richest of the Kel Dennek were the *Ineslemen.* Urvoy described them as pacific, little involved in the war-time revolt and as having maintained a position which had ensured them an easy and early withdrawal. They had escaped the worst consequences of the fighting and had retained large herds. According to Urvoy these numbers some 600,000 sheep and goats, 100,000 oxen and 15,000 camels. Their herds were of enormous value. The markets of Tahoua and Nigeria were open to there *Ineslemen.* On the debit side, they were totally dependant on a political and climatic *status quo.* The sale of livestock was the sole resource of the Kel Dennek. Commerce was not a major occupation, and they took little part in the Azalai salt-caravan commerce of Bilma.

'The rhythm of their life is governed by the rains. When the first violent downpours take place in June, they begin to go northwards following the green herbage sprouting here and there. Towards August they are gathered together around

Tagedda-n-Tasemt, to the west of Air, in order to give their livestock saline water and pasturage. At this time Azawagh is empty. Only a few Bellas are to be found there. Usually in September the move southwards recommences. It is very slow and follows the progressive drying out of the lakes and pools left by the rainy season and the exhaustion of the pasturage. It is only towards December that they have really arrived again at their normal place of habitat. Azawagh possesses numerous wells which unfortunately towards March or April almost run dry. Then it is that the herds gather around the half dozen or so permanent wells. The grass is rapidly consumed and trampled down over a large area. It is in May and June when the cattle sometimes suffer from hunger. With the onset of the first violent rains, the wells are left and there is a search for green grass and the small ponds left by the downpours. Slowly the heavy rains move northwards. Everybody follows and the movement towards Tagedda begins once more. The rhythm is only broken and then barely so, by journeys to Tahoua or to Sokoto to sell cattle and to bring back millet.'

A light hand of authority and minimal loss should logically have predisposed some affection towards the Colonial Power. But this was not the case. Urvoy admits to the hostility of the Kel Dennek *Ineslemen*. 'In spite of their wealth, in comparison with the other Tuaregs, the Iwillimeden of Tahoua are by far the group which is most hostile to us in all the colony of Niger, be this due to pride and rancour among the nobles, or due to religious fanaticism among the 'marabouts'. The coldness of their welcome contrasts with the familiarity of the Tuaregs of the Colony. This curious fact of religious fanaticism should be noted. It is very rare among the Tuaregs, and it is probably due to the *Ineslemen* origin of almost all the Confederation and due to the past, the 'holy war' against the pagans of Adar. Furthermore, they live very much apart from the other Tuaregs of Niger - though this does not mean that everybody would not act in concert against us in the event of War. Their churlish welcome at the wells keeps the Kel Air away from them, for example in their frontier region (Bagam). The majority of the *Ineslemen* notables avoid letting their women-folk be seen, especially by 'whites'. Not normally veiled, they are shut away when a Frenchman is in the camp, or else they conceal themselves with a large mat. In the move towards Tagedda, on their oxen, bedecked with trappings, they wear a great white veil. This contrasts with the freedom of the Kel Geres womenfolk for example.'

In the middle years of the twentieth century it was in these *Ineslemen* camps of Azawagh that some of the most active Islamic teaching was to be found among all the Iwillimeden. Even today the region north of Tahoua is acknowledged to be one of the most important centres of Arabic scholarship. Viewed in perspective the Sanūsī revolt of Kawsen should be seen as erratic, largely outside the natural evolution of Tuareg Islamic ideas. In the heart of

Azawagh among the Ait Awari and descendants of Muḥammad al-Jaylānī, all the upheaval and disturbance of the war years gravely disrupted their life. Yet in the long term it strengthened their Islamic traditions which had been well established over many centuries and which are as alive today as they were before the Christians first set foot in their remote pasturage amidst thickets and undulating dunes.

NOTES

1) Urvoy, *Histoire des Oulliminden de l'Est,* pp. 82, 83.

2) See Finn Fuglestad, *'Les Revoltes des Touaregs du Niger,' 1916-1917,* p. 93.

3) See *Iwillimiden* by Altinine ag Arias, Niamey, 1970, pp. 85-105.

4) *ibid,* pp. 91 and 95.

5) See *P.V.*. pp. 307-308.

6) See Boubou Hama, *Recherche sur l'histoire des Touareg Sahariens et Soudanais,* Niamey, 1967, p. 390.

7) See Henri Carbou, *La Région du Tchad et du Ouadaï,* Paris 1912, pp. 130-131, and E. Evans Pritchard, *The Sanusi of Cyrenaica,* Oxford, 1949, pp. 15-28.

8) See André Selifou, *Kaoussen ou la Révolte Senoussiste,* pp. 58-59.

9) See the dissertation (unpublished) by Muhammad Zbairu Kolo (1972/1973 session) in Ahmadu Bello University, Kano, entitled, 'The Kaoussen Rebellion of 1916-1918 with particular reference to its impact on Northern Nigeria.' I am grateful to Professor M. Crowder for the loan of this dissertation.

10) See André Selifou, *ibid,* p. 55, and pp. 197-200.

11) M. Cortier, *D'une rive à l'autre du Sahara,* pp. 286-289.

12) Regarding In Ṣaṭṭəfan in Toureg history see pages 53 and 114.

13) *agaraf* is fruit of the *tagaraft*/tubulus, generally called cram-cram.

14) On the role of Mūsā ag Amastan in the 1914-1918 war, see Andre Selifou, *Kaoussen et la Révolte Senoussiste,* pp. 189-196, and H. Lhote, *Les Touaregs du Hoggar,* pp. 345-377.

15) Urvoy, *op. cit.,* pp. 95-97.

CHAPTER XIII

IMĀMS OF ABALAGH

The religion of the Prophet is our chosen religion.
The night departs and the day comes.
Deeds done by the virtuous we accept.
They are rivers of clear water.
Deeds which an evil man commits are not
Our religion. They form no part of it.
To forsake our religion is a disgrace,
Something said by the ignorant and the babbler.
It is our duty to teach and to repeat
To inculcate firmly and to recall
Everything which the pious have composed.
The mighty scholars of high status
Are the proofs and evidence of God.
They are His helpers, other men are ignorant
How different is their character and their faith.

Muḥammad b. Muḥammad al-Shafī‘,
(d. 1954) (Poet A)

The village of Abalagh is situated on the main road which links the town of Tahoua to Agades, the Air capital. It is set amidst a flat Sahelian plain of sparse pasturage, acacia trees, cram-crams and spiky bushes. Buildings of size are few, but among its mud houses is one adjacent to the road at the northern exit of the village. It is the property of Shaykh Muḥammad Ibrāhīm of the Kel Aghlāl Within it he has stored his collection of Arabic manuscripts. They are packed in some twenty-five 'canteens', locked within a long bare room to the right of the door.

This house is not the home of Shaykh Muḥammad Ibrāhīm who lives with his brother Shaykh and *Imām* al-Ḥājj Muḥammad b. Muḥammad al-Mu'min. They are the most respected *Ineslemen* of Abalagh district. Their religious, legal and political advice is sought by many Tuareg chiefs, poets or scholars who are campe within easy distance of Abalagh. Some of their visitors are Moors from Mauritania or Kel Intasar from Tagarōst or Gao. The centre of these men of piety and learning is to be found in two or three camp sites within a radius of some seven or eight miles of the modern village. The exact location depends on the needs of the herds of cattle, camels and goats which have declined in number during recent years of drought. The camp sites are not easy to find. One small valley bottom

5. Kel Intasar visitors to Abalagh

6. An *ineslemen* novice in the camp of Shaykh Muhammad Ibrahim of Abalagh

and its trees look very like others, one *egef* or hilly dune is indistinguishable from the next. Even members of the camp at times may be at a loss to guide.

One site for the camp is next to a grove in a dip a virtual wood of gnarled and twisted trees. The Tuareg tents are pitched around an impressive red termite hill. In all directions there are low goat-skin tents, each one of them protected by a fence (*eferag*) of thorn and lopped branches. Each tent, supported on a central T-shaped post, is so pitched that every breath of fresh wind may be felt within it. By the arrangement of matting around the tent, it can be turned to face either east or west at will, depending on the time of day, the position of the sun and shade, or the season of the year.

Shaykh Muḥammad Ibrāhīm is about fifty years old. Although Tamashegh is his mother tongue, he, his brother and other relations are deeply versed in Arabic The bias is towards the Classical language but the *Ineslemen* here are also influenced to some extent by modern idioms. Rarely an hour passes without a portable radio being tuned to London, Cairo or Algiers. Young Tuaregs who have studied Arabic in Algeria, Libya or Egypt come and go during vacations and visit relations

These *Ineslemen* are Kel Aghlāl, a branch of the Kel Dennek. The traditions of their history in earlier centuries has been mentioned in Chapter IX. The Kel Aghlāl are wholly Tuareg in their habits and bear the proud name of 'red' *Imazwaghan.* Many of them are tall and have a lean and sinewy physique. They dress in white and indigo, and they wear a white band above the turban and *lithām*. This band identifies them as *Ineslemen* and indicates their religious vocatio

Daily life, even during the most favourable seasons, can be monotonous and hard. Their life has always been a precarious balance between the fickle climate and the health of their livestock. In the day-time the herds of cows, goats and asses are taken to pasture. A shuttle service of servile labour, girls and boys on donkeys, carries goat-skins of drinking water from Abalagh village to the camp. The sound of the anvil of the smith or the pounding of mortars may disturb the silence of the inner camp. From time to time a little band of *Ineslemen,* or Moorish visitors who are guests of the Shaykh will descend on a certain tent. They may argue religious or secular affairs and drink glasses of sweet tea. At other times they ponder and meditate with bowed heads, sitting quiet and still.

The Kel Aghlāl are puritanical and devout. Yet their view of humanity is free from narrow dogmatism, and their Islamic faith is interpreted in an enlightened and practical way. One example is the Ramaḍān fast, the total observance of which is frequently impractical. Some compromise has to be made. While no food is eaten in daylight hours, glasses of sweet tea are taken by many, and Shaykh

7. Prayer on the march in Azawagh

8. Quranic teaching boards of the ineslemen in Lazaret Camp, Niamey

Muhammad Ibrahim and his brother, though abstemious themselves, do not prohibit others from this minor breaking of the rules.

To many who are familiar with the northern Tuaregs, or with the *Imashaghen,* the way of life of the Kel Aghlāl seems atypical of Tuareg customs. Yet, in many ways, there are echoes of the kind of life led by Izār of Tagedda in the days of Ibn Baṭṭūṭa. Here however, the womenfolk are strictly secluded or their movement restricted.

At every statutory hour the whole *aghoras* (valley bottom) resounds to the invocation of Allah's greatness and unity. The call to prayer is beautifully delivered. A group of veiled men laden with amulets, makes its way to the mosque. The latter is an open piece of ground surrounded by spikey *eferag.* The sole indication of its special function is a suspended skin which is taken down to serve as a prayer mat for the *Imām.*

The most solemn celebrations are reserved for the great feasts such as the *'Īd al-Fiṭr* which marks the end of the fast of Ramaḍān. On a prominence just above the camp Tuaregs gather in a circle and bow in meditation. The *Imām* of the mosque, Shaykh Muḥammad b. Muḥammad al Mu'min, Shaykh Muḥammad Ibrāhīm and relations sit in the middle circle all wearing new indigo robes. A visitor reads the sermon which he holds high in one hand, grasping a spear-like staff in the other. The same sermon is read each year on the day of this feast. After prayer the gathering slowly disperses. There may be a little camel racing but the simple life of the camp is preserved. No drumming is heard, and there is little to indicate that this day differs from any other. Only the thin crescent moon on the horizon and the excitement aroused by its appearance have disturbed the routine of the camp. A few gifts given new clothes worn or slaughter of sheep - it all depends on the state of the Shaykh's resources since he is responsible for the welfare of all throughout the year whatever their status. The struggle to preserve and better the health of the herds pre-occupies the camp, whether the day be a fast day or a feast. Nor will the absence of the Shaykh on pilgrimage and his return alter the cruel realities of a Sahel without rain or a depleted herd. This means less millet and less capital. It threatens the survival of the camp and continuation of studies.

II

The Imāms of the Kel Aghlāl

The Kel Aghlāl are ruled by a family of predominantly patrilineally related *Imāms.* Some of their names have been preserved in the archives of the camp.(1.)

'The tribe of the Kel Aghlāl is one from among the Ṣanāhija. From ancient times their status was of central importance among the other tribes. The reason for this was that it was normal for the *Imāmate* in the region to belong to them.'

The line of their *Imāms,* according to their archives, is:-

Usāma 1)

Isūf (Yusūf) 2) . . . . sister

(died a martyr in the battle of Shimānnaṣen (1814) against the Itisen.)

The son of Isūf's sister was *Muḥammad al-Jaylānī* 3) who held the *Imāmate* after the death of Isūf.

Muḥammad al-Ṣaḥḥū 4) . . . .

(went to Sokoto with Muḥammad al-Jaylānī.)

'Abd al-Karīm (d. 1906) 5)
(See note on *Ineslemen* legal problems on page 202)

Muḥammad al-Shafī' 6) d. 1920)
(ratified the peace treaty with the French.)

Muḥammad al-Mu'min 7)
(d. 1964) (aged 90)
(assumed the *Imāmate* after the death of his blood brother Muḥammad al-Shafī' .*)

Khalīl al-Raḥmān . . . (m) sister . . . . Muḥammad (d. 1954)
(Poet A.)

Muḥammad 'Abdullāh
(Poet B)

al-Hājj Muḥammad b. Muḥammad al-Mu'min 8)
(present *Imām*)

*During this period there was a dispute among the Kel Dennek. Among his rivals was Shaykh Muḥammad al-Fazzāzī who was a Mahdist leader of the fanatical *Murīdīn* who reached their peak in 1927. They were suppressed by the French. Muḥammad al-Fazzāzī, chief of the Ishsherifen was a noted Arabic poet and claimed that he visited Mecca and Medina accompanied by the Angel Gabriel. (2)

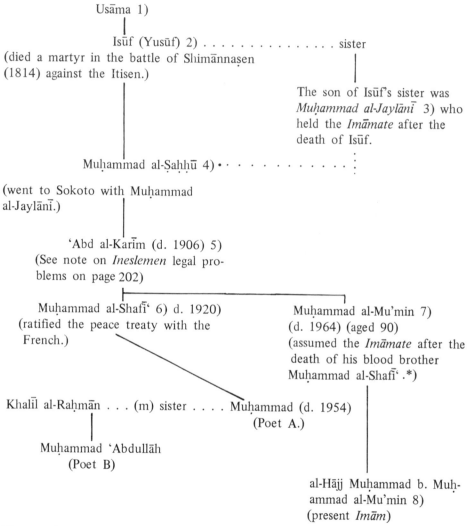

Influences which have shaped the Islamic ideas of the *Imāms* of Abalagh between 1900 and the present day are exceedingly varied. A study of the leading teachers and their pupils not only underline the important role played by Shaykh Bāy and his pupils, but also that of certain Mauritanian and Sokoto scholars. The influence of the Middle East is detectable in the poetry of those Kel Aghlālī scholars who visited the Sudan, Egypt and the sacred places of Arabia. The impression is one of an eclectic Islamic tradition, blending a schooling in the accepted classics of *Sharī'a* law and Sufism yet open to Middle Eastern influences and to some new ideas. The scholars concerned were capable of interpreting their thoughts among the Tuareg community as a whole and not merely exchanging academic ideas with their kinsmen among the *Ineslemen* of the neighbourhood.

Some idea of the recommended reading of the Kel Aghlālī scholars can be obtained by glancing at the list of works which appear in a lengthy poem by Muḥammad 'Abdullāh b. Khalīl (Poet B) al-Raḥmān b. Yūsuf who ranks among the greatest Arabic poets of the Kel Aghlāl of the twentieth century. He was related to the *Imām* Muḥammad al-Shafī' by his mother who was sister to Muḥammad b. Muḥammad Shafī', one of the *Imāms* sons.

The ode begins with the erotic prelude (*nasīb*) employed by the pre-Islamic poets, a recollection of the desert, the loved ones, more particularly 'she who cast the bracelet'; then lightening is suggested, the desert skies and intermittant rain-clouds; the fate of the nomad chiefs, men of virtue debased by the wicked who are described as 'the refuse of the Sahara.' The reason for this sorry state is the decay of Islam, above all the canonic law. Men have sought pleasures which the scholastic life could not afford. Voyages to discover learning were wasted, and the prized books in the libraries were lost for ever. Sufism had been rejected and ridiculed, 'Presence at litanies is a sin, their value is denied and deemed stupidity.' Islamic custom had been rejected in favour of pre-Islamic practices. Where were the springs of Islamic teaching to be found?

There were first of all the two greatest traditionists, Muslim (d.875) and al-Bukhārī (d. 870) These could be supplemented by other sources of the *Sunna* of the Prophet, or by collection of his *ḥadīths* or by works which amplified their content. Certain major works on tradition and jurisprudence had to be included, for example those by Abū Zakarīyā' Yaḥyā b. Sharaf al-Nawawī (d. 1278) and Abū 'Alī Muhammad b. Yūsuf b. al-Qādir al 'Abdarī b. al-Mawwāq (d. 1492) who wrote a commentary on the *Mukhtaṣar* of Khalīl. The other great interest of Sufism could be learnt in such major works as the *Iḥyā' 'ulūm al-dīn* by Abū Ḥāmid Muḥammad al-Ghazālī (d. 1111), in the works of 'Abd al-Wahhāb al-Sha'rānī (d. 1565), who combined both jurisprudence and Sufism in his arguments. Perhaps the most important scholar of all was Ibn 'Aṭā'allāh of Alexandria (d. 1309) whose

Sufi Aphorisms (*hikam*) had been classic reading in Sudanic and Saharan scholastic circles as far back as the fifteenth century. Because of the influence of Shaykh Bāy and his predecessors certain texts of the Kunta were particularly praised. Two were written by Shaykh Sīdī al-Mukhtār al-Kuntī (d. 1811), his *al-Kawkab al-waqqād fī faḍl dhikr al-mashā'ikh wa ḥaqā'iq al-awrād* and his *Naḍar al-dhahab fī kull fann muntakhab.* A third was the biography of this Shaykh and his wife *Kitāb al-Ṭarā' if wal-talā'id* by his son Muḥammad (d. 1826).

Certain major Mauritanian scholars are mentioned. They are Sīdī 'Abdullāh b. al-Hājj Ibrāhīm (d. 1818), and one of the scholars of the Tajakant. Another Western Saharan scholar mentioned is Shaykh Mā' al-'Aynayn (d. 1910), particularly his pan Sufi texts such as *Na't al-bidāyāt wa tawṣīf al-nihāyāt.* Also mentioned are compositions of the scholars of Sokoto. They include *Rimāḥ ḥizb al-Raḥīm 'alā (fī) nuḥūr ḥizb al-rajīm* by the Tijānī *mujāhid* of Futa Toro, al-Ḥājj 'Umar b. Sa'īd Tal (d. 1864), and the works of 'Uthmān Dan Fodio which had been familiar to the *Ineslemen* of Azawagh and Adar since the days of Muḥammad al-Jaylānī.

III

The biographies of Kel Aghlālī scholars of the early twentieth century

Scattered among the family archives of Abalagh are to be found copies of Arabic poems composed by men of letters, and short incomplete biographies which seek to perpetuate their memory and to record anecdotes and details of their teachers. (3) They are occasionally student efforts, but they are none the worse for that. Written in a clear Arabic style, free of the superfluous rhetorical praise found in some books of the Kel Es-Suq, they are composed in the long-standing tradition of these regions where biographical dictionaries have been prized and where fragments of poetic masterpieces have been included, framed in biographical description. The diversity of the studies is made apparent, also the close relationship established between master and pupil, the bond often extremely close by reason of familial ties.

Among these scholars, at one time a student, later a teacher, is a certain Shaykh al-Wālid who died before 1960; he was a companion of the leading scholars of Abalagh, Tchin Tabaraden and In Gall just before and during the Second World War. Pupils of his have left short biographies, and these often give first hand portraits of other scholars who were the most influential during al-Wālid's youth. Biographies of this type are many but they are often lost. They are never published and much of their record is likely to vanish.

'It is our concern and our duty to mention what happened to Shaykh al-Wālid during his blessed life. It is out obligation to do so. Mention will be made of his scholastic upbringing, and what he learnt from scholars, whether by word of mouth or by written text. I shall introduce what is at hand in mentioning his Shaykhs.

Shaykh al-Wālid in his youth began to recite the Qur'ān. He memorized it and perfected his acquaintance with it from his Shaykh and teacher 'Abd al- Ṣamad b. Ḥāmidun. That was due to the concern of his father, the late (*Imām*) Muḥammad al-Shafī'. (d. 1920). He perfected and learnt it by heart, but after that he forgot it due to the violent earth-quakes and the terrors of the affliction which came with the French to our country. At that time he was ten years old. After that he revised the Qur'ān until he learnt it again by heart.

This Shaykh of his 'Abd al-Ṣamad b. Ḥāmidun al-Aghlālī was pious and upright. He knew the book of God by heart. He recited it aloud during the night-time, and in the day-time. He was a tutor. He recited and taught the Qur'ān to young lads from his early years until he grew weak, and he was in his dotage. It was a remarkable thing about him, and I heard Shaykh al-Wālid report it of him, that as he increased in age, he likewise increased the range and compass of his knowledge of the Qur'ān. Shaykh al-Wālid held him in the highest regard and esteem. . . . .

. . . . Then Shaykh al-Wālid began to study the sciences - jurisprudence, grammar and syntax of Arabic, tradition, logic, language and literature and other branches of learning besides these. He learnt them from his Shaykh respected amongst scholars, a man of great understanding and comprehension, Shaykh 'Abd al-Raḥmān b. (Yūsuf) al-Aghlālī - then al-Mallālī - may God be pleased with him. Shaykh al-Wālid remained close to him all his life until he died. He was a respected scholar for his learning, for his piety, his abstinence and his comprehension of jurisprudence and Sufi doctrine and practise. He shunned worldly offices and any connection with princes or with Sultans. He was deeply versed in rare books, he quoted extensively, and he engaged in research both profound and extensive.

Throughout his life he continued to grasp new matters and to perfect such topics, and he would write them down, recording them with a fine hand. His comprehension was excellent, likewise his ability to compose and to express clearly and elegantly. The bulk of his learning depended upon tradition. In this respect he differed from all other scholars of our country, who, in a reactionary and rigid manner, relied upon texts of jurisprudence and upon nought else. He among the rest clung to the tradition of the Messenger of God in order to act by it and from it to derive rulings of the *Sharī'a*. He avoided those who follow their fancies and indulge in them and who use the canonic law in circumstances wholly inappropriate, inapplicable or contrary to its intention, for in that they went to excess, save for a few from amongst them . . . .

. . . . The Shaykh uncovered the concealed, he distinguished the good from the bad. He revealed to the people that there was no alternative but to act by authentic traditions, on the authority of the Messenger of God. God made him a reason for the true guidance of those in our country who had the least connection with learning, and an opener of their eyes to the true path to follow without error or fancy. This is clear from the start to anyone who is prepared to put his writings into practice.

He wrote many books in sundry fields. Some were original works, others commentaries. Despite their small size, yet sensitive and elegant style, they could not be dispensed with, nor superseded by books of length and bulk. Shaykh al-Wālid had debates and correspondences with Shaykh 'Abd al-Raḥmān, in poetry and prose, in every branch and field of learning. I shall record what I can of this after examination and investigation. Shaykh al-Wālid learnt from Shaykh 'Abd al-Raḥmān the teachings of the Qādirīya order, as he did so from many of his Shaykhs, like his Shaykh the Sharīf Muḥammad Maḥmūd b. al-Sayyid Muḥammad al-Amīn b. Jiddu al-Samlālī and like his Shaykh Sayyid A'mar b. Sayyid 'Alī b. al-Shaykh al-Raggādī al-Kuntī and others besides these two. In short, Shaykh 'Abd al-Raḥmān was among the mightiest Shaykhs of al-Wālid. He died - may God have mercy upon him - as recorded by the hand of the Shaykh al-Wālid - may God be pleased with him - on Monday, the 8th of *Jumādā II* in the year 1348 AH (Nov. 11th, 1929).

Among the mightiest of his famous miracles was his frequent prayer to God that He would decree his death to take place on a Monday. It came about as he had so wished. His father died a week later or less than that. Both of them were buried to the east of the village of Kajgar, towards the south. Now it is a huge cemętery. Shaykh al-Wālid composed an elegy for him on more than one occasion, among them being that elegy in which he lamented both him and his Shaykh Sīdī Maḥammad known as 'Bāy'. Its opening verses are:-

I came to the encampments, and I enquired who dwelt there,
Are my neighbours in your midst, are there those who

journey forth mounted on camel saddles?
They answered me that they had left the day before,
And had left behind them the traces of a camp-fire,
and their now deserted place of sojourning.

It is among the most distinguished odes, unequalled in the beauty of its art, the eloquent rhetoric of its opening verses and in the gentleness and sensitivity of its form and pattern. . . . .

He left a son and a daughter by the sister of Shaykh al-Wālid, and they were in his custody until his death. Today his son is our teacher Muḥammad 'Abdullah. He was among the company of the greatest novices of al-Wālid. As for his daughter, she is Fāṭima. Both are now living (1379AH/1960 AD). May God preserve them both and watch over them.

Also among his Shaykhs was Muḥammad known as al-Faqqi b. Bū Bakr al-Aghlālī. He was one among the company of the scholars of our country known for their learning and piety. Under his instruction Shaykh al-Wālid repeated and revised the reading of the *Mukhtaṣar* of Sīdī Khalīl to increase clarity of its contents, since this Shaykh was among those who were famous for knowledge of the exegesis of the *Mukhtaṣar* in the Tuareg language, an explanation and interpretation of it both precise and close to what is to be found in its (Arabic) commentaries. This closeness and aptness was unknown to most of the scholars. As for his death I have found nothing in regard to it. He left behind him a pious and God-fearing company of offspring.

Also among them were his two mighty and noble brother Shaykhs, pearls of the age and lights of the times, God's saint al-Qāsim and his brother Ya'qūb, the two sons of Ibrāhīm Id Daghmaniyān. Al-Wālid derived much profit from their sermons, their counsel and their guidance.

As for Abū 'Ā'isha, al-Qāsim, he was one of the saints of God. He was among those who had amazing psychic vision and perception. He united the *Sharī'a* with the reality of the truth. His energy was beyond description, labouring to learn and to adhere to the letter of the *Sharī'a* and in calling mankind to God. In regard to God he had nought to fear from the reproof of the reprover. At the same time he was severe in his asceticism and abstinence, a devout faster who failed not in his devotions to his Lord. He was a fighter in the *jihād* for the sake of the religion, both with the sword and with the tongue, and, on more than one occasion, he fled to his Shaykh and his teacher, the wonder of the age, the senior *Mujāhid,* Shaykh al-Ḥājj 'Uthmān b. Sambu al-Fūtī. He did so with his wife and his household. This was due to the intensity of his concern for the practice of the religion. He was blind towards the end of his life. To him are attributed miracles uncountable . . . .

As for his compositions I have learnt nought of these save that he correspond-ded and communicated with the scholars of his time such as his Shaykh, already mentioned, al-Ḥājj 'Uthmān b. Sambu al-Fūtī, Shaykh Bāy b. al-Shaykh Sīdī 'Umar al-Kuntī and others . . . .

Brother 'Īsā b. Muḥammadun mentioned with regard to him that he undertook the task of teaching after sunrise until the high forenoon and from the noon prayer until the *'Aṣr* (afternoon) prayer, and that his leader and principal helper, when he lost his sight, was Sīdī Maḥmūd al-Dabbakarī. He was granted his close companion-ship in this world and the next, since he was present at his death, and he died four days after him, and he was buried with him. He also mentioned about him that he was in a place set apart from political affairs since his brother Ya'qūb acted as his deputy. Remarkable about him was that whatever the situation might be he would mention God's name. How could it be otherwise. He was among the *Imāms,* the guides and the rightly guided ones. He died in the year 1344 AH/1925/6 AD. He was buried in the country of Alamāmāg at a spot called In Tamaẓẓūk. Now it is a huge cemetery and it is famous for its *baraka.* The spot is visited by the pious and illumination is bestowed by virtue of his mosque and his presence there in that locality. . . . .

He had offspring. None remain today save one, his grand-daughter, Zaynab.

As for the Shaykh and saint of God Ya'qūb, he was a superior lord and respected, abstemious, pious and God-fearing. He spoke little, but was of great humility and lowliness towards Almighty God. He died in the year 1354 AH/ 1935/6 AD, and he was buried at Tajīgalt. Thus it appears in the historical collection of our maternal uncle Muḥammad Ibrāhīm b. Muḥammad Al-Mu'min. I have seen the following passage written in the hand of Shaykh al-Wālid: - 'Ya'qūb was 87 years old when he died. It was in the year 1363AH/1944 AD. He left behind him a goodly number of descendants.

Among the Shaykhs of Shaykh al-Wālid was the great scholar, example of wisdom and understanding, one given to psychic power, rare spiritual visions and marvellous miracles Mamma b. 'Uthmān al-Kel Akkudī. His saintly miracles were manifested among the elect and the common people. He was truly one of the wonders of the age. Despite the severe unbalance of his personality from which he suffered at the end of his life, he was one who had only to be asked about an important matter, and he would be found to have a sound and intelligent apprec-iation of its import. Such an occasion was when Shaykh al-Wālid one day asked him about the truth of the affair of Muḥammad al-Fazzāzī regarding his claiming to be the expected *Mahdī.* He retorted, "Oh, youth, did you think that I could not fathom this question?" It was the only answer he gave him. This was something strange in his habit for he often would be met by people who would ask him about things which were concealed and hidden from them. He would give them a positive answer regarding the truth of their preoccupations. It came about that those who were ignorant obtained spiritual disclosures from him regarding the truth of occurences. They did so without understanding. This was due to error or fault on their part. He was favoured with power to elucidate dreams and visions. Two persons came to him, and what they saw was one vision. He expressed to one of them the opposite of that which he expressed to the other, yet the affair transpired just as he had predicted.

As for his books I know nothing of authorship, save for what I have seen written by Shaykh 'Abd al-Raḥmān b. Yūsuf al-Aghlālī, then al-Mallālī. It is a poem regarding the duties of ritual ablution and its text was attributed to him. As for his death I have seen in the hand of Shaykh al-Wālid the following passage - Shaykh Sīdī Mamma b. 'Uthmān died on Tuesday, the 12th of *Jumādā I,* at sundown in a village called Danwal near Kafa, westwards, while he was sick or during his famous fits of possession. It was in the year 1352 AH/ 1933 AD.

Also among the teachers of Shaykh al-Wālid was one whose renown filled all the horizons, the one who was the good counsellor of the community the erudite of the era Sīdī Maḥammad (with a *fatḥa* of the *mīm*) b. Sīdī 'Umar b. al-Shaykh Sīdī Muḥammad b. al-Shaykh Sīdī 'l-Mukhtār al-Kuntī, then al-Wāfī in lineage, and from Azawād in habitation. He had no equal and no peer in perceptivity and detailed knowledge of the sciences and perfection of them, combining the *Sharī'a* and mystic truth. He was a servant of God and an ascetic, one who undertook to call humanity to God throughout the day and night. He was among those who energetically travelled with camels both to east and to west to seek out learning. God singled him out by great and mighty *baraka.* May God disappoint us not in the outpourings of His copious flood of learning and the scented breezes of His blessings which He bestows.

This Shaykh was amongst those from whom Shaykh al-Wālid most truly benefited. I have touched on this and have pointed it out where I mention that he journeyed to meet him. Brother 'Īsā b. Muḥammadun said this about him in his commentary to the ode of the great scholar Alūjalī, in which he eulogized the scholars of our country. It is in his commentary to this verse from it, "The Shaykh of Shaykhs, men of knowledge of their Lord. I mean Maḥammad - renowned as Bāy." . . . .

Dozens of his answers have come to my knowledge. He also was the author of a splendid commentary on the traditions. It has no equal. He - may God have mercy upon him - appointed himself to teach and to issue *fatwās* until he changed his habit for the mercy of God and betook himself to a branch hut wherein he read books. He was isolated from the company of men . . . . . . He used to conceal his face, and would be seen only rarely. He was a calligrapher. I have not heard that he recited verse. To him all the people hurried and were assembled.

Such is the text of 'Īsā b. Muḥammadun, "After his death he was succeeded by his heir and his novice, Shaykh Sīdī Muḥammad b. Bādi al-Kuntī, who undertook the important task of collecting his answers. He did so, and he arranged them, systematically and well. He did so under pressure and haste because of the acute need of the people for it, and because the establishment of the faith demanded it . . . . "

As to the date of his death, I have made reference to it - 'ishā'-khamīs ṭak (4) rabī 'i th-thānī 'ām Ḥamshasa (5) māta Bāyu 'an sinni *Kajām.* (6) I mean by this that he died at the time of the evening prayer, Thursday the 29th night of *Rabī' II* in the year 1348 AH / Friday 4th of October 1929. He died aged 63, the same age as the Prophet. Here ends the quotation.

I have already mentioned in the biography of Shaykh 'Abd al-Raḥmān b. Yūsuf that al-Wālid composed a striking elegy for him and Shaykh Bāy. This obviates the need to recall their virtues and qualities. That dual elegy was due to their proximity in age and the fact that they died in the same year. He also said about Bāy in his *takhmīs* on the ode of the scholar Alūjalī wherein he eulogized the scholars of our country.

By him who combined two sciences, the *Sharī'a* and
God's mystic truth,
Refuge of widows and orphans; father, tribal guardian
and protector from abuse.
Succour of humanity, their pole, their meeting place,
and Shaykh of those who know their Lord.

In regard to Maḥammad, famous as 'their Bāy' I have also seen that his novice Sīdī Muḥammad b. Bādi composed an ode in which he praised him. I discovered it in the handwriting of Shaykh al-Wālid saying that he had copied it from the hand of its composer. It begins thus:-

If fate should wound you with its fangs, and you escape
not the slip which injures him who stumbles,
When brothers spurn you in their hate and enemies advance,
As fortune changes - mount in haste your camels with

high humps and tread the open desert waste in search of
victory.
Until you make your camels kneel where spears are cast,
The house of shelter offered by the shelterer.
He who is steadfast, will be extolled enjoying the
glory of the ages.
A sun whose light smothers the darkness of the infidel.
He is master of a light possessed neither by Mars nor
Jupiter.
He is master of the words he speaks, the deeds he does,
and knowledge which his mind reveals.
Bāy - what Bāy! If you fault him, then behold a swelling sea.
Bāy - what Bāy! Should you startle him behold torrential rain.
He is the essence of our ancestral fame, bearing their
legacy of learning and their deeds of pride.
Praise be to God - in sorrow and joy - Invincible Protector
from all hurt and harm.
What a profiter is the striver who attains the master of
the source of sciences and of holy power.
So clasp your hands as long as you may live and grasp
the fire of brimstone if it be within your grip . . . .

As for his miracles they are like the sun at noon-time. I have introduced a little regarding them when I mentioned the journey of Shaykh al-Wālid to visit him. (7) As for his offspring I learnt from my Shaykh and scholar-teacher, most understanding and most knowledgeable Muḥammad Lanā b. 'Abdullāh known as Balkhu al-Sūqī (al-Lamtūnī) the following which I quote, "Let the discoverer of this know that our Shaykh Maḥammad (with a *fatḥa* to the *mīm*) known as Bāy, son of the late 'Umar that of his male offspring the eldest was Sīdī Muḥammad, then Aḥmad, then 'Abdullāh, and our Shaykh, pure and pious and lettered, Muḥammad al-Amīn was the youngest of them. His daughters are Lalla and Mayja. Their protected clients are Khaṭṭāri and Abū Aḥmad and their blacksmith Ṭuwayhir.

Among the teachers of Shaykh al-Wālid was Sīdī Muḥammad b. Bādi al-Kuntī, then al-Wāfī . . . . From him he learnt a number of 'chains of authority'. I shall mention them from the corpus of the *asānīd* of Shaykh al-Wālid. This Shaykh was a mighty scholar. His equal can hardly be found in the midst of the country. He gleaned the sciences, virtue and *baraka* of his Shaykh Bāy. To boast it is enough to refer to his gathering and his arranging of his 'answers'. From them he made a book of systemized chapters, each independant. It is sufficient to mention his peerless works on every branch of learning. He supplied a commentary and versified the *Nuqāya* of al-Suyūṭī. He enhanced it with many branches of learning. He is still alive . . . . . . May God facilitate the privilege of my meeting him and grant me long to live so that I may learn and study from him.

As for his offspring and brothers, I learnt from my Shaykh and teacher-scholar Muḥammad Lanā al-Sūqī the following which I quote, "My Shaykh Sīdī Muḥammad b. Bādi and his brother Muḥammad and his sisters; al-'Āliya and Fāṭima, nicknamed Amma. As for his offspring they are Muḥammad al-Kuntī and his daughters Fāṭima and Khādim known as Hattun. His protected clients are Aḥmad b. al-Marḥūm known as Bamma and his blacksmith Kanni." End of quote.

Sīdī Muḥammad known as Ammak b. al-Bakkā' al-Kuntī, then al-Wāfī, was one of the Shaykhs of Shaykh al-Wālid. He was among the company of those who recited traditions and his knowledge and collection of *asānīd.* Shaykh al-Wālid encountered him once coming from the country of Air. He knew him in the company of Shaykh Bāy . . . . . . He is still alive according to my information. I heard Shaykh al-Wālid mention a long time ago that he was one of the outstanding novices of Shaykh Bāy, and that he appointed him as his deputy, so that he could pray the *Ramaḍān* night prayers (*tarāwīḥ*), and that Shaykh Bāy had a *ḥizb,* a section of the Qur'ān which he taught for the people after the afternoon prayer in the month of *Ramaḍān.* His novice followed him in the reciting of his text. Shaykh Bāy would make a statement while he would explain its commentary to the people.

Among his teachers was Abū Bakr, renowned by his nickname Būbī with a *bā'* as its first letter or a *gāf* Gūbī of Sokoto who was among the greatest and mightiest of the scholars of Sokoto. I have mentioned something of his biography in the journey made by Shaykh al-Wālid to Sokoto. As for his death I have no information in regard to it . . . .

Among his teachers was the lettered, scholarly and percipient Shaykh Wālī Yaḥyā al-Nawawī b. al-Wazīr 'Abd al-Qādir al-Ṣukkutī. He was among the company of his Shaykhs in the transmission of *ḥadīth* and traditions. I have written down those 'chains' of authority he learnt from him. I have briefly mentioned his biography when I cited the second journey of Shaykh al-Wālid to Sokoto. As for his death I have no information regarding it. I have heard from Shaykh Muḥammad 'Abd al-Raḥmān b. Ajdūd al-'Alawī al-Shinqīṭī that he frequently profited from him. This was when he met him in Sokoto. Each one of them benefited from the other. I have seen that Muhammad 'Abd al-Raḥmān aforementioned was the author of a *takhmīs* upon his ode rhyming in the letter *jīm.* It was among his miracles in the Arabic language. Why not when it was said of him that he had memorized the lexicon? There will follow some of that which I have discovered of his poetry in my collection of books and documents. It is from the collection brought by Shaykh al-Wālid and from his pupils and novices when he visited him in Sokoto.

He also learnt from Wālī Yaḥyā b. al-Wazīr 'Abd al Qādir . . . . . . Among the companions of Shaykh al-Wālid was the great scholar, man of understanding and much travelled Muḥammad Alūjalī b. Sayyid al-Bakkā' al-Aghlālī who was among those who enjoyed his special friendship. Much correspondence, in prose and verse, elegant discourses, literary feats and witty exchanges took place between them. Among these were poems about tea (8) (*at-tāy / shāhid*). From them are two verses which Shaykh al-Wālid sent in reply when Muḥammad Alūjalī wrote to him alleging that he had given him some leaves of tea which were not of a good kind or flavour . . . . Also on this subject are the following verses said by Muḥammad Alūjalī:-

Dissension in religion came about because of him who
introduced the use of tea.
Its sessions swept the land, but with it came neglect
In thinking of our Lord and in pondering man's destiny.
Vulgar jest can take away the virtues of prized qualities.
Superstitious yarns are feeble in their merits.
Tea is a greater looter of wealth than raids of mounted men.
It leaves a son penniless after he possessed all he
ever wanted.
But if one day he makes a firm resolve and gives up the
base delights,
Then that will be a day which cures the malady of the bowels.
Anxieties, sorrow and hidden sicknesses will be relieved.
It is a beverage which removes your need for goodly fare.
Yet there is no better way to feast a guest, be it in
town or village, desert or in the open pasturelands.

IV

Arabic poetry of the Kel Aghlāl

Arabic poetry is encouraged by the families of Abalagh. Tchin Tabaraden to the west, a nomad centre, also has its own poets and Arabic scholars. (9) Much of this literary activity stems from the traditions of Tadamakkat, Tagedda and the spiritual retreats of Air. The Abalagh poets express their Islamic beliefs in verses of 'beseeching' (*ibtihāl*), the topics of which are restricted yet are sometimes frank and stark in utterance. (10) Many poems are short, and the longest ode is rarely more than fifty verses.

Among the most gifted of the Abalagh poets must be counted al-Ḥājj Muḥammad 'Abdullāh b. Khalīl al-Raḥmān (Poet B) whose poem about the texts which the *Ineslemen* study has been summarized. He is the author of a yet incomplete but comprehensive *dīwān* of all the poetry of the scholars and heros of Abalagh entitled *al-Qawl al-fāriq min tārīkh abṭāl al-Ṭawāriq*. Having performed the pilgrimage and having spent some time in centres in the Arabic East his poetry has been influenced by ideas which are rarely found in the Sahel of Niger. The pull of the Arabic East is an important one. It is more marked here than it is in the poetry of the Moorish West. The following ode lamenting the decay of faith has ideas which clearly show the Tuareg authorship of the Arabic verses:-

Our great Sahara has customs false and base which
Contravene a *Sunna* proud and glorious.
All we observe is the letter of the law and tribal customs.
We are like a people who have camped unceasingly in one
wādī.
If the people forsake a duty, like the pilgrimage,
We follow them, yet they indeed have contravened a duty.
If they wear the veil (*lithām*) its wearing soon becomes
an obligation.
It is a garment black in colour and exclusive. It permits
no ritual ablution.
To journey forth, one day, such is our boast.
Thereby we hope for power but we are abased not glorified.
Our endless voyage is God's Saharan tribulation.
Oh, men of intelligence, concentrate and think!
With sober minds of reason and intelligence which are yours.
There is God's book. It has condemned blind faith without
thought.
Thought has surpassed and outshone pearls in spotless beauty.
I believed the human mind to be the supreme creation.
By it God revealed the faith and its observance.
How majestic is its power!
Those lands which are inhabited save for our country
Progressed. Their advance was rapid thinking with the mind.
They attained a prominent state on lofty heights,
While we were backward or retarded due to sterile custom
Amidst a community which God's book says,
Possessed what it deserved of treasures stored.'
It evolved in habitations in the wilderness, but it grew up
On deepening ignorance, denying us the power to think
and to perceive.
Many a youth of ours longs to awake and stay alert
But the wasteland has made him simple, blurred his memory.
By my father's life, to travel, always on the move, is
indeed a quickening,
Reminding us of resurrection and the assembling on judgement day.
The desert sun does not equip a nation
Seeking a corporate life in a community, or to build in freedom.
I have asked God, my Lord, for an abode more permanent -
Or else it is His will that I endure life patiently.

Among the most common of all these Tuareg Arabic poems are those described as *rithā'* or *marthiya,* that is to say an elegy and eulogy combined, and emotional expression of the loss felt by one scholar for the death of another.

Here is one, also composed by Muḥammad 'Abdullāh b. Khalīl al-Raḥmān (Poet B) for Shaykh Muḥammad Lanā b. 'Abdullāh 'Balkhu' (11) al-Kel Sūqī al-Lamtūnī, who 'died aged 60, before the sunset on Friday the last day of *Ṣafar* 1349/26th July 1930. His tomb lies to the west of Jabal Ingal in a locality called Awalawal':-

Is it because of a deserted camp whose traces are erased
That you tarry in a hidden trap of extasy, of love,
A place where tears are shed?
You ask about the one who halted in its open spaces.
My place of covenant with her - Asma' - wearing her
dainty shift.
A maiden who restores one silvery haired to radiant youth.
Such is her manner - the daughter who has dark tresses.
When she unveils her neck, alone and carefree,
Her beauty distracts the thought from strings of dangling onyx.
Oh, heart, forsake the recollection of fair maidens
and their company.
You are in a moment of separation.
Have you not heard? It seemed that our beloved teacher
Was only yesterday in the pangs of death.
Muḥammad Lanā, his origin from kinsmen of the Lamtūna.
He achieved distinction and was noble in his birth
And every quality he possessed.
His reputation was of highest praise, yet he was lowly.
He was among those few who were abased only to be exalted.
After the 'maternal uncle' (Muḥammad b. Muḥammad al-Shafī')
he was renowned for knowledge and for abstinence.
He was, for us, one who was unique, one solitary who
Compensated for a gathering of men.
Chaste was his ascetic life, how patient in his solitariness.
His remoteness from all worldly things was his true nature.
He inclined to the pious, he yearned for that host
Who glorify the Almighty in the Seven Heavens.
Every problem he divined with sharpest thought.
If one day you came to him to solve a question
In hospitality you would stay amidst fertile vales.
How full he was of joy, upon his countenance was a
frank delight.
A companion's heart, free from parsimony and all hardness.
For us, people of the veil (Kel Tagilmus) his was a nature
Wherein benefits and godly things have now been lost.
We deprecate our men of learning. We flee their portals,
And we disdain to knock upon their doors.
Our scholar lived his life held in low esteem
And knowledge shone forth from him though in darkness.
The day of separation was of grave concern to us.
It left behind a spacious rent beyond repair.
In one dark night we returned to ignorance of learning
and of science in every branch.

Faith, grammar, syntax and canonic law.
Nights spent in research in books, after his death
Were nights spent in research in bogus saws and slanderings.
After his passing to another world, our brethren's zeal
was spent in worldly gain, boasting of hoarded goods.
Lord of Mercy, prepare for our Shaykh treasures of grace
Cleansed from marks of fire or trace of soot.
When clouds of mercy should, one day, bring rain, then
Order them to wash his tomb repeatedly.
Blessing be upon the secrets of existence and its light
Upon Muḥammad, chosen one, whose task was God's alone
Also upon his family and his Companions, for we have
Been fashioned to love them and to offer praise,
Be it in prose, blank verse or poetry, and extended ode.

The Islamic tradition of the Niger *Ineslemen* is a living tradition but it will survive only as long as the *Ineslemen* survive. It could be stimulated by the traditions shared in common with their fellow-countrymen of other ethnic groups in Niger and with the Islamic ideas emenating from Algeria to the north and from Libya, to the east. There are Tuaregs in both these Arab countries, but in Niger, as in parts of Mali, the *Ineslemen* draw upon a legacy of scholars who among their number include the founders of their tradition in the early Middle Ages.

It is curious that an almost excessive preoccupation with mortality and the hereafter should be a literary stimulus. Fatalism is not applicable in this context. It is difficult to justify from Islamic texts, nor can it explain the violent zeal of Tuareg 'Mahdīs'. Perhaps the *manes* worship of the ancient Libyans may have continued as a subconscious influence on their poetic imagination. Thus the statement of Herodotus (12) that among the Nasamones men who took oaths lay their hands upon the tombs of those considered to have been pre-eminently just and good, and in so doing swearing by their names, may be matched by those sentiments of the Tuareg descendants.

However, it would be wrong to think that only in *Ubi Sunt* the recollection of deceased scholars and warriors, or regret at the passing of the age of faith religious emotions is kept alive. Scholars and *Imāms* still living and at Abalagh and elsewhere are the contemporary exponents of this belief and maintain close association with the living (See Appendix B) The following verses of Muḥammad 'Abdullāh b. Khalīl al-Raḥmān, composed in Khartum as an elegy for his maternal uncle Shaykh Muḥammad b. Muḥammad al-Shafī' in 1954 concerns itself with the future and foreshadows the disasters which were to befall the whole Tuareg community, among them the *Ineslemen* of Abalagh in their tents and thickets surrounded by dying herds of cattle in the Sahel drought.

Your sky is cloudy. Its happy stars have departed from it.
Your earth grieves in wretchedness. Will you not tend it?
In the sky there are stars which foretell rain, but
they lament in sorrow.
Wherever lightening flashes, and the thunder rages,
At first the earth's shoots, its adornment
Are dry and of meagre benefit, pale in stem and shoot.
Our days as they advance encounter handicaps which
block their progress.
You know that the life of this world is one of change
and of upheaval.
Mens' palaces can be found in it, so too their sepulchres.
By the life of my father there is great heat and passion
in my soul.
Can shock and passion fiercely burn due to the ardour of
its flame?
Has an irreparable loss afflicted the faith of Aḥmad?
Some seem pleased. Its event to them was sweet.
'Yes', they observed, 'Muḥammad - spirit of 'the Great One'
Is a major influence, a power for good, and it guides.
But worldly life is so confined in scope.
God the Merciful was responsible for it. Yet He does
not enrich it.'
I spoke to them, 'What you first said is sound, that I concede.
Your comments afterwards - well - who can testify?
They said, 'Man lives here, then he is forgotten.'
Your sky is cloudy. Its happy stars have departed from it.
On the horizon, tents of Ifrīqiyā have begun to disappear.
When their centre posts collapsed they were without support.
Oh, Community of the Prophet, such is your recompense
The favour of the Lord is faced with disbelief.
Grace, when you disbelieved in it
Mounted heavenwards towards the watery bower of Paradise.
The days of that peerless one, after his departure to
another world
Were dearly sought for by the envious.
The world, only with labour, bestows a goodly lord.
One who tends a steed, as he once did for men
And led them.
He was a *Rukn* and a *Qibla* in the land. (13)
Its lions were led by him through trials and tribulations.
He was a Shaykh for scholars. But after his decease
The bonds of ignorance round men of learning squeezed
yet tighter.
In his time the life of the country prospered.
But after his death, its banners were new furled.
Such is truly death, for the world's joy dies with it.
The deserted camps of the Prophet's religion are a
place remote.
The troops of his community intensify their weeping.

Our fancies toyed with a divine *Sharī'a* until its bounds
no longer mattered.
Where is the one we hope will splint and mend our fractured bones?
Men of reason among us have lost their hold.
Where is the one who after al-Shafī' and his son
We can address and say, 'The emissaries of the world
have come to you.'
I thought the women of the universe were barren, and those
who nursed had breasts which swelled and then ran dry.
If they mentioned a day, such sorrows were those things
they mentioned,
Weak and feeble, despite the heritage of our father.
We are like women but with bracelets unadorned.
In the (Ephesus) cave the dog slept after the awakening
of the Sleepers.
While the Sahara desert's slumber grew yet deeper.
There is not amongst us one who is wise nor wakeful,
by whom the world may recover and covenants be fulfilled.
Our 'redness' (as Imazwaghan) is lost. It has been
humbled, likewise shamed are women whose cheeks were of
a beauty unsurpassed.
Oh, grief. Life in the desert is a plague and torment.
Even if its milk flowed in abundance, its hides plentiful,
And if it brought advancement and our increase,
Your land would still remain in sorrow and in misery.
I am not the man to shepherd it.

NOTES

1) In a note given to the author by Muḥammad al-Mukhtār quoting Shaykh Muḥammad Ibrāhīm of Abalagh.

2) Referred to in several Tamashegh poems published by F. Nicolas in *Bull. de l'IFAN'* Tome VI, 1-4, 1944.

3) The texts are located in collection *A*.

4) *ṭak - degh (dég)* - the Tamashegh word meaning 'in'.

5) Probably H - m - s - sh - 8-40-300-1000 = = 1348 AH.

6) Probably K - J - m - 20+3-40 = 63.
See Dr. H. Gwarzo 'The theory of Chronograms as expounded by the 18th century Katsina astronomer, mathematician Muhammad b. Muhammad.' Centre of Arabic Documentation, University of Ibadan, *Research Bulletin,* Vol. III, no. 2, p. 116-123.

7) A portion missing in the texts copied in collection A.

8) Both words *'at'ei (thé)* also found in the Moorish Ḥassānīya dialect, and *shāhid (*Ar. *Shāy*) are in current use in Tamashegh in Abalagh district.

9) Appendix B p. 205 and collection *A. N.*, manuscript 1167.

10) See the poems on pages 191, 194, 195.

11) See page 47. Rodd refers extensively to a chief called Belkho in *P.V.*, pp. 25, 50, 75, 146, 191, 243-244, 305-6, 436, 444.

12) Herodotus IV, 172. See also Cortier, pp. 290-291, regarding consultation of the dead.

13) See page 146. 'He (like Mecca) was the person towards whom all among his community turned their gaze.'

CHAPTER XIV

THE SCRIPTURE OF THE GLAIVE-GIRT CAMELEER

'What will not be will never be, the potential will
come to pass,
What is potentially there, in time, such will be.'

From a poem by Muḥammad 'Abdullāh b.
Khalīl al-Raḥmān al-Aghlālī.

Those who know the Tuaregs well have often claimed that they are unduly lax and superstitious and somehow alien to the ethos of the Muslim world. This view is not shared by my Tuareg friends. Shaykh Muḥammad Ibrāhīm of Abalagh is versed in history and has ample texts in Arabic to prove the Muslim piety of Tuaregs from many classes and tribes. Professor al-Qāsim al-Bayhaqī and al-Ḥājj 'Abdu Malam Mūsā, both knowledgable of the Arab world as well as the lands of the Tuaregs, are of the opinion that their kinsfolk are neither more nor less 'religious' than any other Muslim people. The Kel Es-Suq have been complimented by their Arab neighbours. Lettered Arab merchants from Tuwat or Moors from Timbuctoo quote the pious verses of the Kel Es-Suq with admiration.

The flame of zeal has sometimes burnt low between periods of enlightenment. A devout *Anislem* may be narrow-minded and superstitious. His colleague may be of an enquiring outlook, alert, open to new ideas yet equally religious.

The full story of the contribution of the Tuareg lettered to the Islamic life of the Sahel will never be known. Early books have vanished, and chronicles which once recorded Islamic practise and faith are so scattered that to hope to see more than an outline is unrealistic. Much of the Islamic tradition was and is oral. Some documents survive outside the Sahel, in Cairo, France and perhaps in Tripoli and Istanbul. Oral traditions and archaeological research remain alternatives in helping to piece events together. A detailed study of Islamic groups and *Ineslemen* communities may tell us something of the historic factors at work in past ages.

Yet there is enough evidence to show that the Tuaregs in Azawagh, Tadamakkat (as-Sūq), Air and Tagedda were talented, sophisticated and open to influence from Morocco, Tunisia, Egypt and Arabia. They were able to found towns and communities of a settled or semi-settled nature, and they were able to employ their skill as caravan organisers, to use to their advantage the local presence of salt or copper.

In the Sahel they were to become owners of large herds of cattle and innumerable clients which contributed to the necessary leisure needed by the *Ineslemen* in order to study, write or formulate laws for the whole of the Tuareg community.

The flexibility of Tuareg social systems enabled the Massūfa, Lamtūna and other alien elements from Tuwāt, the Fezzan and Morocco who settled in Tadamakkat, Tagedda and Agades to be absorbed in Tuareg society. They learnt Tamashegh and the *Ineslemen* employed the language to furnish elaborate commentaries and abridgements of mystical poems and treatises and the minutae of texts of jurisprudence culminating in a Tamashegh version of the Mālikī legal manual, the *Mukhtaṣar* of Khalīl. The Tuareg towns and Sultanates and major geographical regions were the crossroads of the Sahel. It would be false to conclude that the Islamisation of the Tuaregs was synonomous with 'Arabisation' - whatever the latter meant in a pre-nationalist age. Arab or non-Arab is an absurd dichotomy in the context of the cosmopolitan culture of Sahelian Islam. The growth of Tuareg political institutions came about by culture contact in all directions. It evolved naturally in their own community, particularly among the *Ineslemen* and in its turn had an influence on the *Imashaghen* and on adjacent Sahelian societies which lived side by side or came under Tuareg political control.

The Air Sultanate owed much in nomenclature and administrative methods to Mamluk Egypt. Formal profession of recognition between Sultan and subject and ultimately to a Cairene Caliph, referred to as *bay'a,* appeared again and again in texts or in Tuareg investitures. The investiture of the first Mamluk Sultan in Egypt by the collective decision of the *Amīrs* and the ability to seat and depose Sultans is echoed in pages of the Agades Chronicles. The servants of the Sultan, 'men of the pen', 'men of religious duties and offices', and 'the men of the sword' were all represented in the Agades Sultanate. The military men of the latter were the *Imashaghen* who were 'tribes of the King'. It is possible that the 'wars of the Kel Imeglalen' to whom the ruin of As-Sūq is attributed may refer to wars among the military élite, for this Tamashegh term can mean 'people of the swords of chivalry', and idea which could have been copied from the Mamluk East. The debt to Mamluk ideas is revealed in the correspondence with Al-Suyūṭī. The division of Air into fiefs and the attempt to model the Sultanate land-tenure on Mamluk lines seem clear from the documentation which has so far been discovered.

Islamic culture had been diffused by the Massūfa from Walāta to Tagedda in the fourteenth century. They retained matrilineal forms of succession, more particularly a man's inheritance by his sister's son. No contradiction between this and Islamic principles was then generally raised by jurists in the communities concerned. This custom survived in the Air Sultanate until the sixteenth century, if not later. Even in the strictest *Ineslemen* groups today some preference in the female line remains.

The great advocate of rigid patrilineal succession was undoubtedly al-Maghīlī whose teachings swept the area of Tagedda, Gao and adjacent areas in the beginning of the sixteenth century. His replies to Muḥammad Askia are forthright on this issue and were uncompromising. (1) The Kel Es-Suq and the other Ishsherifen were compelled to favour a patrilineal system if only for lineal reasons. Their prestige and existence as a prominent *Ineslemen* group demanded it. Ruses to equate matrilineal lines with those of male eponyms were extensively employed. They appear so late in their texts that the process must have been a relatively recent one, within the last four hundred years. Fāṭima, the Prophet's daughter, and 'Alī, his son-in-law, were useful in symbolically binding the two forms of succession. Other *Ineslemen* were of Mauritanian origin, the Kel Aghlāl for example. They were descended from the Lamtūna or the Lamṭa. A great deal of variety or compromise between the choice of succession - either Arabian or Tuareg - had been observed among them since the eleventh century if not earlier.

The *Ineslemen* intermarried with Arab and non-Arab Muslims. The fact that they were able to retain so much of their Tuareg life testifies to their ability to select or reject customs which either suited or were irrelevant to their social life and its needs. Arab heros and tales of town foundation or religious expeditions were to be rephrased by them or re-interpreted. The thesis that patrilineal principle and 'Arab' influence are intimately or indissolubly linked in the Islamisation of the Tuaregs is unproven, and many exceptions show it to be a theory which cannot be accepted.

Islamic influences endow the *Ineslemen* with a particular facility in mixing with the Arab peoples which adjoin the northern borders of the Sahel, and with the Egyptians and the Saudi Arabians. Scholars from the latter have recently visited *Ineslemen* groups to examine Arabic documents, Tuaregs have studied at Al-Azhar University in Cairo, or have held teaching posts in Algiers, Tunis and Libya. In finding translators, interpreters and secretaries in the Arab world, Niger for example has discovered that those least wedded to French colonial education, most advanced in Arabic studies both Classical and modern, were most often to be found among the *Ineslemen* of Azawagh or in parts of Air.

Ineslemen who cherish the best of the past heritage, so relevant for a possible future, could have useful ides to offer. Others, sad to say, see no value in progress and are bitter foes of the twentieth century. In some groups the *Anislem* is viewed with suspicion, even contempt. At best he is portrayed as an ambivalent and rather ineffectual figure. He mediates and is consulted but he seems to take little active part in positively shaping the future of the group or the tribe he is supposed to serve. There is a belief that one sacrifice made, however worthy, demands some compensation to the devil. The death of one if it draws upon the powers of the supernatural invested in the *Ineslemen* may require the ultimate price. There is a balance in nature which is distinct from the moral law, and it must be respected if social relationships are to be preserved. Fixed bounds are set, and it could be fatal to transgress them.

A tale, found among the Iwillimeden, tells of a mother and her son. The latter became acquainted with a girl to whom he became deeply attached. One day they journeyed in the company of a griot whose playing excited much dancing and singing. At the height of the rejoicing a serpent bit the boy. His mother, his girl friend and the griot were in despair when they saw him grow sick and his body become weak. They consulted the *Anislem* who was seated among his novices They besought his help to save the life of the boy. The *Anislem* pondered. He ordered that a fire should be lit, and he told the mother that if she fell on the fire her son would live, and she would not be burnt. His mother advanced boldly but the heat was fierce and overcame her. Three times she made the attempt but failed. The girl came to the *Anislem.* She asked him whether it was only the boy's mother who could risk the flames. 'No, anyone,' he replied. The girl leapt into the fire. The fire went out, and the boy arose cured of his snake-bite and restored to full health. The girl was unhurt. The *Anislem* spoke, 'A price must be paid for the cure of the boy. Some restitution must be made to the serpent for the loss of his poison. The price must be either the death of the mother or the death of the girl.' With this awful choice the story ends in a dilemma. The *Anislem* could only interpret the law of nature, he could not plead for the lives of any one of the participants. The question is posed to the audience to whom the tale is told. The Tuaregs who listen must decide. The spectators have the ultimate choice, but this choice is difficult since the slaying of the serpent is not one of the options. Were it to be slain, then the boy's mother would surely die . . . . . Such is the eternal dilemma of life, and the *Ineslemen* have only limited powers to control it.

The *Ineslemen* are believed to control the rain. They can either bring it or restrain it. The Ishsherifen in particular have this power. Certain among them are given the nickname or title of *Egag,* a word which denotes the thunder-cloud and by extension rain. Aḥmad (Akhmad) Egag who was one of the Kel Es-Suq, but whose activities took him to Air, was among the most famous of them. An *Egag* maintains an equilibrium. He can prevent a total drought by prayers or by other acts of intercession which help to assure regular and seasonal rainfall. By it, the life of the herds and flocks which live on the pasture is preserved. Yet he is also able to ensure that the rain does not fall to such excess that the earth is flooded, and the tents and herds are washed away. He is conceived as a cloud or as a celestial sponge in years of extreme drought or inundation.

The limitations and options open to the *Ineslemen* are far from clear or uniform. They may be governed as much by the stars as by the Almighty. They may depend on magical forces which have little or no direct connection with moral laws or the supreme power in the universe. It is the task of the *Ineslemen* to discover laws which may not be apparent. To do so they have delved deep into the archives of the Islamic and ancient world. They have copied books or made abridgements and have borrowed ideas. In a future full of uncertainties, their own future is the least certain of all.

How much of the *Ineslemen* Islamic legacy in hidden texts will survive is doubtful. Even now rare books are being discovered in copies or in original format. How much remains to be discovered is unknown. In the Sahel and the Sahara legends are woven about holy books as they are almost about everything which is rare and prized.

Among the Kel Aṭaram there is a widespread tale about the cave of Gīdma. At no great distance from Menaka, near the border between Mali and Niger, there is a rocky terrain in which caves may be seen. One of them is called Gīdma. It has a narrow mouth but upon entry the walls of the cave steadily become wider and higher and lead into a hall-like chamber; on its sides are engraved Tifinagh and Arabic inscriptions. No intruder should venture beyond this chamber, for to do so would lead him into an unending labyrinth of tunnels. He would lose himself and perish.

The chamber is not empty. In it there is a vast library of the Kel Es-Suq who have deposited their precious books there. Loose pages are tied and wrapped in covers of leather, skin or wood. Their leaves are filled with verse and prose written in black or coloured inks, all in the archaic Kufic script of the people of Tadamakkat. Few have seen these books, but many are those who believe them to be there - either a piece of exaggerated reality or a secret wish - the books of Gīdma symbolize the scriptures and the memories and the wisdom of the glaive-girt cameleer.

NOTE:-

(1) See *As'ilat al-Asqiyā wa ajwibat al-Maghīlī* edited by 'Abd al-Qādir Zabādīya, Algiers, 1974, pp. 57-62.

APPENDIX A

A note on Ineslemen legal problems

The *Imāms* of Abalagh are not wholly preoccupied with teaching a small group of the *Ineslemen.* They are involved in practical every day issues, and since they are totally responsible for the welfare of the artisans and other servile members of their camps they are obliged to make judgements on legal problems or to consult other scholars as to how these may be resolved. Their role in this respect differs in no way from that of the Kel Es-Suq, the Kunta or other Sahelian pastoral nomads. Nonetheless their relatively close proximity to Sokoto and Hausaland has made them rely on those quarters for help in untangling complex legal issues. As has been seen, this consultation was a marked feature of the relationship between Muḥammad al-Jaylānī and Muhammad Bello. At that time the Dundaye district of Sokoto had many Adarawa Tuareg refugees. They needed a special judge for proceedings in Tamashegh.

One legal case is to be found in a letter sent by the *Mujāhid* 'Uthmān b. Samba to the *Imām* of the Kel Aghlāl, 'Abd al-Karīm b. Muḥammad (d. 1906). The father of the latter had gone to Sokoto with Muḥammad al-Jaylānī, and his son maintained close links with the scholars of that city.

'Greetings to the blessed Shaykh and *Imām* 'Abd al-Karīm b. Muḥammad and all with him. I have received a letter the subject of which is a debate which has taken place in your midst. It concerns a man who married his slave woman to one of his slaves. Then that master began to make love to her in secret while she was in the protection and sole possession of the slave, her husband. She bore a child in those circumstances. Then that slave left her, and she married another slave. Then the master removed her from her last husband with the intention of taking her as his concubine. She refused. The master threatened to sell her and her daughter. So she consented, and he took her as his concubine. The master claimed that her daughter whom he had begotten while she was in the protection and custody of her first husband was his own. Then he died. A dispute arose between the heirs regarding the daughter. Was she daughter of the slave, her mother's husband, and therefore his, or was she daughter of the master who had claimed that she was his, thereby becoming a free person and an inheritor? This is what your letter informed me . . . .

God knows best. This girl according to the interpretation of the jurists (*fuqahā'*) of the apparent intention and content of the *Sharī'a* cannot be a true daughter of this master and an heir of his by the mere claim which he made. I do not say that she is not a daughter of his in reality but in the circumstances wherein he committed the act because this act of his is an infringement of the *Sharī'a* since the preservation of lineage is an obligation in the *Sharī'a* established so by consensus. It is said because of that God made adultery and fornication unlawful, and He prohibited free and illicit contact and association with women so that men would not be like brute beasts, and so that none would be unjustly treated by another. He who marries off his slave girl must not approach her in order to have intercourse with her since it is unlawful for anyone to approach a woman who is married while she is protected and guarded by her spouse even though she be his slave girl, because of what I have already said to you - namely, that the preservation of lineage is a legal obligation, and it is unlawful for two men to join together in one woman in intimate relationship.

The jurists said, that "chaste women who are guarded and protected" means those who are married and have husbands. Then God Almighty said, "Save that possessed by your right hands." The jurists said this verse refers to women captives taken in infidel territory (*dār al-ḥarb*). Intercourse with them is lawful after purification, even if they are married, since their capture in *dār al-ḥarb* destroys the marriage union. A group of jurists said, "Save that possessed by your right hands.," means possession by marriage rights. So it is unlawful for anyone to carnally approach a woman when she is married save after she has left the protection and custody of her husband and after her purification. He who acts to the contrary and who commits forbidden things and who shares other men's womenfolk, then his offspring is the son of him who has sole protection and safeguarding of the woman according to the *Sharī'a,* since the Prophet said, "The offspring belongs to the bed." Every child is in this category. He can only belong to the husband who protects and safeguards. Between the two run the rules of inheritance. The husband is never free of it save by the curse or the likes of it when the marriage is dissolved. The origin of this is the tradition of the Prophet which I have already quoted. It is an authentic tradition. Ibn 'Abd al-Barr said that the *ḥadīth,* "The offspring belongs to the bed" is among the most authentic narrated on the authority of the Prophet. It has come down on the authority of some twenty or more persons among his Companions. One of the jurists said, "The rightful claim to the son is that of the natural father," is an absolute statement only in respect of the 'free woman'. As for the slave-woman, then the avowal of paternity is not that of the master unless he acknowledges it personally or, let us say, by trustworthy testifiers. What I have told you is this, "The offspring belongs to the bed" is a matter for the spouse who possesses the protection and custody and safeguarding. This is what we know from the jurists . . . . . .

The situation as that presented to me regarding this problem of yours over this girl - God alone knows best - the uncertain position regarding her case at this time . . . .

This girl most clearly would appear to be of the master as he so alleged. However, I do not say that she should inherit him, because that is not firmly established and because he would be committing that which is unlawful in the *Sharī'a,* since he accosted his slave woman when she was married and she was with her husband. Undoubtedly God Almighty said in His mighty book that they should preserve their sexual parts for their spouses or "that which their right hands possess. They will be blameless." But that applies also to the unmarried among slave women on account of that which I told you, namely that the preservation of lineage is an incumbent duty in the *Sharī'a* by consensus. I do not say either that this daughter is an 'inherited slave women' because this master made the claim himself; he alleged and confessed that she - the offspring - was his own, and she was the daughter of his slave women.

Hence I have said that you should be in an undecided position in regard to her problem, then if you find able physiognomists attach her to either one or the other and let her be his on account of that. This is what has occurred to me regarding this problem of yours over the affair of this girl. God Almighty knows best of the true reality in all affairs.'

APPENDIX B

Poetry collected by Muḥammad agg Dā'ūd of Tchin Tabaraden. (A.N. No. 1167)

In the name of God the Compassionate, the Merciful, the blessing and peace be upon the noble Prophet. This is a poetic composition by one of the lettered. It is beneficial and is a reminder to the one who cares for his religion and his good manners:-

The 'little slave' of his lord, al-Bashīr, 'the joyful messenger', the repentant towards his Lord, the Mighty Decreer, has said:-

In the name of God, praise be to God, the blessing upon
the Prophet.
To proceed - this is a counsel given and perchance to
be praised,
So pay regard to it and show concern, Oh, Muḥammad! (1)
It will be of help for both the young and old.
If they memorize it neither shame nor disgrace will
rest upon them.
Within its contents there are obligations, celebrated maxims.
Say and act according to them.
Do not pray as if it were a game.
Pay serious heed. It is an act accomplished well.
Be punctual on the hour, be not remiss, and with regard
to prayer's ablutions be not changeable.
In prayer behave not as a soul perplexed. Be wise in
adopting the postures of the prayer,
Especially in your bowing and your standing, also in
prostration, Oh, young man!
Place your hands opposite your ears, and keep away the
stomach from your thighs.
Do not fall down like a camel when you bow your knee.
Place not your hands opposite your buttocks.
Pick not the ground, like the pecking of a cock.
Such is the action of the careless weakling.
If you arise or if you sit, keep calm or still before
the task in hand.
Glance towards the right in uttering the *salām*. (2).
Raise not the head as though in salutation to the public.
Between your two prostrations, move not an index finger,
and when you give your *salām*, refrain from indicating
with the hands.
Belch not on purpose. The rite of prayer is not an
incoherent act.
Such is wisdom gleaned by one who has heard the words
of *al-Shabrakhītī* and the *lawāmi'*. (3)

Raise not your hands before you utter the first 'God is great'.
In prayer be not for ever rubbing and scratching,
refrain from yawning and giggling, for
Such is evidence that this man in prayer, is inattentive when he prays.

Piety towards one's parents:-

Be resolute. Devote your will to performing filial acts especially towards your mother, then her mother.
Show not obstinacy towards your parents. Anger is heard and then abates.
When they have ended their reproof, apologize in words both soft and smooth.
Imitate God's word, 'Your Lord has decided'.
Make your heart free and open, like the boundless space.
If you find one who is more experienced than you in some affair, yet you know the contrary to be sound, display not disbelief, listen to him well,
Until it is as if he were about to make a gift to you.
Act likewise if you hear him tell an old wives' tale. (4)
listen to him as though it were a marvellous thing
which you had never come across or it had never crossed your mind.
This is polite behaviour and good manners. Act accordingly.

How to behave in the Assembly

Attend not a gathering where the foolish sit, retire and keep apart. Sit beside those who are intelligent and alert.
If necessity demands the sufference of fools, add not to their number.
Face the fellow sitter, do not stare intently.
Listen to his discourse, though it a repetition be.
Interrupt not his speech even though it weary by irrelevant digression, or by a reminiscensing.
Outwardly you will be listening, while inwardly you will be reflecting, humble and content.
When speaking pay close attention. Control yourself,
for fear lest you may slip and thereby err.
More often it is your duty to be silent, especially when those of age or dignity are in attendance.
If you speak, be informative and constructive. Do not repeat yourself.
Avoid insinuation and falsehood, boasting, argument and oaths.
Do not litigate, be restrained in jest, in laughter and
in brash request.
Too much heedlessness and entertainment are among those

things which incur the wrath of God.
In a polite assembly substitute the finesse of circumspect address.
For every word which, if addressed direct to a participant will seem uncivil, rude or harsh.
If you recite grammar, add not a fancy *Hamā* before the one whom you address, in second person; and this before the man who is intelligent. (5)
Sleep not in a gathering. Such is a disgrace; since, without exception, 'He who sleeps knows not.'

How to treat dependants

Be not like the man who is sharp and bitter whenever you hold forth against dependants.
Their obedience, in my view, is best acquired by the rule of affection, rather than by the common dictum, 'fear is best'.
For the Prophet commanded you to be one who evokes love in your family.
Abuse not slaves - neither man nor woman - and treat womenfolk with clemency and kindness.
Descend to their level in intelligence. Allow for this in what is said.
Enjoy their company - how much in the Prophet's life and word is thus evoked.

How to treat the rest of humanity

Converse kindly with the whole of humanity, set no bounds, be it the lowliest of mankind.
Harbour not evil thoughts regarding men, beware of their outward aspect and their circumstance.
Be a companion only to the pious, the friendship of the wicked leads astray.
Avert your gaze from acts forbidden, restrain your hearing from sinful deeds.
Buy not, sell not, in debt, save in dire necessity and something trifling in amount.
He who asks for it is hateful among the people and bearing it is the way to bankruptcy.
Be not among those who know 'the facts', who disclose 'the secrets'.
Appear not 'dark', sham not blindness. Mankind will find that man unfathomable, impenetrable.
Yet be not so spotless in heart, so 'white' that all men know you, life brings no surprise.
Be not among men a man of varied hue. Constant change of mind is not the insignia of the faith.
Rather, be in a state which is equitable and steady,

open-hearted, free in expression towards every Muslim.
Boast not of favours nor herds you have been given,
thereby surpassing other folk.
Since all you have been given was given in trust,
keep them with gratitude and in all humility.
If you go to water be not one who argues and disputes,
harbouring rage, nor one who pushes or who comes to blows.
Drink not a containerful unlawfully. In your watering,
follow in the footsteps of the noble.

The visit paid to brethren

The visiting of brothers - say - a favour asked, if it
be not burdensome.
Enter not a dwelling without permission. Act in accordance
with Qur'ānic dictate.
If you enter, do not be nosy and pry about with the eye
in that house. Do not speak too much.
When you depart speak not of secret matters which you
have seen or heard from its occupants.
Do not outstay your welcome when you visit, for folk
have private matters in their homes.
Unless some special purpose has arisen, be off when
you have fulfilled that purpose.
If you are between households, conceal a sorry secret,
show not partiality.
If you travel, look not for ever here and there, and when
speaking be not overpowering.
Speak not just to use your voice, or to mix with others.
Towards mosques let your steps be frequent.

Correct behaviour when travelling

Beware of travelling too much. You will decrease the
blessing of old age.
Preserve and treasure the best purse. Be like a fugitive
in the mysterious unknown,
Who while there is contented by one whom he makes happy.
Then off he speeds towards the highest peak.
If you can, pass not the night as a guest. Choose a
homely lodging among men.
If you are afflicted by a companion who is a bore,
whether he sleeps, dresses and eats his nature ever
will be contrarywise.
If you forbid or command he will say 'so and so'.
He will drink much and eat much and be a lazy-bones.
He will neither carry baggage nor will he herd the camel.
Any jest which may pass from your lips will anger him,
such is the dourness of his nature.

Whenever flies may fly, his tongue is cross, bitter, sharp and vulgar.
He, due to his gross ignorance, reckons himself to be among the people who are cultured and well-bred.
His heart is the heart of a king, his condition is that of a pauper.
He is but a crafty knave.
The one who gives him aid and sustenance, is regarded by him as one who gives short measure.
Yet lower your wing for him, cover his ways by goodly behaviour on your part.
Forgive him over food and drink,
treat him like the remainder of your friends.
Impose no work nor labour on his shoulders, thereby you conceal the sloth within his nature
Be philosophical be composed and cheerful in the face of every evil in his foul nature which becomes apparent.
When'er this person favours you with a blessing, praise those favours and bless him for it.
Then you appear agreeable in his thoughts, so it would seem that you could never act without him.
Be wide in the *bāʻ* (6) in the allotment of your benefits; his nature disdains a quantity which is small.
And if this bore is one whose presence clings, then journey with him for a life time,
Since life's duration is a pathway short, and the doing of good in its entirety is summed up by patience.
Be cautious lest you have the temperament of the sponger and the bore, a man base and shameworthy.
Believe not yourself to be superior to that bore, nor the wrong-doer, nor the most ignorant man.
Virtue lies in entering into Paradise, and in escaping from the fires of Hell.
Today, that is a fate hidden from us, since we are in a state which hovers between fear and hope.
We will ask for our hope to be fulfilled and for safety from every terror of the future.

How to treat a neighbour

If one day a neighbour is not found praising noble acts, then you will find him faithless,
Alleging that you hold him in contempt, or that you cheat him of his due.
He always seeks for what you have, deeming little the giving of your favour.
So be wary of him! Pay no heed to his allegation.
He who is always in need is one whose eyes are blind.
Cease not your good works and know that what is yours you owe to God alone.

Seek no reward from any other, for a man is rewarded
according to his intention.

How to treat a guest

If a guest comes in the winter, neglected and weak due
to lack of nourishment,
His family in a similar plight, and having nothing
for their comfort,
Then let him be a burden to be carried.
Spread wide the arms and treat him in a way becoming
to the hospitable.
As for God's guests, wayfarers, meet them with a welcome
and with joyful news.
With the utmost effort bestow bounty, whether it be
drink or food or with a lodging.
For in respect of hospitality has been revealed, 'He who
believes in God . . . . . .' . (7)
It is a *ḥadīth,* which everybody knows.

The etiquette of eating.

Of that which is next to you eat.
Add it not a morsel, but measure it to an average size.
Do not stare at a fellow eater and be careful lest
you waste the food.
Guide not the sauce or gravy towards you and speak as
little as you can during your eating.
Cheat not your partner, even by a morsel, and turn not
a morsel over in the hand,
Unless your companions are close friends. Amongst friends
garments are put aside.
Grip the vessel firmly, and keep your head away from
its lip.
Be not one who mixes dishes - or drink, or one who is
observed to put on airs.
Be not an upturner of a vessel in the presence of slaves.
God is the One Who is responsible for my ending,
likewise what I have stated at the commencement of my verse.

To conclude I ask God to beautify it

Govern affairs according to the dictate of the *Sharī'a*
If it be lawful and permissible follow nature's dictates.
Attribute not evil to a thing connected with an affliction
endemic to this age.
Beware of rash experiment and the horoscope. Good and
Evil are beheld by God.
No bad omen or evil luck exists, save that divined by
God's religion or else it will be found wicked, marring

manly virtue.
Do not show preference to some necessity for cleanliness
over the sacrifices and payment of the *fiṭr zakāt.* (8)
The right of the Creator has preference over the rights
of His created even if he be exalted.
Beware lest you forget God's holy book the Qur'ān.
He who is forgetful comes back empty handed.
Always practise its recitation. The more it is increased
the sweeter it becomes.
Be occupied in learning. It is a lasting treasure -
success, pride and power.
Provided at the outset it is free from personal ambition.
Act in accordance with what you know, else it will be a
proof and argument against you and a weary burden.
I seek protection in the name of God, the King, from
seeking favours by requitals.
To enjoy health and security in life and a happy passing
in the hour of death,
A happy life in the present hour, and a protection
from fears and terrors in the hour of doom.
And kindness and joy when I am alone at the moment of
my entering the tomb.
Know that the ways of upright conduct are difficult to
gather in a book.
But here is enough for a man who comprehends, so measure
against what I have said those things unmentioned.

I ask my Lord that I may be attentive, a 'renewer' of
the religion, the Prophet being my guide.
With a long life of happiness - both for myself and
everyone who hears my admonition.
By the title of Muḥammad (Ṭāhā), the chosen one, the
best of humanity upon whom be the most excellent blessing and the peace of God.

NOTES

1) The name of the youth to whom the counsel is addressed.

2) The *salām* (benediction) is uttered during the course of the statutory prayers. See the *Encyclopedia of Islam* under *Salām - Ṣalāt.* The poet has in mind the end of the prayer where the *taslima al-'ūlā* is performed. The worshipper while seated turns his head to right and to left and says, 'Peace be upon you and God's mercy.'

3) Burhān al-Dīn Ibrāhīm b. Mar'ī al-Shabrakhītī who died in 1697 and was famous for his writings on Mālikī jurisprudence.

4) lit. 'chewed by the calves.'.

5) The poet presumably refers to the Arabic equivalent of *nonne ('amā)* which takes the form of *hamā* and *hamā* as variants. See Wright, *Arabic Grammar,* Vol. I, pp. 282-284.

6) *bā'* - measure of the two arms extended.

7) Probably that which refers to the duties and rewards of the true Muslim given in the *Ṣaḥīḥ* of al-Bukhārī, Chapter of *Jihād,* 4.

8) The poor tax paid at *'Īd al-fiṭr* marking the end of the month of fasting, *Ramaḍān.*

APPENDIX C

The reply of the Ḥājj of Tadeliza to Ḥadāḥadā and Ḥamidtu

(See pages 128-134 for translation)

وإذا اعتنق [illegible] مزارا … [illegible] مزارا

فقالوا [illegible] قرارا … واعتنوا [illegible] فرارا

فلم تزل أموالهم [illegible] … [illegible] وشاكيفا

وقد علمتم أن [illegible] الظلم … تمعن جارا لم يخف بالظلم

كما يقول ربنا الإله … في محكم التنزيل فيه نهاه

[illegible] من لم يكن قد ظلما … يكن فقير أمره لم [illegible]

تالله يا أخي لقد غررتم … بأن جيشنا منه ما رأيتم

إلا بغية ما اعترفتم أولا … وتركتم الثاني قد عولا

ثم تردون الظلم عنكم … بل قيل إنما يأخذ [illegible]

ثم [illegible] الأعلاما … تنشعجون منه الانتقاما

[illegible] عرامه … [illegible] سيرامه

وإنهم [illegible] العنوة … تجمع من [illegible] العيش

أن [illegible] الفساد … ويجعل [illegible] للجهاد

وسعى

[illegible]

وفيهما فليجتنب شكوكهما [illegible] الامير جعلتما

فما خلا الذي فيه من العدوان والظلم والفساد والطغيان

وإنما يكشف ذا الأمرا يشكو إليهم فيزيلوا المنكرا

وغير الاشتكاء بالبنان زيادة الفساد والعصيان

[illegible]

فما اشتغلتما ولا غزوتما وعلى الإسلام فهذا غزوتما

قد وجب الجهاد عنكم فلتما مع الأمير لينتني فعلتما

ذاك الذي هو الجهاد قد نزل نص عليه العلماء الكبرى

ألم يكن نصب الإمام واجبا وأنه فرض الجهاد واجبا

[illegible]

وطاعة الإمام فرضا وجبا وفي كتاب الله [illegible]

لبثاو معروفك ذا وقصرا   جمعته في كل بيت كذ...

فعاك خواك بالتخميس صورت   في القوافي جاء بالتضمين

ثم الإجازة مع الإكفاء   واضرب السناد والإيطاء

وغير ذاك جلا من عيب على   ضرائر الشعر كواك ما فهم

وما لغو بالموزون والأعراب   فرجأ اذا بلغة الأعراب

والله ما تنظم أخي قلت جير   ولم يكن لديك علم الشعر

فحضت فخرا ما ذربت فكرا   ولم تحصل لك الكلام بفكر

أخلة بربا حزو تنقابها أصابها البرون   ...

ورجة ما جاء في القوافي   ما أوهمت غير تموام الناس

وكم له من بعد علم ينثر   للشعر ميزوية قد تخبر

داهله صانعة ذوو البراعة   فذا رغفوا ما طاوعوا اليراعه

فأين تخضرموا الكلام   أو يتعاطى صناعة النظام

وَالعُلَماءُ أَجمَعوا عَلَيهِ

وَلا يَروعَكُمُ العِلمُ بِالسودانِ ... خُروجُكُم عَن طاعَةِ السُلطانِ

الأَعلَمُ مَذهَبٌ لا ... ... اِن ثَبَتَتِ الجَورُ ... العِزوانِ

تِلكَ الطَريقُ الظُلمُ وَالرَدى ... أَبطَلَها قَولُ نَبِيِّ الهُدى

كَذاكَ في مَعنى حَديثٍ ... ... وَمَن عَصى الأَميرَ فَهُوَ قَد عَصى

الشُكرُ ... ... وَالأَمرُ حَتمٌ اِن ... بِالمُسلِمِ

خُصوصُ رَحمَةٍ لِلأَنبِياءِ ... نورُ المُسلِمينَ وَالأَولِياءِ

وَلا يُرى في الشَرعِ ما أَعتَدوا ... وَالخُلَفاءُ مِن بَعدِ هؤُلاءِ

... قيموا الجُمَعَ ... ... بِأَهلِ بِدعَةٍ ... وَالعيدُ وَالجِهادُ ...

... الدُعاءُ الصالِحُ ... وَعِندَهُم عِلمٌ ...

... كَنى الفُروعِ ... أُصولٌ ... وَالشَرعُ

... ما عَجَبا ... وَعالِمٌ ...

... قَد وَهوا ... إِذكَرها ...

وَالأَرضُ تَنقُصُ مِنَ الأَطرافِ ...

تمت القصيدة بحمد الله وحسن عونه
نظم الفقيه العلامة محمد بن احمد
ابن حامد المعروف بأمّه تيغغ
نوّر الله قبره ورحم السلف وبارك في
الخلف على يد الفقير الى الله ذاك البائس
ابن الشريف ابرهيم بن الشيخ ...
... رحم الله لنا ابائنا واشياخنا
واخواننا وجميع المسلمين والمسلمات
امين ... عليك ... صالحة
بحسن الخاتمة والستر الذي ...
حيا وميتا والخير ...

A SHORT GLOSSARY
OF RECURRENT TERMS AND PROPER NAMES

More specifically of Islamic beliefs and institutions among the Tuaregs.

T = Tamashegh. Ar. = Arabic

Amenukal (pl. *Imenukalen*)(T). A title used for supreme and independant chiefs of large Tuareg political units. There is difference of opinion regarding its precise significance. Theories vary from 'the owner of the land', 'chief not subjected to another chief', '*Amenu/Imenanan* (Imāms?) of the country'. See Nicolaisen, *E.C.P.T.*, pp. 393-395.

Anestafidet. (T) The supreme chief of the Kel Away of Air. See Nicolaisen, ibid, pp. 416-418.

Banū Hilāl and Banū Sulaym. (Ar.) Specifically the title refers to groups of Arabian beduin who were pushed or emigrated into the Sahara, the Maghrib or the Sudan from the eleventh century onwards. In Sahelian traditions the Banū Hilāl have either become a convenient patrilineal Arabian ancestry for diverse groups, or a collective title for Muslim heros in a cycle of epics which have been adopted and diffused by Muslim peoples for social and religious reasons.

Baraka (Ar.) Literally, blessing or benediction and spiritual power which is possessed by certain *Ineslemen* and which can be absorbed in food, drink or in other ways by the laity. Among Tuaregs, *Elbaraka* (T) is a mystic power, of magic properties. It is possessed by the Sultan of Agades and is present in the bones of his predecessors, see Nicolaisen, ibid, p. 416.

Bay'a (Ar.) An oath of allegiance given to a Caliph. A ceremony by which the leader of the people physically, or in a figurative way, took the hand of a new Caliph as a mark of homage. It was also given to the Caliph's local representatives. In Tuareg country, the Sultan of Agades claimed to have a right to it.

Bayt al-māl (Ar.) 'The Public Treasury'. In Tuareg and Sahelian countries the wealth is donated in the form of *zakāt,* alms, tithes, taxes on income, ***kharāj,*** a land tax to which all Muslim landowners and cultivators were liable, and the *jizya*, or poll tax on non-Muslim subjects.

Bella. Former slaves or slaves of the Iwillimeden.

Buzu. Former slaves or slaves of the Air Tuaregs.

Eṭṭebel (T) means the symbolic drum of authority, drum chief, drum group. The insignia of a Tuareg drum-chief is known as *eṭṭebel* (Ar. *ṭabl*), and the word also denotes drum-groups among all the Tuaregs. See Nicolaisen, *ibid,* pp. 438-439.

Fātiḥa (Ar.) Specifically the opening chapter of the Qur'ān, but in Tuareg Islamic beliefs the *Elfatekhan* (T) denotes a prayer made to obtain the Almighty's favour. It is specifically recited when the *Amenukal* is chosen by the *Ineslemen* and the elders. In Agades the Ishsherifen recited it.

Fiqh (Ar.) The Islamic science of law and jurisprudence. Among the Tuaregs the sources of jurisprudence (*uṣūl al-fiqh)* relate to key text books and manuals such as the *Mukhtaṣar* of Khalīl and other works (see pp 180-181) On local matters, *fatāwī (*s. *fatwā*) have been issued, formal opinions of a jurist on a specific legal matter. Examples of these may be seen on pp. 49, 50, 202-204.

Iklan (s. *Akli*) (T) Slaves or dependant labour who were mostly if not entirely of negroid stock, taken during raids or bought from slave dealers. 'Freed slaves' in Air are often called *Ighawalen* or *Buzu.* There are numerous categories of 'slaves' among the Tuaregs, and the whole subject is being investigated. At the time it may be said that 'slaves' are a class rather than an occupation and are broadly divided into those who are dependant or independant of their masters.

Imām (Ar) a title denoting the leader in prayer, Caliphs, doctors of Islam, and among the Tuareg *Ineslemen* a leader, a Sultan or a chief of a sect or a tribal group when his office combines a religious and secular function. The title *Imām* may lie at the root of the name of the noble *Imenan* of the Kel Azgar, see Nicolaisen, *ibid,* pp. 393-395.

Imashaghen (var. *Imajeghen,* s. *Amajegh*) (T). The supreme Tuareg class of nobility. It corresponds to the *Ahaggaren* among the northern Tuaregs.

Imghad (s. *Ameghid*) (T) Vassals rather than serfs. This class exists in all groups save the Kel Geres, and they are the most numerous, slaves excluded.

Ineden (s. *Ened*) (T) Blacksmiths who are found in all Tuareg groups. They make weapons, implements and ornaments.

Ineslemen (s. *Anislem*) (T) The religious class established after the introduction of Islam. In most Tuareg groups there are 'tribes' of *Ineslemen* under their own chiefs. Their status may vary from that of vassals to that of a status comparable with noble Tuaregs.

Ishsherifen (T) *Shurafā'* (Ar.) Tribes which claim descent from the Prophet. The term is often synonomous with *Ineslemen.*

Iwillimeden (T). The major confederation of Sahelian Tuaregs, now divided into the Kel Aṭaram (West) and Kel Dennek (East). They reside in Mali and Niger. They may number some 160,000, but a total of some 95,000 slaves and ex-slaves should be deducted from this total.

Jihād (Ar) Frequently intended to signify a holy war against unbelievers, but interpreted by many scholars as a fight for righteousness, both inwardly and outwardly, and a synonym for moral re-armament. There were several Tuareg *Mujāhidīn* of note in their history, more particularly during the *jihād* in Hausaland in the early years of the nineteenth century.

Kel Es-Suq (T) A 'holy tribe' like the Ifoghas, but who claim descent from the Prophet through Ibrāhīm al-Daghūghī and the Idrīsids of Morocco and who are among the important of the *Ineslemen.* They claim to have dispersed from the city of Tadamakkat, now ruined but said to exist in the remains of Al-Sūq (Ar. the 'market') in the Adrar-n-Ifoghas of Mali. They were allegedly expelled from it by the Songhai ruler Sunni Ali, but this is disputed.

*Kel Tademaket (*var. *Tadamakkat)* (T) who also claim to have come from Tadamakkat but were expelled from it by Karidenna the founder of the Iwillimeden confederation. Nowadays they are several tribes and groups around Timbuctoo and Lake Faguibine. Important among them are the Tengerregif and the Kel Intasar who claim descent from 'helpers' (Ar. *Anṣār*) of the Prophet and who were in that district prior to the arrival of the bulk of the Kel Tademaket.

Kunta (pl. *Kanāta*) An arabaphone Saharan confederation centred in Tuwāt, Mauritania, Mali and Niger who claim descent from 'Uqba b. Nāfi', the conqueror of Africa, through Sīdī Muḥammad al-Kuntī who lived in the fifteenth century. The Kunta were the chief propagators of the Qādirīya Sufi order (see *Ṭarīqa*) in the Sahel in particular during the life of Sīdī al-Mukhtār al-Kuntī (1729-1811)

*Kusayla (*var. *Kasīla)* 'the Berber' was a historical character who was notorious for the death of 'Uqba b. Nāfi'. In the Sahel he has come to personify the pre-Arab Berber population, a sheep shearer, the ancestor of some of the *Imghad*, a Muslim traitor, even an ancestress among some of the Tuaregs. In Sahelian mythology he is the slayer of 'Oqba al-Mustajāb while he was at prayer or delivering a sermon at Walata.

Lemta (Lamṭa). A Saharan nomad confederation of unknown antiquity which appear frequently in medieval Arabic texts. It is claimed that many Tuaregs descend from the *Lemta.* See Nicolaisen, *ibid,* 411-412.

Mahdī (Ar.) The 'rightly guided' one, the restorer of true Islam who towards the end of the world will conquer the world for the faith. A series of leaders who claimed this title, or were believed to be such. characterized Sahelian Islam, Tuareg Islam included, between the sixteenth and twentieth centuries.

Al-Maghīlī, Muḥammad 'Abd al-Karīm (d. circa 1504) was a key figure in the infusion of Islamic beliefs among the Tuaregs. He taught in Tagedda, Air, Gao and Hausaland. His doctrines were principally of a fundamentalist or legalistic Muslim Mālikī orthodoxy but tempered by Sufi ideas. He was in favour of a strict application of the *Sharī'a.* Four key ideas of his were important for the Tuareg *Ineslemen,* (1) the *Mujaddid* (see below), (2) the status of the sinner and the nature of unbelief in a semi-pagan environment, (3) venal scholars who deformed Islam both in doctrine and in practise, (4) patrilineal succession.

Mujaddid (Ar.) 'a renewer'. This doctrine later contained the belief in a series of learned and pious men, all renewers, who would be precursors of the *Mahdī* (see above). The appearance of a great *Mujaddid* in Takrūr was frequently prophesied. The first reformer *Mujaddid* was, by consensus, the Caliph 'Umar b. 'Abd al-'Azīz (717-720 AD). The twelfth *Mujaddid,* the *Mahdī* himself, was to have appeared at the end of the twelfth century of the hijra - the late eighteenth or early nineteenth century AD. Ideas of this kind were to the fore during the Sokoto *jihād.*

'Oqba al-Mustajāb is a semi-mythical hero of the Sahel. He is held to be the Muslim conqueror of Africa, and to have founded noted cities including Qayrawān in Tunisia, Walāta in Mauritania, Al-Sūq (Tadamakkat) in Mali, or to have accompanied Karidenna as a religious counsellor when he formed the Iwillimeden confederation in the seventeenth century. 'Oqba died in battle in Algeria or was martyred in the pulpit in Walāta. Elements of the lives of 'Uqba b. Nāfi', 'Uqba b. 'Āmir and the romance in the *Futūḥ Ifrīqiyā* of 'pseudo' al-Wāqidī are discernible in this hybrid hero.

Qāḍī (pl. *Quḍāt*) (Ar.) a judge who according to canonic law of Islam (see *Sharī'a)* has to decide cases involving criminal and civil law. The office is held by certain *Ineslemen* among the Tuaregs or by Arabs, Moors and other lettered Muslims in their midst.

Ṣadaqa (Ar) In general, alms giving and charity but sometimes employed as synonomous with *Zakāt,* the legal poor rate. *Ṣadaqa* more specifically indicates voluntary alms-giving but among the Tuaregs it also denotes tribute paid to chiefs and *Ineslemen* and is laid down as a specific fee. See Nicolaisen, *ibid*, PP. 428, 432, 434, 438, and in *Folk*, Vol. 1, 1959, Copenhagen, p. 127.

Ṣanhāja (pl. *Ṣanāhija*) A group of Saharan and Sahelian peoples who claim to be patrilineally related and of ancient Arabian origin. Among the most noted of them are the Lamtūna, Gudāla and Massūfa who are scattered in the whole Sahel. Certain of them are to be found in Niger, among them the Inussufen of Tagedda, some Lamtūna and other minor groups. The Kel Es Suq, Kel Aghlāl, the Ifoghas and the Barkuray sometimes claim to be Ṣanhāja as do many *Ineslemen* who wish to stress ties with the Muslim community.

Sharī'a (Ar.) Canonic Islamic law administered by a *Qāḍī*. In theory the *Sharī'a* was established in centres such as Tagedda, Agades and in important Tuareg centres of Islamic practice. However, *'urf*, customary law, influenced by many pre-Islamic Tuareg social customs and institutions is followed in many cases. Attempts by Tuareg reformers to impose the *Sharī'a*, for example that of Muḥammad al-Jaylānī, were short lived, partially effective and owed a good deal to outside influences.

Shaykh (pl *Shuyūkh*) (Ar.) denotes an elder or head-man (*Amghar* in Tamashegh). Among the *Ineslemen* it is more often applied to Kunta, Kel Es-Suq or other scholars who are learned in mysticism and in jurisprudence. The *Ishshikhen* (var. *Echchikhen*) (T) are a religious class in Damergu. Their title is similar in signification to *Ineslemen* but not to Ishsherifen who are specifically patrilinealy related to the Prophet.

Sulṭān (Ar.) It is possible that the first bearer of this title was first appointed by the Saljūq rulers in Asia Minor in the eleventh century. The office was known by the Tuaregs of Air and Tagedda in the fourteenth century since those in Tagedda and the Air Massif are given this title in Arabic documents. The Tuareg Sultanate today is centred in Agades. The title is almost the same as *Amenukal* or with *Amīr* or *Imām* which are sometimes preferred by the *Ineslemen* in their writings.

Sunna (Ar.) Among the early Islamic schools of jurisprudence (*fiqh*)it meant the generally approved doctrines of the practice and custom of Islam, interpreted according to the views of Islam's four main law schools. From the time of the Imām al-Shāfi'ī (d. 820 AD) it denoted the precedent set by the Prophet.

al-Suyūṭī, Jalāl al-Dīn 'Abd al-Raḥmān (d. 1505) was one of the very greatest scholars of the Mamluk age. His ideas had a great impact on Takrūr and among the Tuareg scholars of Tagedda and Tadamakkat, many of whom studied with him in Cairo or studied his works. He differed from al-Maghīlī (see above) because (1) he was more flexible and liberal in concession to local customs, (2) his mystical and astrological tendencies were far more pronounced, (3) he issued a number of *fatwās* to Takrūr, answered questions and wrote letters to rulers in Agades, Katsina and elsewhere. He offered a second opinion to those of al-Maghīlī. He eased the investiture (*taqlīd*) of rulers from Takrūr by the Caliph in Cairo.

Ṭarīqa (pl *Ṭuruq*) (Ar.) Literally a 'path', (*Abareqqa* in Tamashegh) applied to a Sufi brotherhood. The important orders of the Sufis among the Tuaregs are the Qādirīya, which entered the Central Sahara with the Kel Es-Suq, the Kunta or independantly, the Khalwatīya, strong in Air and Hausaland; the Tijānīya which was established in the nineteenth century, the Sanūsīya which was brought into the area just before the first World War and formed a powerful inspiration for the Tuareg revolt in Air and Damergu under Kawsen.

Tawshit (Air T) (var. *Tawset* or *Tawsit*). signifies a palm or base of the hand from which fingers issue. It indicates a tribal unit or lineal structure a matrilineal unit where all members claim descent from a common ancestress. See Nicolaisen, *ibid*, pp. 140-141.

Tégéhé (T). Persons who descend from sisters and female cousins of the maternal line. It also denotes a confederation of drum-groups (see *Eṭṭebel*). Among the Iwillimeden it denotes a political confederation. See Nicolaisen, *ibid*, pp. 396, 402, 433.

BIBLIOGRAPHY

Abadie, Colonel M. *La Colonie du Niger,* Paris, 1927.

Barth, H. *Travels and Discoveries in North and Central Africa,* 5 Vols., 1858.
Travels in North and Central Africa, London, 1890.
Travels in Africa; Timbuktu and the Soudan, London, 1890.

Bates, O. *The Eastern Libyans,* London 1914. (1970)

Benhazera, M. *Six mois chez les Touareg du Ahaggar.* Algiers, 1908.

Bernus, Edmond and Suzanne *Du Sel et des Dattes.* Etudes Nigeriennes, No. 31. Niamey, 1972.

Bernus, S. *Henri Barth chez les Touaregs de l'Aïr,* Etudes Nigeriennes, No. 28, Niamey, 1972.

Bivar, A.D.H. and Hiskett, M. The Arabic Literature of Nigeria to 1804: A provisional account, *Bulletin of the School of Oriental and African Studies,* XXV, 1, 1962.

Bivar, A.D.H. *Nigerian Panoply,* Department of Antiquities, Nigeria, 1964.
The Arabic Calligraphy of West Africa, *African Language Review,* VII, 1968, 3-15.

Boubou Hama *Recherche sur l'Histoire des Touareg Sahariens et Soudanais,* Niamey, 1967.

Bovill, E.W. *The Golden Trade of the Moors,* London, 1933.

Cissoko, S.M. Famines et épidémies à Tombouctou et dans la Boucle du Niger du XVIe au XVIII siecle, *Bull. de l'IFAN,* xxx, Sér. B., no. 3, 1968, pp. 806 - 821.

Cortier, M. *D'une rive à l'autre du Sahara,* Paris, 1908.

Cuoq, J. M. *Receuil des Sources Arabes concernant l'Afrique Occidentale du XIIIe au XVIe Siècle (Bilād Al-Sūdān)* Editions du Centre National de la Recherche Scientifique, Paris, 1975.

Delafosse, M. *Haut Sénégal - Niger, I-III,* Paris 1912.

Denham, Dixon and Clapperton *Narrative of Travels and Discoveries in Northern and Central Africa,* London, 1826.

Duveyrier, H. *Les Touareg du Nord,* Paris, 1864.

Fuglestad, F. Les Revoltes des Touaregs du Niger 1916-1917, in *Cahiers d'Etudes Africaines,* No. 49, Vol. XIII, 1973, pp. 82-120.

Gautier, E.F. *Sahara Algérien,* Paris, 1908.

Hiskett, M. *The Sword of Truth,* C.U.P., 1973.

Hodgkin, T. *Nigerian Perspectives,* C.U.P., 1960.

Humwick, J. "Notes on a Late Fifteenth Century Document concerning 'al-Takrūr', *African Perspectives,* ed. C.H. Allen and R.W. Johnson, C.U.P., 1970.

Ibn Battuta *Textes et Documents Rélatifs à l'Histoire de l'Afrique,* Faculté des Lettres et Sciences Humaines, Dakar, 1966.

Jean, C. *Les Touareg du Sud-Est,* l'Air, Paris, 1909.

Last, M. *The Sokoto Caliphate,* London, 1967.

Leo Africanus *Description de l'Afrique.* Edition translated by A. Epaulard and annotated by E. Epaulard, Th. Monod, H. Lhote and R. Mauny, Paris, 1956, 2 Vols.

Levtzion, N. *Ancient Ghana and Mali,* Methuen, 1973.

Lewicki, T. *West African Food in the Middle Ages,* C.U.P., 1974.

Lhote, H. *Les Touaregs du Hoggar,* Paris, 1955. Contribution à l'Etude du Touareg Soudanais, I and II, *Bull. de l'IFAN,* B, XVII, 1955, pp. 334-370, and 1956, pp. 391-407.

Martin, B. G. "A short History of the Khalwati Order of Dervishes" in *Scholars, Saints and Sufis,* ed. Nikki Keddi (Berkeley, University of California) 1971.

Marty, P. *Les Kounta de l'Est, les Berabich, les Iguellad,* (1918-19), II : *La Région de Tombouctou, Diénné, Le Macina et dépendances.* (1920). Revue du Monde Musulman.

Mauny, R. *Tableau géographique de l'Ouest Africain au Moyen Age,* Mémoires de l'IFAN, Dakar, 1960.

Nicolaisen, J. *Ecology and Culture of the Pastoral Tuareg,* National Museum, Copenhagen, 1963.

Nicolas, F. *Tamesna, Les Ioullemmeden de l'Est ou Touareg "Kel Dinnik".* Paris, 1950. Contribution à l'Etude Twâreg de l'Air, *Mémoires de l'IFAN,* X. Paris, 1950.

Palmer, H.R. Notes on some Asben Records ("Agades Chronicles"), *Journal of the African Society,* 9, 36, July, 1910.

The Bornu Sahara and Sudan, London, 1936.

Richardson, J. *Travels in the Great Desert of Sahara,* Vols, I and II, London 1853.

Richer, A. *Les Ouilliminden,* Paris, 1924.

Rodd, F.R. *People of the Veil,* London, 1926.

Salifou, A. *Kaoussen ou la Révolte Senoussiste,* Etudes Nigeriennes, No. 33, Niamey, 1973.

Trimingham, J. S. *A History of Islam in West Africa,* London, 1962.

U.N.E.S.C.O. *Nomades et Nomadisme au Sahara,* Recherches sur la zone aride, XIX, U.N.E.S.C.O., 1963.

Urvoy, Y. Chronique d'Agadès, *Journal de la Société des Africanistes IV,* pp. 145-177, Paris, 1934.

Histoire des Populations du Soudan Central, Paris, Larose, 1936.

Zeltner, Fr. De Les Touareg du Sud. *Journal of the Royal Anthropological Institute XLIV,* pp. 351-375, London, 1914.

INDEX

Bold numerals refer to illustrations

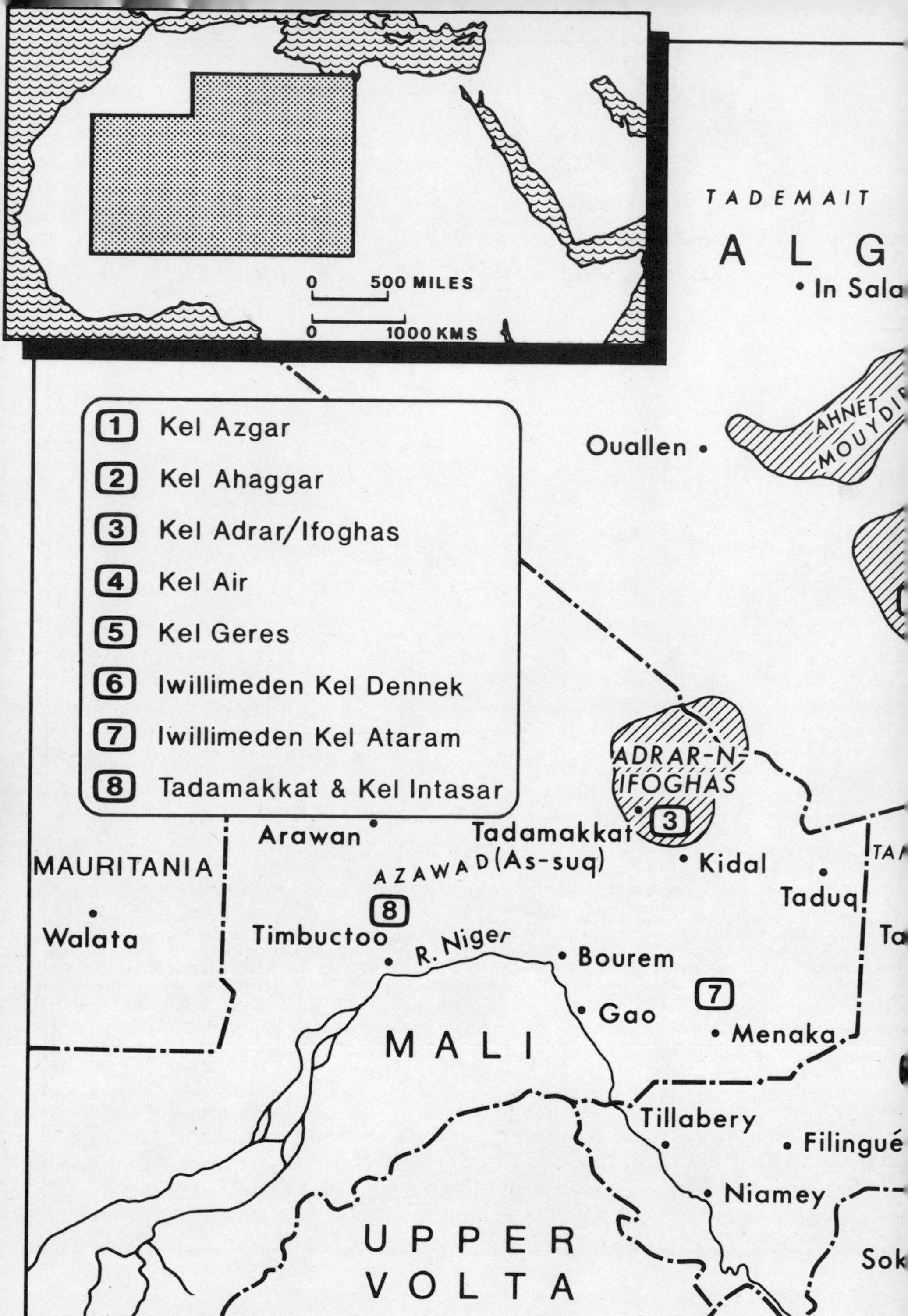
0 500 MILES
0 1000 KMS
1 Kel Azgar
2 Kel Ahaggar
3 Kel Adrar/Ifoghas
4 Kel Air
5 Kel Geres
6 Iwillimeden Kel Dennek
7 Iwillimeden Kel Ataram
8 Tadamakkat & Kel Intasar
TADEMAIT
A L G
In Sala
AHNET
MOUYDI
Ouallen
ADRAR-N-IFOGHAS
3
Arawan
Tadamakkat
AZAWAD (As-suq)
Kidal
Taduq
MAURITANIA
Walata
8
Timbuctoo
R. Niger
Bourem
7
Gao
Menaka
MALI
Tillabery
Filingué
Niamey
UPPER VOLTA
Sok